The BEST

Cambridge Restaurants in and around Cambridge

including Saffron Walden, Royston, Ely and Newmarket

2000 EDITION

by Neal E. Robbins and Louise Tucker

Illustrations by Tom Morgan-Jones

INSIDER GUIDES

www.cambridgeinsider.com

A Cambridge Insider ® book

This edition was first published in October 1999 by
The Cambridge Insider Ltd
PO Box 311
Cambridge UK
CB4 3FG

ISBN 0 9537183 0 1

Printed and bound in Great Britain by
Thanet Press Limited, Margate

Designed by Harris Design Associates, Cambridge

The BEST

Cafés·Pubs·Clubs
Restaurants
in and around
Cambridge

**This book is one of many you can buy from
The Cambridge Insider. Others include:**

Cambridge Secrets

The new edition of the sell-out independent consumers'
guide to Cambridge-area goods and services. By Kate
Paterson. (forthcoming) £6.99 (see ad page 168)

Cambridge

This handsomely illustrated book presents the
architecture, history and traditions of the city. By Douglas
Ferguson, Dona Haycraft and Nick Segal. £25

The Gardens of Cambridge

Practical information and evocative descriptions set
against the background of the colleges. By Richard Bird
with photography by Dona Haycraft. £5.95

The Cambridge Loo Review

A humorous guide to the conveniences of Cambridge. By
W.C. Rolls with illustrations by Tom Morgan-Jones. £2.99

You can order on our website:

www.cambridgeinsider.com

*or you can also contact us by e-mail:
info@cambridgeinsider.com
by fax: 01223 527603 or phone: 01223 462233*

**Look for quality where you see
the wavy-haired reader**

INSIDER  GUIDES

to the people at cafés, pubs, clubs and restaurants
who work very hard
to bring us good food and entertainment

Making the difference
in our community

By purchasing this guide, you are helping the Q103 Appeal. The Cambridge Insider Ltd, publisher of the *Best Cafés, Pubs, Clubs and Restaurants in and around Cambridge*, kindly donates 5 percent of the £5.99 purchase price, or about 30p for each book, to the Q103 Appeal.

This money helps the Q103 Appeal to relieve suffering amongst local people. The Appeal – unlike any other charity in our region – has one objective: to quickly meet the needs of individuals and groups who need our help and who live in the area covered by this book. It works all year round to raise funds. Over the past four years, the Appeal has raised more than £100,000 and made donations to over 50 local charities.

The Appeal would like to hear from you. If you can run an event to raise money, please contact us. To learn more about the Q103 Appeal or make a donation, contact:

The Q103 Appeal Office
PO Box 103
Histon, Cambs CB4 4WW
Tel: 01223 235255
Fax: 01223 235161

Thank you, and The Cambridge Insider, for
helping to make the difference
in our community.

registered charity no 801876

CONTENTS

Contents

This is a guide for visitors, tourists <u>and</u> residents. For those passing through, it helps get the most out of a short stay with quick information on where to go to get the best. Equally, this guide is meant to enrich the lives of people who live in Cambridge and the surrounding area, including Newmarket, Saffron Walden, Royston, Huntingdon, Ely and all the villages between. It describes the full range of good restaurants, pubs, cafés and clubs available to them, providing complete information on each in a handy, easy-to-access format.

Unlike a guide meant for a national readership, this book is focused on a geographic area anyone already in the Cambridge area is likely to use. There are more than 240 entries, providing clear options in every category and cuisine. It is organised by location and type and has indexes, two maps and handy ratings to make it easy to zero in on the best choice for a particular time and need.

With each book come 34 tear-out discount vouchers worth over £140 – many times the cost of the book – entitling you to everything from free bottles of wine with a candle-lit dinner to a cappuccino with a sandwich. The vouchers are valid until 1 October 2001. This gives you lots of extra reasons to get out and enjoy the great variety of food, drink and entertainment available in this part of England.

We wholeheartedly recommended every place in this book. The 'Insider Choice' symbol earmarks those places that we most highly recommend, making it easier to decide which choice suits you best. But note that in a guide like this, including many different kinds of establishments, it has been important not to compare, as they say, apples and oranges. We have rated and broken down the entries of special distinction into roughly comparable categories in the list that follows this introduction, so that a café or a city pub is not compared with a country pub or a gourmet restaurant. The entries are ranked by number with the 'ties' indicated.

For all the entries, our definition of 'best' has been simple: Would we go out of the way for this place? Would we recommend it to a friend? If the answer was positive, we tried – within the limitations of our space and time – to include it. We made these decisions based on personal, anonymous visits to many hundreds of possible choices. In every case we paid for our own drink or meal. No favours were accepted. We decided on independent editorial grounds alone which places deserved to be part of the select few in this book. The places chosen were given the opportunity to offer a voucher only after we had decided to include the entry.

We set certain criteria. Each establishment had to provide a clean, safe and welcoming environment for everyone. Where food is served, we looked for fresh ingredients, careful cooking, preparation in a reasonable amount of time and civility of service. We always looked for good value food or drink – at the price – and when the food went beyond the ordinary, we let you know. Beyond that, we looked for places with interesting character, attractive atmosphere or that extra touch of warmth that turns an ordinary pub, restaurant or café into a place of refuge.

Naturally, our views on the 'best' necessarily contain an element of subjectivity. So you may find useful the indexes at the back, which give you selections based on 20 functional categories. Looking for a romantic dinner? See 'Business Lunch/Special Occasion'. Need a dog-friendly pub for your pooch? See 'Pets Allowed'. Dining on a budget? Go to the 'Budget Eating'.

We give you a further basis for choice. With the cooperation of the local branches of the Campaign for Real Ale (CAMRA), we have noted those pubs that the local groups recommend. If you are looking primarily for good beer, the CAMRA logo on selected entries indicates that these pubs meet their high standards.

Every entry includes a text commentary, accompanied by a quick list of the basics on price range, location and information like credit card use and hours. We did our best to go beyond the 'facts' and capture the spirit of each and every entry in the book. This, we hope, is what makes this book different from others of its kind.

We have also done our very best to make sure the entries were accurate and up to date at the time of publication. Naturally, however, things change. We reported on what was the case when we visited. Everything may not be exactly the same on your visit. Indeed you may see a place though different eyes. Why not let us know? Did we get it right? Have we chosen the right places? Is there anywhere we've missed that you'd like to see included? We hope that you will contact us with the reply mail card or by other means to share your views so that they can be reflected in future editions.

Neal E. Robbins
Editor and Publisher

Entries are listed by location and then alphabetically by cuisine or type.

INSIDER CHOICE, indicated by this symbol, appears next to the names of the entries that are on the list of the 'very best' on pages 9-11.

 A rosette on the left of entries highlights those top rated in a category in the 'Insider Choice' list.

SPECIAL FEATURES are listed in gray (**budget**) under the entry name. These correspond to index category lists beginning on page 224 and give extra information.

The Free Press
garden/patio, pets allowed, veg choice

❖ *DISCOUNT VOUCHER - FREE PUDDING*

7 Prospect Row
Cambridge CB1 1DU
Map ref: back E 6
Telephone: 01223 368337
Open Mon-Sat: noon-2.30pm,
6-11pm; Sun: noon-3pm,
7-10.3-pm

No smoking
Children who behave admitted with parents
Prices: pub food under £5

On a shaded backstreet, the black and white fronted Free Press looks small, even inconspicuous. But this little pub, inside hardly large enough to park two Fords

OPEN: gives the days and times of trading. If these do not coincide with food service hours, more information is provided.

CREDIT CARDS: unless otherwise stated, the listed outlet accepts major credit cards. Credit card use is noted only if none are accepted or we have been informed that a card or cards are not accepted.

SMOKING: unless otherwise stated, smoking <u>is</u> permitted. <u>No smoking</u> means no smoking anywhere. <u>Non-smoking area</u> means smoking is forbidden in a designated area, but permitted elsewhere.

DISCOUNT VOUCHER: provides information on the discount available. Look at the back, from page 235 to find the coupon, with terms and conditions.

PRICES: these are the top and bottom prices of the major menu categories or key items, usually the main course in the case of a restaurant.

CAMRA LOGO
(for pubs only): this pub is specially recommended for its beer by the local branch of the Campaign for Real Ales (CAMRA).

INSIDER CHOICE Our 'Insider choice' of the very best is below. The establishments are ranked. Rosettes ( ) highlight the top entries.

INSIDER CHOICE

🏵	1. Don Pasquale	(Italian)	57
🏵	1. Trattoria Pasta Fresca	(Italian)	64
	2. La Mimosa	(Italian)	59
	3. Pizza Express (Jesus Ln)	(Italian)	61

🏵	1. Efes	(Mediterranean: Turkish)	67
🏵	1. Panos	(Med-Greek: French)	70
	2. Al Casbah	(Mediterranean: Algerian)	65
	2. Anatolia	(Mediterranean: Turkish)	66
	2. Varsity	(Med: Cypriot/French)	71

🏵	1. Golden Curry	(Indian/S. Asian)	75
	2. Tandoori Palace	(Indian/S. Asian)	80
	2. Bengal	(Indian/S. Asian)	72
	3. Cambridge Curry Centre	(Indian/S. Asian)	73
	3. Pipasha Restaurant	(Indian/S. Asian)	78
	4. Maharajah	(Indian/S. Asian)	76
	5. Victoria Tandoori	(Indian/S. Asian)	81

🏵	1. Dojo	(East Asian: Pan-Asian)	85
🏵	1. Peking	(East Asian: Chinese)	87
🏵	1. Charlie Chan	(East Asian: Chinese)	82
	2. Sala Thong	(East Asian: Thai)	88
	3. Bangkok City	(East Asian: Thai)	82
	3. Chopsticks	(East Asian: Chinese)	84

Cambridge – Bar Restaurants

🏵	1. Browns	97
	2. All Bar One	94

Central Cambridge – Pubs

🏵	1. Eagle	104
🏵	1. Maypole	107
🏵	1. St Radegund	112
	2. Mitre	109
	3. Bath Ale House	102

Cambridge – Neighbourhood Pubs

🏵	1. Cambridge Blue	118
🏵	1. Free Press	126
	2. Portland Arms	132
	3. Bar Moosh	116
	4. Panton Arms	131
	4. Boathouse	117

ABOUT THE CAMBRIDGE INSIDER

This book was prepared over a 5-month period by The Cambridge Insider, which many will recall as the name of a newsprint magazine published from September 1997 to October 1998. Though honoured with much praise, the magazine was unfortunately not paying its way and had to close. The company behind it, The Cambridge Insider Ltd, was to be merged in November 1998 into a publishing/internet firm in the city. This merger was reversed in April 1999 and The Cambridge Insider Ltd re-emerged as an independent company. Now dedicated to guide publishing, The Cambridge Insider Ltd produces lifestyle publications for the general public based on good writing, thorough research, attractive presentation and reasonable prices. We uphold the following principles:

• Openness to new ideas, imagination and innovation

• Serving the general reader, whose trust and faith in our publications is of paramount importance to us, by providing honest, balanced and independent journalism.

•Operating as a responsible citizen of the community.

About the authors:

•Neal E. Robbins is a journalist, editor and former professor of journalism who served as a news agency and newspaper correspondent in Asia and Europe.

•Louise Tucker is a writer and teacher, a former English lecturer and an avid eater.

•Tom Morgan-Jones shot to prominence with his drawings in The Cambridge Insider magazine and the Cambridge Loo Review and has since had his inky messes appear in the national press. More recently he babysat for Billy Bragg to great acclaim and is currently working on a couple of fabulous children's books.

Central Cambridge
Cafés and Restaurants

"...and just look at the garden."

a typical house whine.

Auntie's

dessert, sandwich

INSIDER CHOICE

1 St Mary's Passage
Cambridge CB2 3PQ
Map ref: back D 3
Telephone: 01223 315641
Open Mon-Fri: 9.30am-6pm
Sun: noon-5.30pm

No credit cards
Non-smoking area
Prices: tea £1.20, jacket potatoes
£3.95-£4.75, cakes £2.35-£4.35,
sandwiches £4.75

Auntie's has the best tea room location in the centre of Cambridge, just steps away from the main tourist attraction, King's College Chapel. It complements this with tea room fare served in an 'auntie's' living room setting, complete with wooden cabinets holding displays of china. On sunny days, you can sit at tables on the broad walkway which Auntie's shares with Great Saint Mary's Church rose garden.

the best tea room location in the centre of Cambridge...

Auntie's tends to be busy. The traditionally dressed waitresses (1950s-type, black knee-length uniform with big white bows and collar) do a good job of meeting the demands of afternoon crowds tired after shopping or tourism, but satisfying everyone can be an uphill battle. You can't come in for just a cuppa at midday. The minimum charge is £2.50 from 12-4:30pm.

For £6.25, you get the full cream tea with scones, jam, cream and egg-cress-and-mayonnaise sandwich. As with the rest of the menu, the grilled sandwiches, jacket potatoes and cakes, the food is a bit pricier than the competition, but tasty and of excellent quality.

Basil's

budget, sandwich, student hangout

17 Magdalene Street
Cambridge CB3 0AF
Map ref: back C 2
Telephone: none
Open Mon-Sat: 9am-5pm

No credit cards
Prices: espresso £0.85,
sandwiches £1.30-£2.45,
baked potatoes £1.90-£3.25

I like Basil's. It has character of the fin-de-siècle sort. An ancient shop front opposite Magdalene College, its old 5-digit telephone number remains like a badge of honour in black and white letters on the sign above the door. You get a dial tone if you try it. Basil's actually has no telephone. The owner gave it up. Too many people called at noon to sell things. That sums up the attitude here – laid-back, so much so that on entering, you may wonder if the place has been abandoned.

Often no one mans the front sales counter. Old boxes are piled behind the glass countertop, and behind it two score tins with bulk tea and coffee for sale have peeling paper and sticky tape labels. Couches covered with India-print sheets dominate a front shop about as big as a pair of parking spaces.
Shelves array an eclectic assortment of coffee machines while little mounds of coffee beans and tins do for a shop window display.

higgledy-piggledy... homely and laid back... just what you came for

But all is not as it seems. When roused by the door buzzer, the shopkeeper emerges momentarily and shows you down the spiral staircase, where, at the half dozen tables covered with green jungle print plastic tablecloths, Basil's does a brisk trade. You'll find students and office people enjoying a cup of espresso, sandwich or the popular freshly-made soups, often with boom-box on at volume. The cake and mocha I had were rather good. Higgledy-piggledly Basil's may be, but homely and laid-back is what you get and, especially at the price, that is just what you come for.

CB1 Internet Café

student hangout

INSIDER CHOICE

32 Mill Road
Cambridge CB1 2AD
Map ref: back F 6
Telephone: 01223 576306
Open Mon-Sat: 10am-9pm,
Sun: 11am-7pm

No credit cards
Entertainment: poetry
readings, games
Prices: coffee £0.80- £1.30,
sandwiches £1.40-£1.85,
cakes £0.70-£1.25

CB1 opened in 1995 to become the first cyber café in the country outside London. But for snags in opening, it would have been the first cyber café in Europe. The pioneering venture was the brainchild

a popular and very friendly café... students especially find the tightly packed café tables congenial

of Daniel Sturdy, who envisioned a shop for second-hand books, but one with coffee and computers. The mix was working in the computer cafés on the US West Coast, he reasoned, why not in Cambridge, the high-tech frontier town of England? CB1 quickly caught on, with students forming the mainstay.

Today, it remains popular. People sit quietly reading, play chess or simply talk over a cappuccino at the close café tables. You can come in alone and start up a chat or come in with friends to feel jolly and close. All sorts

Central

of people use the computers. There are about a dozen terminals, a few on the ground floor and most in a small basement room down the stairs at the back. Superfast internet access is 10p a minute and the computers also have word processing software and printers. If you are new to the web, the staff will help you get started.

CB1 serves snacks, coffee and tea, but no meals. But while you can't feast, you can feast your mind. The used books on the walls are there to peruse and, if you want to continue reading at home, you can buy them.

Grinders Gourmet Coffees

dessert, open early, sandwich

47 Lion Yard
Cambridge CB2 3NA
Map ref: back D 4
Telephone: 01223 301689
Open Mon-Fri: 7.45am-6pm, Sat: 7:45am-6.30 pm, Sun 10:45-5.15pm

No smoking
No credit cards
Prices: espresso and coffee drinks £1-£2.80, toasted ciabatta and crisps £3.10, baked goods £.0.90-£1.75

Grinders is a coffee-plus, pick-and-choose sort of place, serving the full range of espressos, unusual toppings and

coffee-plus, pick-and-choose sort of place...

a wide range of syrup-flavoured coffees (anything from fruit flavours to vanilla, hazelnuts and Irish cream). They use a basic coffee blend made up of mountain beans from Brazil, Uganda and Colombia, making a good cup that goes well with the toasted ciabatta or one of the several good cakes and cookies on offer in the plushly decorated shop. Feel free to linger. The staff makes you feel welcome.

Henry's

children, dessert

INSIDER
CHOICE

5a Pembroke Street
Cambridge CB2 3QY
Map ref: back E 3
Telephone: 01223 361206
Open Mon-Sat: 9am-5pm

No credit cards
No smoking
Children welcome
Prices: coffee £0.80 a cup, tea from £1.05 a pot, cakes £0.65-£1.55

For anyone desperately seeking the perfect cup of tea, filter coffee or hot chocolate, search no further.

Henry's shop draws on a stock of some 90 teas and 30 varieties of coffee (also sold by the pound if you want to take some home). It serves such exotic drinks as Amaretto-flavoured coffee, African Kibo Chagga coffee and teas of every ilk – from fine Indian Assam to

Kenyan Pekoe and smoked teas – even Argentinian maté and good quality Japanese green.

Tea is served by friendly, helpful staff, in good china and by the pot. Depending on what you order, it starts at £1.05 (yielding two cups) and gets more economical if larger pots are ordered, while coffee costs £0.80 a cup, or £1.15 for a cafetière, depending on the sort. There is no espresso, but the hot chocolate (£1.05) apparently won a local critic's top rating. Beverages are served, along with a choice of locally baked cakes and biscuits

For anyone desperately seeking the perfect cup of tea, filter coffee or hot chocolate, search no further

in a small tea room of the doily-quaint sort. This attracts all sorts, but especially tourists, mums with babies and shoppers.

Among the visitors are some avid tea pot enthusiasts because Henry's does a good trade in collectable ceramic teapots – such as one fashioned as a red telephone booth or a little black and white piano with Mickey Mouse on the lid – at prices up to £130 each. Does tea taste better if you drink it out of a piano?

Indigo Coffee House

budget, sandwich, student hangout

INSIDER CHOICE

8 St Edwards Passage
Cambridge CB2 3PJ
Map ref: back D/E 3
Telephone: 01223 368753
Open Mon: 10 am-7pm,
Tue-Sat: 10am-11pm, Sun: 11am-6pm

Non-smoking area
Prices: espresso £1.20-
£1.50, bagels £0.60,
baguettes £2.40-£2.45

By every measure, Indigo is the smallest café in Cambridge, with places for just 22 patrons on its miniscule two floors. It is also the newest, having opened on 15 August 1999 in the narrow people-only street just opposite King's

the students have already discovered that no place in Cambridge is cosier

College. Good things come in small packages, which is why you'll find at Indigo huge, colourful bucket-sized 'just like on Friends' (the TV series) cups, making its espresso ounce for ounce a rather good deal. The students have already discovered that no place in Cambridge is cosier and few have the personality of the coffee matron, Claire Hawkins, whose long-held dream has been to open a coffee house named Indigo. So this is a good place for dreaming dreams within dreams.

Central

The Little Tea Room

children, dessert, terrace, veg choice

❖❖ *DISCOUNT VOUCHER - FREE DRINK*

No 1 All Saints Passage
Cambridge CB2 3LT
Map ref: back D 3
Telephone: 01223 366033
No smoking

Open Mon-Sat: 10am-5.30pm,
Sun: 1-5.30pm
Credit cards except Am Exp
Prices: tea £1.20, jacket potato
£3.95, cakes £2.10

One tea room just a few steps off the well-beaten path around the Cambridge sites offers an extra dash of beauty, tranquillity and tea-roomishness: The Little Tea Room.

You'll find it tucked behind All Saint's Garden. You cross under a white brick archway and enter a small courtyard, where on sunny days tables are set out in the **offers an extra dash of beauty, tranquillity and tea-roomishness...** cool semi-shade. Inside two smallish, well-kept rooms, all the tables are adorned with silk flowers and the shelves hold knick-knacks and a rainbow of tea sets – all for sale. One of these, a handsome deep blue flowered tea service, is used for the tea, adding a certain *je ne sais quoi*.

The Little Tea Room service is polite and prompt. A cream tea (tea, scones and clotted cream) is £3.75, without an obligatory egg, cress and mayonnaise sandwich, which sells separately for £2.35, putting the food at par as far as town centre prices go. The tea rooms overlook the tree-shaded All Saint's garden, site of the Saturday Craft Market, one of the few that require everything on sale to be made by the sellers.

Living Stones Coffee Shop

children, urban peace

St Andrews St Baptist Church
43 St Andrews Street
Cambridge CB2 3AR
Map ref: back E 4
Telephone: 01223 566030
Open Mon-Sat: 10am-4pm

No smoking
Children's play area
Wheelchair access – all areas
Prices: tea £0.80 a pot for one,
£1.50 for two,
jacket potatoes £1.80-£2.70

Something happens when you walk in off the street into this side annex to St Andrew's Street Baptist Church. The bustle drops away, you put down your bags and all of sudden realise how shopping frazzles your nerves. It's not only the quiet lightness of the space in the former churchyard. It is more than the organ music that wafts into the room from the adjoining church. The feeling stems from the lack of crowds, noise and hype.

You can enjoy your drink or light snack – a soup, sandwich or jacket potato – and a selection of fresh cakes made by the shop, with a bit of serenity. One visitor wrote in the guest book that Living Stones was 'an oasis of peace' in a commercial desert.

Living Stones was... 'an oasis of peace' in a commercial desert

The coffee shop is run by the church as a form of low-key outreach. You wouldn't know it though. It is basically just another coffee shop with some Christian literature available in one corner. You have privacy, but if you want to chat, the volunteers will gladly do so, and judging by the remarks in the visitor's book, this is something that many people have appreciated over the years.

Museum Café

urban peace

1st floor
Fitzwilliam Museum
Trumpington Street
Cambridge CB2 1RB
Map ref: back H 3
Telephone: 01223 332900

Open Tue-Sat: 10am-4.30pm,
Sun: 2.15-4.30pm
No credit cards
No smoking
Prices: large tea £0.90, coffee £0.70,
muffins and pastries £0.65-£1.10

This is the Museum Café, one of the most refreshing stops on our tour. Here, you will have a rare opportunity to experience art, to bring it to your lips! You'll recall that small painting by Henri Fantin-Latour, White Cup on Saucer? That picture of a single cup, all in white, with spoon resting on the saucer is what we remember most of the 'master of white'. We have modeled our cups on those very cups, and you can have your coffee or tea in them today.

a stylish place to recover from museum legs right inside the museum

The coffee shop is not really on the tour, but it seems like it could be. They really do have look-alike tea cups and they do look a lot like the ones in the picture painted in 1864. That makes you want to turn the cups around and gaze at them from every angle. The coffee and tea are the ordinary sort, of course, and you will find no treats worth walking a mile for (Mars Bars and cellophane-covered muffins being standard). The room itself is quite pleasant, suspended, as the bands of windows make it seem, amid the trees. Designed by David Roberts and built in 1975, it adds a touch of international architecture to the grand 1848 museum building. What's nicest is that there is a stylish place to recover from museum legs right inside the museum.

Central

Starbucks

dessert, open early, student*, urban peace*

Top floor, Waterstone's Bookshop*
6 Bridge Street
Cambridge CB2 1VA
Map ref: back C 3
Telephone: 01223 360545
Open Mon-Sat: 9am-7pm,
Sun: noon-5pm

18 Market Street
Cambridge CB2 3PA
Map ref: back D 3
Telephone: 01223 328574
Open Mon-Fri: 8am-8pm,
Sat: 8am-9pm, Sun:10am-6pm

Unit 2, The Quay
Cambridge CB5 8AB
Map ref: back C2
Telephone: 01223 303445
Open: Mon-Sat 8am-8pm,
Sat-Sun: 9-6pm

No smoking
Prices: coffees, espressos,
blended coffee drinks etc
(from small to large)
£1-£2.80, brownies, bagels,
sandwiches etc. £1.25-£3

Starbucks took Cambridge by storm in summer 1999, claiming three sites. They caught on immediately, demonstrating that Cambridge is hungry for good coffee. The shops have different characters. The Market Square site is a bustling centre, bright and modern, with a surprisingly pleasant seating area in the basement. It carries the full line of Starbucks' coffees and coffee paraphernalia. The Quay site is small, a handy place for a cup on the go, while our favourite is the most hidden away, formerly called the Seattle Coffee Co, on the top floor of Waterstone's Bookshop.

This is US-style choice. You can have your coffee the way you like it...

The Starbucks in Waterstone's is located at one end of a big room full of shelves on the top floor of this multi-floor bookstore. It is the only one that offers a bit of peace and quiet. On a typical day, you see students on the stools at the wooden table island, scribbling in notebooks or perusing magazines (worn copies of Dazed, The Face and today's Guardian lay about). Separate huddles converse at the low round tables. Everyone speaks in hushed tones, some looking at books or the art exhibits Waterstone's puts on for patrons.

At any Starbucks, choosing takes some effort. The coffee comes as espresso, cappuccino, macchiato, con panna, iced, as a freeze, with everything in short/tall/grande or single/double sizes. The cakes and cookies are a notch above most, a bit refined in style. (In a nice environmental touch, you can take home the coffee grounds to use as compost if you ask nicely.) This is US-style choice. You can have your coffee the way you like it.

Arjuna Whole Foods - Take Away
budget, vegetarian

12 Mill Road
Cambridge CB1 2AD
Map ref: back F 6
Telephone: 01223 364845

Open Mon-Fri: 9.30am-6pm,
Sat: 9am-5.30pm
Hot take away from noon to about 2pm
Major credit cards
Prices: stew £2, soup £1, cake £0.70

At the back of this cooperative health food store, hot wholesome vegetarian take away meals are sold at very good prices. For £2, you get a big ladleful of stew, like mild vegetarian chili, or more exotic but always flavourful choices – all 100% veg – over a heap of whole-grain rice. Mixed salad with the house oil and vinegar dressing or good freshly made

wholesome vegetarian take away meals are sold at very good prices

soups like Sweet Corn Chowder make a nice second course for £1. Along with this, try the vegetarian and vegan savouries – mushroom and tofu pie (£1.09) or the delicious spinach bhaji (£0.48), and complete the meal with sweets like carob brownies or the carrot cake (£0.70). This is the healthiest take away lunch in Cambridge. And you can pick up fresh organic vegetables or muesli while you're there.

Café Metro
budget, dessert, open early, sandwich

57 Hills Road
Cambridge CB2 1NT
Map ref: back I 6
Telephone: 01223 304304
Open Mon-Fri: 8am-6pm,
Sat: 9.30am-4pm

No credit cards
non-smoking area
Prices: soup £2.30, omelettes
£3.50-£4, salad, quiche, etc
£2.95-£3.95, filled baguettes
£2.20-£2.40, take away discount

Café metro is appropriately named. You imagine the same sort of bustling place in European cities, catering to the working, traveling public with quality espresso,

The... shop... offers an array of pizza breads, cakes, filled baguettes and patisserie (all made in-house)

quiche and baguettes. The open, two-tiered shop, decorated with blue tiles, ceiling fans and potted palms offers a tempting array of pizza breads, cakes, filled baguettes and patisserie (all made in-house). The sandwiches use fresh fillings and are made with a French dough that has a fine flavour. Café Metro does a brisk take away business, giving big discounts and is near the railway station.

Central

The Café – Woolworths

budget, children, dessert

13-15 Sidney Street
Cambridge CB2 3HJ
Map ref: back D 4
Telephone: 01223 357168
Open Mon-Thu: 9am-5pm, Fri-Sat:
8.30am-5pm, Sun: 11am-4pm

No smoking
Wheelchair access-all areas
Prices: lunch courses £3.75,
jacket potatoes £1.95-£2.95,
snacks £2.25, child meal
£1.85, cakes £0.80-£1.75

Woolworths' friendly turquoise-clad tea ladies in boaters serve up a good basic meal, with choices like fish and chips, meat pies (£3.75) or cake and coffee (£1.85). This

**inexpensive
eat-in food in
central
Cambridge...
students like
the prices as
do pensioners**

is one of the most inexpensive eat-in food in central Cambridge, and you dine in an open, well-lit space on Woolworths' first floor. The atmosphere can only be described as Woolworthian: there's a sort of white noise of general racket (they ought to patent it really) that oddly makes con-

versation easy, and yet allows kids free rein. The buffet-style eatery is a favourite with mums and dads out shopping with babes, as the adults can eat calmly while the babies exercise their lungs – and no one even notices. Students (who can make just as much noise) like the prices as do pensioners. Definitely good value.

Canadian Muffin Co

**budget, children, dessert,
open early, sandwich**

❖ *DISCOUNT VOUCHER - FREE CAPPUCCINO*

7 Bradwells Court
Cambridge CB1 1NH
Map ref: back E 4
Telephone: 01223 324544
Open Mon-Sat: 6:30am-6pm,
Sun & bank holidays: 10am-4pm
Non-smoking area

No credit cards
Outdoor seating
Prices: muffin £1.20-£1.40,
baguette/bagel/sandwich
£1.20-£2.90, baked potatoes
£1.50-£3.50, salad £1.50-£3,
Take away/students 10% off

Apart from walk-ons in old children's rhymes, muffins – often known as tea cakes – have never made it as big in

**These handfuls of
organic flour, with...
oat bràn, buttermilk,
fresh fruits, nuts and
vegetables are really
good... healthy foods**

England as in Canada. But their fortunes may be rising. The Canadian Muffin Co is on a mission to redefine muffins for the British palates as 'cup-shaped sweet bread rolls usually

eaten hot with butter' that make a great snack.
  I entered the store's ordinary shop front in Bradwell's Court full of skepticism. Improve upon an

old standard? Unlikely. The aroma of freshly baked muffins soon softened my view. In the counter display, I was greeted with an array of browned muffins with appetizing names like Rhubarb, Ginger and Toffee Apple. The store offers sandwiches, soups and potatoes and has a repertoire of over 80 varieties of muffin, including a dozen savoury types like Pesto & Olives or Pizza.

Sampling a hot blueberry muffin completed my conversion. These handfuls of organic flour, with ingredients like oat bran, buttermilk, fresh fruits, nuts and vegetables are really good. In terms of basic ingredients, they qualify as really healthy foods – low in fat and refined sugar, high in fiber and complex carbohydrates. This is a good breakfast or snack that you can enjoy on-the-go or in the pleasant upstairs room, which, thankfully, has no background music.

Cazimir

INSIDER
CHOICE

budget, dessert, sandwich, student

13 King Street
Cambridge CB1 1LH
Map ref: back D 4
Telephone: 01223 355156
Open Mon-Fri: 8.30am-5.30pm,
Sat: 8.30am-7pm, Sun: noon-5pm

No credit cards
non-smoking area
Prices: sandwiches
£1.95-£2.95, espressos/
coffee £0.95-1.85
Take away discount

I'll never cease to marvel at how a bit of paint and personality turn what might be just another café into a café of note. Located in a modern row of shops on King Street, this little glass-fronted rectangular box of a café overflows with warmth. Just inside the

This little glass-fronted rectangular box of a café overflows with warmth...

door, the freshly painted orange walls suggest something a bit lively. The exhibits of paintings on sale (most were soft abstract oils when I visited) draw you over for a look.

The clientele sit round the wooden tables and chairs eating sandwiches and drinking teas and coffees out of big, brightly coloured cups. My apple tea came in a gigantic gold cup with aqua (not turquoise) saucer that Mr T. Conran himself would admire (and no doubt he had a hand in the making of it).

But one comes into a café to eat, and in this respect Cazimir – named by the owner after her Polish hometown – comes into its own. You can get a lovely feta, olive and tomato baguette (£2.50), the Polish Sopocka, smoked pork loin with mustard (£2.85) or the best seller, the Polish Sausage with mozzarella and gherkins (£2.55). The cheesecake (£2.95 a slice), made by the owner from her own recipe, is reputedly fabulous.

And if you want to take a bit of Poland home, Cazimir sells packages of imported Polish delicacies.

Central

CB2 Internet Bistro

budget, dessert, open early/late student, veg choice

INSIDER CHOICE

❖ *DISCOUNT VOUCHER - FREE BOTTLE OF WINE*

5-7 Norfolk Street
Cambridge CB1 2LD
Map ref: back D 7
Telephone: 01223 508503
Open daily: 8am-midnight
Non-smoking area

Entertainment: readings
Credit cards except American
Express, Diners Club
Prices: breakfast £2.65-£4.95, lunch
£2.95-£3.95, dinner £10.95- £15.95

CB2, offspring of the original Cambridge Cyber Café, CB1, refines the cyber café idea with great success. It builds the concept of a lovely student haunt into a splendid free-and-easy café for a broader clientele. This

a splendid free and easy café for a broader clientele... you eat well and inexpensively

comfortably refurbished old shop also attracts a lot of students but a more mature clientele can feel just as comfortable in its large, two-storey space.

As in CB1, people come in for the super-fast internet access (but this time on classy iMacs), to check their email or surf the web for 5p to 10p a minute. The staff will help you get on line and provide instruction. The café crowd here also peruse the wall-to-wall shelves holding thousands of second hand books. Founder-manager Daniel Sturdy (father of CB1) expertly chooses the used titles for sale or exchange and he buys books too.

But the best part is the food. At CB2 you eat well and inexpensively. This is the best of café fare with lots of original touches. Coffee and half-price refills go for £1, with anything from an excellent caffe latte to cioccolata con panna for under £2. Try the delicious 'smoothies' like seabreeze or berries (£2.50) or the vegetable juices (£1.50). There is also a range of alcoholic beverages.

The food is light and tasty. The baked potatoes and toasted ciabattas, the latter served with house salads, make a fine snack, while you can get somewhat pricier evening meals with choices like 'confit of guinea fowl' and 'baked fillet of brill' that are as delicious as the fancy names. The dinner menu changes monthly.

This is good food without fuss and rush. At CB2 you can't help but want to stay a while, read a book, have another cappuccino...

Clowns

budget, dessert, open early/late, student

54 King Street
Cambridge CB1 1LN
Map ref: back D 4
Telephone: 01223 355711

Open daily: 8am-midnight
No credit cards or cheques
Prices: espresso from £1, croissant
£0.70, ham & cheese with salad £4.50

Bright pictures of clowns in all shapes and sizes are
plastered on the walls and ceiling. This is the harvest of
the yearly contest held by the café. Prizes go to the the
best artwork, and the square, wood-trimmed café is the
winner's gallery. The jumping, smiling, colourful
clowns, plus a few paper puppets
and poems, foster cheeriness that
puts everyone at ease.

> **popular with students... the good Italian food appeals to the budget eater**

Clowns is popular with students,
especially foreign students, who
often come in groups to talk at the
mushroom tables. It's the sort of
place you imagine they'll have pleasant memories of
some day, of hours whiled away.

The good Italian food, served in buffet style, appeals
to the budget eater. £4 buys a sizeable lasagne portion.
It's £5.95 with a salad. Everything is made fresh. Toasted
sandwiches and quiche (round-about £2) are popular, as
are the big £1.50-a-portion desserts like baclava and
chocolate cake. The staff serve them with a smile.

Coeur de France

dessert, open early, sandwich

39 Burleigh Street
Cambridge CB1 1DG
Telephone: 01223 518322
Map ref: back D 6
Round Church Street
Cambridge CB5 8AD
Map ref: back C 3

Telephone: 01223 518323
Open Mon-Sat: 8am-5.30pm,
Sun: 8am-3.30pm
(8am-5pm Round Church)
Prices: baguette £2.40-2.95,
coffee £1-£1.20
Take away discount

Good bread is essential to making a good sandwich.
Though many a shop sells baguettes in Cambridge, only
a few use really good bread. Coeur de France bread has a

> **he... bread has a vely consistency, eshness and flavour**

lovely consistency, freshness and flavour. The bread
and pastry dough is imported from France, then baked
daily at the café. Either shop will make you a good, inexpensive sandwich. They also sell soups and French-style
pastries like pain au chocolat and delicious-as-they-look
bright strawberry, kiwi and orange custard tartlets.

Conservatory – Arundel House

urban peace, parking

Arundel House Hotel
Chesterton Road
Cambridge CB4 3AN
Map ref: back B 3
Telephone: 01223 367701

Open daily: 9.30am-10pm
No smoking
Hotel car park at back
Prices main courses: £5.95-£7.95

Try to picture this: you, quietly calm, sitting in a plush rattan chair in a big and airy glass conservatory. Overhead, a fan slowly circulates, and the bright daylight is filtered by the green overhanging leaves of ceiling-high potted plants. A cup of good coffee and a big pot for refills rests handy on the table alongside a fresh scone.

one of the best-kept secrets in Cambridge... quiet... a place to get away from the bustle

That's what it is like at the Arundel House Hotel Conservatory, one of the best-kept secrets in Cambridge. Not a vast number of people know about this place so it rarely gets crowded. What you are likely to find is quiet. Being at the back of the hotel, away from the street, the Conservatory is wonderfully peaceful. There is no smoking and use of mobile phones is forbidden. This is a place to get away from the bustle, to be by oneself, to meet for a discreet chat or to relax.

For £1.25 you get the biggest pot of tea or coffee around, properly prepared so that the tea actually brews and the filter coffee is fresh. Tea cakes and desserts are served all day, and, if you feel so inclined, the menu offers a full range of meals – from ciabatta sandwiches to salmon salad at meal times. You can even order bottles from the large hotel wine list. Can you picture yourself now?

Copper Kettle

budget, children, dessert, student

4 King's Parade
Cambridge CB2 1SJ
Map ref: back E 3
Telephone: 01223 365068
Open Mon-Sat: 8.30am-5.30pm,
Sun 9am-5.30pm

No credit cards
Children welcome
Prices: £1.30 cappuccino,
slice of cake £1.90,
cakes £0.90-£2.30,
hot courses about £5

Unbeknownst to the world, The Copper Kettle is Cambridge's secret of success. Being a prime fueling station for its students and many a senior academic, you overhear the famous Cambridge discussions (As I was saying, oh yes, and ninethly....) along with an incredible amount of pure twaddle. It must surely be the victuals at this café that are responsible for the Great Thoughts that have made this city world renowned – at least for the past few decades. (Cambridge does pre-date it by a tad). Therefore we commend to you one of the best spots for eavesdropping and a really good, cosy place for inexpensive, hearty grub.

a really good, cosy place for inexpensive, hearty grub

You get a good view of King's College and chapel, a £5-or less hot meal – lasagne and the roast beef with Yorkshire Pudding, veg and potato are among the hearty staples – and a big selection of pastries. Make your choice at the cafeteria-style counter and take a seat in one of the wood-panelled stalls or the oak chairs and tables. Then ready your mind for high thoughts (your own or others). On cold days the place generates such ferment that the windows get positively steamy. Of course, no one is at all certain how much of that is brilliant thinking and how much is just hot air....

Corner House Restaurant

budget, children, pizza

7 King Street
Cambridge CB1 1LH
Map ref: back D 4
Telephone: 01223 359962
Open Mon-Fri: 11.30am-2.30pm,
5-9.30pm, Sat-Sun: 11.30am-9.30pm

No credit cards
Take away
Prices: full breakfast
£4.57-£4.95, main
courses £2.50-£4.25,
wines £5.95-£6.45

Every table at the Cornerhouse Restaurant is equipped with placemats, one neat medium-sized bottle of ketchup, a glass dispenser bottle of vinegar, a pair of salt and pepper shakers, a sugar bowl and a drinking glass stuffed with folded paper napkins. This, plus knife, fork and spoon, of course, is what you need for the hearty

Nothing trendy here, just good value... come in for the remarkably modest prices and plain good food

hot meals served to you by a polite waiter in a white shirt and black bow tie. The food served in this dark wood-panelled, neatly maintained dining room is of the chips-with-everything café sort – roasts, omelettes, fish – with choices reflecting the legacy of the previous Greek owner – moussaka, kebab and such – and more recently pizza, courtesy of the new Italian owner. And it's cheap. Roast Pork? That'll be £3.59. Moussaka? £3.75. A bottle of wine? £5.95-£6.45. Nothing trendy here, just good value. Students, pensioners and families come for the modest prices, comfortable stall-style tables and plain good food.

Central

Haagen-Dazs Café

children, dessert, open till late

Market Passage
Cambridge CB2 3SN
Map ref: back D 3
Telephone: 01223 721833
Open Mon-Thu: 10am-10pm,
Fri-Sat: 10am-11pm, Sun: 11am-11pm

Non-smoking area
Outdoor seating
Prices: £1.95 one scoop,
chocolate sundae £4.30,
espresso £1.10

In great scoops, over waffles, on fruit, with cakes and pies, in squat and tall sundae glasses, Haagen-Dazs serves gourmet ice cream at its shop in the narrow and picturesque Market Passage. The attraction of the café is its handiness to the centre, a street-side café ambience and, of course, the way a score or so varieties of ice cream come with chocolate, butterscotch (etc) sauces, with chunks of cookie, nut crunch, maple syrup, whipped cream. I must say my pecan pie with vanilla (£3.60) met with approval, as did the sundaes the children ate with great relish. They do serve a light sorbet shake at £3.20, for the calorie conscious.

Martin's Coffee House

budget, dessert, open early, pets, sandwich, student, veg choice

INSIDER CHOICE

❖ *DISCOUNT VOUCHER- FREE COFFEE OR TEA*

4 Trumpington Street
Cambridge CB2 1QA
Map ref: back H 4
Telephone: 01223 361757

Open daily: 7.45am-5pm
No credit cards
Prices: tea £0.60, jacket potatoes
£1.70-£2.95

In the fraternity of cafés frequented by students, Martin's occupies a special position as the oldest and certainly among the most loved. A bit worn it may be. A gallery of events notices adorn the fading wallpaper above 1970s high-backed wooden stall tables. It may be a bit crotchety (at least the sign says, 'Children left unattended will be sold as slaves,') but that's the way people know and love it. For some 40 years Martin's Coffee House has served inexpensive food. Ex-students and former patrons are forever coming back in and remarking to the staff that the place is 'just like it used to be'.

The customers are still students, academics, tourists.

They come, just as previous generations, for a cozy place to chat, to sit out in the garden on warm days, and, not least, for the budget food (unless it has been more than 20 years since their last visit). Martin's serves a top notch espresso and cappuccino, along with Columbian coffee. You get freshly-made cakes and a good breakfast for £3.70 (the usual – bacon, eggs, tomatoes, sausages, beans, toast, jam and coffee or tea). A jumbo hot chocolate sells for £1.95. There are sandwiches, jacket potatoes and hot meals served cafeteria style.

Beware. If you drop in you too may come back years later to see if it's 'just like it used to be.'

Nguyen's Street Stall
Unusual places to eat, veg choice

Street food stall
Silver Street Bridge
Cambridge
Map ref: back F 2

Open: lunch on warm days
No credit cards
Prices: eggrolls £0.90-£1, satay £2

What's this? I saw two young women walking away from a hot dog stand on Silver Street Bridge by the Mill Pit biting elegantly into spring rolls! Investigation revealed that the stall had a sideline in Vietnamese food.

A few moments later I was sampling spring rolls which came in a choice of three fillings: meat or veg- **Thi K N Nguyen and his wife... make eggrolls the traditional way** etable, at 90p a shot and crab for £1. The vegetarian filling includes bean sprouts and the wrappers are crisp and fresh-tasting, the fillings succulent and not greasy. How come? They are made by people who know how. Stall owner Thi K. N. Nguyen and his wife, who came to this country 17 years ago, make the eggrolls the traditional way. Using wrappers made of wheat flour, not rice flour as in Vietnam, is about the only adaptation.

Octagon Lounge
dessert, sandwich, urban peace

❖ *DISCOUNT VOUCHER- FREE AFTERNOON TEA*

De Vere University Arms Hotel
Regent Street,
Cambridge CB2 1AD
Map ref: back F 5
Telephone: 01223 351241

Open daily 10am-11pm
Prices: baguettes £3.10-£3.50, baked potatoes £3.50, tea £1.85, coffee £1.85-£2.10

Central

As far as elegant comfort goes, you can't beat this central rotunda. The room is a focus of the hotel dating back to 1834. Recently tastefully refurbished and modernized, the high-ceilinged room is outfitted with colourful soft armchairs that are just the ticket for a relaxed meeting or chat. It is popular with friends and businessmen who want a quiet, casual place with tea, snacks and no need to book.

As far as elegant comfort goes, you can't beat the rotunda...

Pret A Manger
open early, sandwich

19 Petty Cury
Cambridge
CB2 3NA
Map ref: back E 3
Telephone: 01223 315000
Open Mon-Fri: 8am-5.30pm, Sat: 8.30am-5.30pm, Sun: 11am-5.30pm

No credit cards
No 17.5% VAT on take away
Prices (eat in): sandwiches/
baguettes £1.17-£3.25,
salads £3.16,
desserts £0.60-£1.69

This Pret A Manger looks much like all the others. The refrigerator cabinet along one wall is filled with interesting sandwiches – Thai chicken, super club, hoummos and red pepper wrapped in a tortilla. It has good desserts – cakes, mousse, yoghurts – and a range of £0.99 coffees. You can take your meal out or eat at the indoor counters with high stools. Promising no additives or chemicals, Pret A Manger pretty much lives up to its motto 'top quality at top speed'. If a quick sandwich on the run is what you want, Pret A Manger has got your number.

If a quick sandwich on the run is what you want, Pret a Manger has got your number

Savino's
dessert, open early, sandwich

INSIDER CHOICE

3 Emmanuel Street
Cambridge CB1 1NE
Map ref: back E 4
Telephone: 01223 566186
Open Mon- Sat: 8am-11am,
Sun: 10am-6pm

Take away
Prices: sandwiches £3.90-£4.85,
pain au chocolat £0.85,
espresso £1

I don't know what it was – the aroma of the caffe latte, MTV glowing on the big screen above the refrigerated drinks cabinet or just the friendliness of the place. But as soon as I came into Savino's, perched myself on a stool and took a sip of my coffee, I forgot completely why I had come in – to do a review. A newspaper provided for customers on the countertop attracted my eye (It was the day a big pop star had revealed all – and I don't usually read the Sun) and I just took a deep breath and took a break.

I did recover after a while and looked around, finding an altogether pleasing Italian-style café bar. Bright, with a cheerful staff casually chatting with the customers, Peter Savino promises everything you buy is of excellent quality. This is not an idle boast. The sandwiches cost a bit more than elsewhere, but here the ciabatta bread and pastries are imported from Italy and baked freshly every day. Only genuine mozzarella, provalone and Parma ham are used. The coffee is Illy brand, which makes a distinctly more flavourful cup.

> **Savino's promises everything you buy is of excellent quality. This is not an idle boast**

Most of all you get a little personality, which in these days of packaged restaurants is most rare. The sandwiches have family names. 'Alla Luca' (£3.90), after the owner's son, is, of course Luca's favourite, with Parma Ham, mozzarella, virgin olive oil, oregano and tomato. There's also an 'Alla Tara', for his daughter, and 'Alla Sara'. And now that I've said nice things about the café, there'll be an 'Alla....' Just kidding.

Scudamore's Boat Yard
children, dessert (ice cream), garden, unusual places to eat

Granta Place
Mill Lane
Cambridge CB2 1RS
Map ref: back F 2
Telephone: 01223 359750

Open weekends only April, May and September, daily June, July and August: 10am-7pm

If the weather's good and you're just looking for a pleasant, inexpensive place for an ice cream, snack, coffee or tea, then stop here. Scudamore's Boat Yards sets out plastic tables and chairs under a big leafy tree at the top of the mill pond under Silver Street Bridge. This is a good cheap place to enjoy the view of the Common and the punts. Ice cream is £1 a scoop or £3 for sundaes.

> **a good cheap place to enjoy the view of the Common and the punts**

This is also the launching point for punting trips up the river to Grantchester, which is one of the most delightful experiences Cambridge has to offer. It is quite a trip.

Central

Tatties Café Restaurant
budget, children, dessert, sandwich

11 Sussex Street
Cambridge CB1 1PA
Map ref: back D 4
Telephone: 01223 323399
Open Mon-Sat: 8.30am-7pm,
Sun: 10am-5pm

Outdoor seating
Children welcome
Prices: jacket potatoes £1.95-£6.25,
full breakfast £5.95, espresso £1

Since 1981 Tatties has served baked potatoes in these high-ceilinged rooms bathed in daylight from the big shop front windows. The speciality comes a score of ways, with baked beans, cheese, butter, and more.

baked potatoes... make a good filling meal and keep the price of a meal a minimum

They make a good filling meal and keep the price of a meal down to a minimum. You can also get a range of baguettes (£1.95-£3.95) on bread baked fresh daily and huge breakfasts – with double sausages, eggs, tomatoes, bacon and coffee or tea for £5.95.

A lot of people come in for drinks and a dessert. Tatties sells a seriously tempting American Blackberry Cheesecake and a big selection of humongous ice cream sundaes and creations. Although Tatties gets busy at midday, service is prompt at the cafeteria-style counter. This is food with character and you can get in and out without taking too long.

Terrace Bar - Garden House Moat House Hotel

INSIDER CHOICE

garden, parking, urban peace

Garden House Moat House Hotel
Granta Place, Mill Lane
Cambridge CB2 1RT
Map ref: back H 2
Telephone: 01223 259988
Open daily: 10am-11pm

Prices: afternoon tea £3.95,
sandwiches £3.75-£3.95,
omelette £5.95, desserts
£1.95-£2.25, espresso/
cappuccino £1.95

The management at the Garden Moat House have recently started to overcome a severe shortage of names. The Restaurant used to be called The Restaurant. Now it's The Riverside Brasserie. The Lounge now is the Terrace Bar. A rose is a rose is a rose etc and The Terrace Bar, by whatever name, makes a good quiet place to relax. It has deep fabric chairs, low tables and,

one of the finest vantage points on picturesque Cambridge

for a hotel, a wide not-too-costly menu, plus bar service.

What most distinguishes The Lounge is its view of the hotel garden along the River Cam. Sitting back on one of the armchairs, you see the green grass and trees through the full-length windows. If the weather is warm (or if the outdoor heaters are out on cool evenings), you can sit in the garden at the wooden tables (not picnic tables) each with a peach sun umbrella. From the garden you can see more, beyond the trees, onto the Common, the mill pond and the river. This makes it one of the finest vantage points on picturesque Cambridge.

Trockel Ulmann und Freunde INSIDER CHOICE

dessert, pets, sandwich, student

13 Pembroke Street
Cambridge CB2 3QY
Map ref: back E 3
Telephone: 01223 460923
Open Mon-Sat: 9am-5pm,
summer hours (July, August): 10am-3pm

No credit cards
No smoking
Prices: baguettes £1.50-
£2.50, cakes £1.40

The name sounds a bit like a 60s Euro rock group, but Trockel Ulmann und Freunde is a café with exceptionally good cakes, sandwiches and four different home-made soups. Rather than regulars like carrot cake, you'll find Poppyseed Apple or Avocat Liqueur. The best part is that these moist, flavourful goods

> **rather than the plain old fillings, you are likely to find sandwiches a cut above: mozzarella and sun-dried tomatoes for instance**

are really home-made by the German couple who own the café. The baguettes, on the other hand, are imported daily from exotic Shelford. It's proper bread, and, rather than plain old fillings, you are likely to find sandwiches a cut above: mozzarella and sun-dried tomatoes, for instance. You won't get fancy coffees or drinks, and the café no long sells German wines like it did some years ago, but Trockel Ulmann und Freunde (named after a café in Germany) is among the cosiest cafés around. Perhaps it's the friendly staff, classical music or arty posters, but I think it's something about sitting on the high stools leaning over bright red, yellow and blue tables as daylight pours in through the big front windows.

Central

Cambridge Lodge Hotel & Restaurant

garden, parking, special occasion

139 Huntingdon Road
Cambridge CB3 ODQ
Map ref: back (just above) A 1
Telephone: 01223 352833
Open Mon-Fri: 7-9pm, Sat: 7-9.30pm,
Sun: 12.15-1.45pm (open for weekday
lunches for parties of 10 or more by
arrangement)

Non-smoking area
Children welcome
Booking advised
Prices: (children half
price) weekdays 2-3
courses £14.90-£20.50,
Sat £20.50 (set menu),
Sun £10.95-£15.95

The meal at The Cambridge Lodge begins when you make your way either to the garden – if it be summer – or to the well-appointed lounge. Sitting in the walled, mature garden of this mansion imparts a sense of serenity that sets the mood for dining. Equally, in the lounge, with its comfy chairs and sofas, you just naturally sit back. It helps that the mock tudor Cambridge Lodge is a modestly sized, intimate place – the garden, flowers trees and all, covers not more than a tennis court; the lounge is about as big as a parlour.

the walled, mature garden of this mansion imparts a sense of serenity that sets the mood for dining

You can order your meal from the lounge or garden, and then relax with a drink until your choice from the classic French and English cuisine is prepared. The menu changes daily, with a typical example listing starters such as curried carrot and courgette soup, cornets of ham and French-style tossed salad. A typical main course selection might be pan-fried lamb's liver, roast loin of pork and charcoal-grilled sirloin steak. There are always vegetarian options, like a filo pastry spring roll or stir-fried vegetables, along with a choice of desserts, sorbets and cheeses.

This is served in a comfortable hotel dining room, with a well-set table, linens and attractive glassware. This makes a meal an event – and the good food completes the picture. I feasted on an elaborately prepared trout, with all the trimmings. This had attractive garnishes and sauces. The food was rich and flavourful. The style is traditional, which goes well with the solicitous service and decor.

The Galleria
**business lunch, terrace (balcony),
open early, special occasion**

33 Bridge Street
Cambridge CB2 1UW
Map ref: back C 2
Telephone: 01223 362054
Open daily: 8am-10.45pm

Credit cards except Diners Club
Prices: lunch courses
£4.95-£7.95, dinner £7-£13

If the day is warm, you can sit out on the lovely balcony
at the Galleria. Right over the River Cam, the balcony
tables afford the best view of passing punters on the
River Cam. Most seem to
be having a ball, giggling,
wobbling, splashing and
bumping into one anoth-
er, and occasionally top-
pling into the water. It's
just as much fun (and a
lot more dignified) to
watch while partaking of the refined Galleria menu
(recently revamped by a new chef). The show opens
early, providing a range of classy breakfasts like Eggs
Benedict (£3.95), which in case you've never enjoyed it
is muffin with poached eggs, sliced ham and hollandaise
sauce, or Salmon Royale (£4.95), scrambled eggs with
salmon and chives. These are available at lunch, along
with a light continental menu – more café, than restaurant – ciabattas with chicken, steak or chargilled marinated vegetables; chicken or vegetable stir-fry, which you
can also eat in the airy and bright interior or out on the
pavement tables.

> sit out on the lovely
> balcony at the
> Galleria. Right over
> the River Cam, the
> suspended tables
> afford the best view of
> passing punters

When the sun begins to set, the Galleria takes on
more the air of restaurant rendezvous, the sort of place
friends or couples can dine before an evening out. The
evening menu offers substantial and classical choices
like chargrilled squid (£4.50) and lambs' shanks with
spinach and marinated artichokes (£11).

Rocket Salad

Hobbs Pavilion Creperie & Grill

budget, children, dessert, terrace, urban peace, veg choice, wines by the glass

INSIDER CHOICE

❖ *DISCOUNT VOUCHER -CHILDREN EAT FREE*

Parker's Piece
Cambridge CB1 1JH
Map ref: back E 5
Telephone: 01223 367480
Open Tue-Sat: noon-2.15pm, 6-9.45pm

No smoking
No credit cards
Prices: main dishes
£4.95 -£11.50

The setting is perfect for a film: a cricket pavilion looking over huge grassy Parker's Piece. The drama begins with a panoramic shot of the sunny lawn, with people on its long walkways stepping around the locally famous 'reality check' lamp post (planted squarely in mid-path for dreamy people not looking where they are going). Then, dramatically, a medium shot zooms in on the fashionable crowd sipping wine and eating pancakes on the elegant veranda.

for over 20 years owners Stephen and Susan Hill have served brilliant, original and tasty pancake concoctions

This scene is Hobbs Pavilion Restaurant – creperie and grill – where for over 20 years owners Stephen and Susan Hill have served brilliant, original and tasty pancake concoctions drawing from Franco-English traditions. (Perhaps inspired by an 1838 banquet for 15,000 on the Piece to celebrate Queen Victoria's coronation.) A meal on the veranda is classic, of course, but eating inside is delightful too. The cosy dining area is light and airy, with chairs and tables that are simple and rustic, like the pavilion, named after cricket hero Sir Jack Hobbs, who opened the reconstructed building in 1930.

For anything from £4.95 to £8.95, there are choices like Dijon Chicken or hot chillied lamb, and vegetarian and vegan selections, such as leek, ginger, cashew and cheese or specials like chillied aubergine with yoghurt. A pancake is an ample main meal, and may be complemented by the soup of the day (like a buttery and delicate cream of lettuces). There are main-course salads and £7.95-£11.50 chargrill selections, and an eclectic wine list, including vegetarian and organic wines. Vegetarians have a good choice. Most people can't resist the desserts. The delicious sweet pancakes, £3.85-£5.75, are wrapped around ice cream that Hobbs makes in-house, with chocolate sauce or creme de menthe liqueur.

This is seriously good food, modestly priced, making Hobbs Pavilion a restaurant of special distinction.

Loch Fyne Fish Restaurant & Oyster Bar

business lunch, special occasion

37 Trumpington Street
Cambridge CB2 1QY
Map ref: back F 3
Telephone: 01223 362433
Open daily: 9am-10pm

Weekend booking advised
Prices: £0.90 (one oyster),
main courses £6-£16.95,
£29.50 (lobster platter)

It is always such a joy for foodies when a new restaurant opens in Cambridge. Especially when, like the Loch Fyne Oyster Bar, situated in the 500-year old Little Rose pub, it has a radically different character.

The restaurant and bar are extremely attractive: lots of pale wood tables and simple decor. In the daytime the whole restaurant is sunny and light and at night the bustle is very inviting. The bar is definitely a draw for a glass of chilled white wine and an oyster or two. Sensibly, you can buy oysters singly (£0.90) as well as in multiples of three. The more you buy the cheaper it gets. And they are exquisite, with a wonderful, full flavour and creamy texture.

The flexibility of the menu makes Loch Fyne ideal for large groups and the indecisive, as well as the oyster-lover

Oysters are what Loch Fyne do best but the rest of the menu offers lots of other seafood and fish, which can, depending on the choice, be either fabulous or fair. My Loch Fyne Ashet (half portion £8.95 main portion £14.95), a cold platter with four different salmon preparations, juxtaposed a wonderful Bradan Rost (salmon roasted in the smoke kiln) with a good smoked salmon and an indifferent gravadlax. Service is a little patchy... some of the staff (and not, it seems, the most experienced) know what they are doing and others are lost. In wine terms, Loch Fyne has recognised what the French have always known: that Loire white wine is perfect with shellfish. One of the cheapest bottles on the list, the Gros Plant (£10.95), is also one of the best for this sort of food.

Loch Fyne is great for oysters and white wine lovers and a good place to try lots of different flavours. It isn't cheap (unless you're having a couple of oysters) but since the menu encourages customers to select any combination of starters and main courses, in any order, you can still try what's available on a budget. The flexibility of the menu makes Loch Fyne ideal for large groups and the indecisive, as well as the oyster-lover.

Central

Midsummer House Restaurant

business lunch, garden
special occasion

INSIDER
CHOICE

Midsummer Common
Cambridge, CB4 1HA
Map ref: back B 5
Telephone: 01223 369299
Open Tue-Fri, Sun: noon-1.45pm
(last orders), Tue-Sat: 7-9.45pm

Booking advised,
essential for dinner
Prices: £19.50 for 3-course
lunch, £39.50 for 3-course à
la carte (lunch and eve),
3-course Sunday lunch £25

I was prepared to be disappointed by this extremely highly-rated restaurant. I wasn't. Midsummer House is everything it claims to be and more, offering exceptional food, a lovely location and perfect service.

The House is almost in a world of its own: stepping through the conservatory you enter an enclosed garden, with parasol-shaded tables, flowers, mirrors and a tiny fountain. Here you can sip apéritifs whilst looking at the menus and trying an olive or caper. Once the ordering is complete and the table readied, customers are led into the elegant creams and blues of the interior, ready for the show to go on.

> **I was prepared to be disappointed by this extremely highly-rated restaurant. I wasn't. Midsummer House is everything it claims to be and more...**

For it is a show. The waiters and maître d' work in symphony to ensure that everything is performed to the highest standards. Even the serving of a simple slice of bread is done with panache. After the grand beginning the food is in danger, as in many places, of being a bit-player but it is definitely the star. Clean, classic and real flavours predominate: there are no superfluous garnishes or gimmicks. A strong French influence is evident in chef Daniel Clifford's style of cooking: prime ingredients like rabbit, foie gras and lemon sole are the focus and sauces and vegetables are used to highlight and enhance them.

What is interesting about Midsummer House is that many consider it expensive. But quality is not cheap. And, if you consider that a 3-course lunch costs £19.50 and that the main course is thus around £10-£11 Midsummer House is no more expensive than most restaurants. The wine list is also accessible, covering the whole gamut, from £12.95 to £250. Many of the house choices are under £20 and lots are served by the glass.

If I was going to be finicky about anything I would say that on a hot summer's day the conservatory resembles a humid greenhouse and needs either a few more open skylights or the blinds pulled. And, at times the service was a little too grand for comfort. However, my overall sense is that Midsummer House is close to perfect.

No. 1 Kings Parade

business lunch, dessert, special occasion, unusual places to eat, wines by the glass

❖ *DISCOUNT VOUCHER - FREE DESSERT*

The Cellars
1 Kings Parade
Cambridge, CB2 1SJ
Map ref: back E 3
Telephone: 01223 359506
Children welcome until 9pm
Groups of up to 90 welcome

Open Mon-Fri: noon-3pm,
6-11pm, Sat: noon-11pm,
Sun: noon-10.30pm
Music: live Thursday eve
Prices: light lunch £3.95-£7.95,
dinner courses: £9.95-£17.95
optional 15% service charge

No. 1 Kings Parade is hard to judge from the street. On the corner opposite King's College, all you see is a glass front with a door and a stairwell. The restaurant is in the cool cellars below. On entering, it takes a minute to get used to the light, but once your eyes adjust, you see the brick floor and vaulted ceiling of this bar-restaurant create an intimate, cave-like space in a 350-year-old basement cellar.

No. 1 King's Parade has a lot to offer, not least a central location. It has more range than first meets the eye

This is a bar <u>and</u> restaurant, which means you get a broad range of choice – from cappuccino (£1.80) to fruit juices to spirits, vermouths and especially fine wines, which are sold by the glass and by the bottle.

The spirit carries over into the dining. You can enjoy menus such as the 'summer express lunch' featuring light lunches like fish and chips (£6.95) or sandwiches such as smoked bacon and tomato (£5.95). The dinner menu offers delicacies like genuine Sevruga Caviar (£25 for 30g) and entrées ranging from pastas starting at £9.95, whiskey cured salmon gravadlax (£10.95) or an 8oz fillet of scotch beef for £16.95.

No. 1 King's Parade has a lot to offer, not least a central location. It has more range than first meets the eye and whether you come for a drink or for dining, the staff treat you in the same, friendly way. The fare may not be the most inexpensive around, but it is very good. Most of all the atmosphere is informal, with a buzzy, lively feeling at lunch and candle-lit atmosphere after dark.

Rainbow Vegetarian Café

budget, children, dessert, student, vegetarian

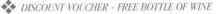

INSIDER CHOICE

❖ *DISCOUNT VOUCHER - FREE BOTTLE OF WINE*

9a Kings Parade
Cambridge CB2 1SJ
Map ref: back E 3
Telephone: 01223 321551
Open Mon-Sat:11am-11pm

Children's menu
No smoking
Prices: main courses £6.25,
cakes £2.25,
drinks £1.35-£1.65

Vegetarian food can be an us and them matter. But not at Rainbow Vegetarian Café. Attracting a mostly non-veg crowd, the café sells good food that happens to be vegetarian.

> **Attracting a mostly non-veg crowd, the café sells good food that happens to be vegetarian**

What's more they cater to about every dietary need that comes their way – vegan, gluten free, nut-free, low fat and are very carefully to list the ingredients of everything they serve. This is a practice that a lot of people – veg or non – would like to see other restaurants adopt too. It costs nothing and puts a lot of people at ease.

While the vegetarian selection at most restaurants is simply a meatless item, Rainbow makes food that is good on its own merits, often drawing from ethnic traditions. Take a favourite, the Latvian Potato Bake, a big portion of potatoes, mushrooms, carrots, garlic and herbs topped with cheese or the Mexican specialities with tortillas. This is not just meatless food – these are foods meant to be made this way – and using good basic foodstuffs (including free range eggs). Of course, you can also get the local fare in the form of cakes, including the best carrot cake in town, lager, cider and organic wines.

All this is served by a long-serving and friendly staff in cosy, unfancy basement lodgings across from King's College.

Restaurant 22

special occasion, veg choice

INSIDER CHOICE

22 Chesterton Road
Cambridge CB4 3AX
Map ref: back A 4
Telephone: 01223 351880
Open Tue-Sat: 7-10pm

Booking advised
Children: none under 10 unless
particularly well-behaved
Prices: 4-course set meal £23.50

It would be easy to miss the gourmet restaurant at Mitcham's Corner – not only because you would not expect to find one there. The converted house has maintained enough of its air of residential privacy to fool the casual passerby. The single word 'restaurant' next to the front door is in the style of a house name plaque; only a small menu outside and the words 'Dining Room' woven discreetly into the stained glass suggest anything other than suburban domesticity beyond. 22 is the sort of place known by its reputation.

the meal mixed traditional French and English cookery in a delightful way... surroundings were relaxed and the service uniformly excellent

As you climb the few steps up to the green front door the residential feel is so strong that you can't help wondering whether you should knock first. The exterior, however, ultimately works in the restaurant's favour; once inside, it is all soft and homely – even cosy – and you feel like a welcome guest. The main room, the size of a typical living room in a Cambridge terraced house, has the traditional Victorian feel of formality – with full table settings, flowers and folded napkins. Some people dress up and others come casually – both feel fine.

The £23.50 fixed-price menu consists of a monthly set of choices, excluding service, with optional fish and cheese courses for £6 extra. There are always four starters and four main courses, including a vegetarian option in each. The meals are designed by the owner David Carter, who teaches cookery at Cambridge Regional College and recruits his chefs from his students.

To begin, I ordered delicious grilled sardines with garlic and rosemary and my partner a duck flavoured with Armagnac, which though tasty, didn't have the rich flavours either of us were expecting. This was followed by a fresh mixed leaf salad, and then came the main courses. I had the daube of beef with roast aubergine and thyme mash, while my partner had honey-roast chicken with yoghurt and lime oil. This she said 'came well up to expectations,' while my beef was beautifully cooked, if a tad too salty. The desserts – we had a bitter chocolate and chestnut tart and a lemon mascarpone

Central

cheesecake – were both exquisitely presented and excellent.

Overall, the meal mixed traditional French and English cookery in a delightful way. We had a great evening. The surroundings were relaxed and the service uniformly excellent. The food was very enjoyable with flavours that might not be bold, but made me want to come back.

The Riverside Brasserie

business lunch, parking, special occasion

INSIDER CHOICE

Garden House Moat House Hotel
Granta Place, Mill Lane
Cambridge CB2 1RT
Map ref: back H 2
Telephone: 01223 259988
Open daily: 12.30-1.45pm,
7-9.45pm

Non-smoking area
Booking advised at weekend
Children welcome
Prices: starters £3.95-£5.50,
pasta £8.95, fish specialities
£10.95-£12.95, featured
dishes £9.95-£19.95

What are the elements of elegance? I think I found them here. The newly refurbished interior of the high-ceilinged Riverside Brasserie (formerly 'The Restaurant') is truly spacious, with wrap-around full-wall windows looking over the hotel garden, the River Cam and beyond, adding to the sense of openness. Acres of room separate the white linen-covered tables, each set with broad blue glass plates

the chef has some principles – and they come through. The Riverside Brasserie is clearly an extraordinary restaurant

and matching water goblets so big you might need both hands to pick one up. The cutlery is precisely placed on a linen napkin of vast proportions, while the well-cushioned chairs all have arms. Sofas at tables in the centre are piled with pillows upholstered in subdued reds and golds coordinated with trendy copper and brass lamps and ornamentation on the wine cabinet and entrance. This is tasteful decoration that sets one at ease.

They call this a brasserie to give it a continental feeling, but what strikes is the predominance of light dishes – pastas, fish and chicken. The starters include appetising choices such as a 'punt of mussels', a large bowl of mussels with white wine, shallots and cream (£5.50) or Potato Crab and Cheese Strudel on Plum Tomatoes and Basil (£4.75). There are five fish choices, and featured dishes ranging from Braised Lamb Shank (£11.95) to a vegetarian Aubergine and Tomato Bake

(£8.95). Six different pasta choices include the Linguine with Spinach, Goat's Cheese and Pine Nuts (£8.95), which is what I tried. This was a big portion of pasta mixed with olive oil. Spinach, slices of half-melted goat's cheese and a sprig of parsley gave it an artful look. It was served with the attention one would expect in exclusive clubs.

But what most pleased about this dish were the flavours. This was not, as so often is the case, sauce swilled around pasta yielding one muddy flavour. You could taste the spinach, the linguine and the oil. You could whisk in a bit of the strong cheese as you pleased. As in good music, the elements were distinct, individual and clear, not all alike.

This dish suggests that the chef has some principles and they come through. The Riverside Brasserie is clearly an extraordinary restaurant with quite ordinary prices.

Roof Garden Restaurant
business lunch, terrace

Cambridge Arts Theatre
St Edwards Passage
Cambridge CB2 3PJ
Map ref: back D/E 3
Telephone: 01223 578930
Open Mon-Sat 10am-10pm, closed
some non-performance evenings

Hot food served: noon-9pm
Children's menu
Outside terrace seating
Prices: main dishes £6.99-
£12.95, desserts £3.75-£4,
minimum £10 per head
6-8pm, when fully booked

Come to the Roof Garden for the wonderful lightness of the big open space. An arching, modern glass roof and walls surround the dining area, where the floors are wood-tiled and the walls a minimalist white. Potted plants growing to above head height break up the rows of café tables. The music – usually jazz or something classy – and the colourful theatre posters complete the modern feeling. On warm days, you can sit outside on the terrace. It's upmarket, casual and comfortable.

> Come to the Roof Garden for the wonderful lightness of the big open space

This is an in-town rendezvous place. Situated in the Arts Theatre, it also makes a convenient place to eat before or after a show. The selections are somewhat limited and can be pricey, but are well-chosen and quite well-prepared. Choices like Supreme Chicken with Stilton and wine sauce and Caesar Salad are politely served by waitresses in white continental-style aprons.

For a pre-theatre drink, espresso or pastry, try the O'Briens Café on the ground floor. The First Floor and Founders rooms can be booked for large groups.

Central

"venue"

business lunch, open till late, special occasion, wines by the glass

 INSIDER CHOICE

❖ *DISCOUNT VOUCHER - FREE KIR ROYALE DRINK*

66 Regent Street
Cambridge, CB2 1DP
Map ref: back F 5
Telephone: 01223 367333
Open Mon-Sat: noon-3pm,
6-11.30pm, Sun: noon-10pm
Credit cards except American
Express and Diners Club

Non-smoking area
Wheelchair access inc toilets
Booking advised at weekend
Entertainment: evening jazz and
classical, (£1 cover charge)
Prices: £4.95-£15.95, 2-course
set lunch £9.50, 2-3 course set
dinner £12.95-£15.95

Cambridge is a small town. "venue", however, is a big city restaurant. There is nothing magic about what it offers: good food, impeccable service, interesting wines and a customer-oriented attitude. What is special is the way it presents what is, to my mind, an unbeatable package.

Walk in through the front door of this modern restaurant and you are confronted by a somewhat clinical interior. Wood floors, pale wood tables and chairs, white walls. Look again and you spot a column of pink,

What is special is the way it presents what is, to my mind, an unbeatable package

a bright red wall, an orange chair. At the back of the room a black piano sits, strangely unobtrusive, next to a microphone. Finally, by the bar, completely blacking out all those white thoughts you had a few seconds ago, there is a massive bright flower arrangement. No pastels and greens here: these are primary colours let loose with all the restraint of a kindergarten fingerpainting class.

The food follows the same style. Like the decor, it has a classic structure: high quality ingredients and finely tuned techniques. But it also lets rip with a vengeance, allowing taste combinations that you might have questioned until now: seared yellow fin tuna with sweet potato chips; rocket and parmesan soup with red pesto; malibu and coconut brûlée. You will be taken round the world and back again, both in terms of the menu and the wine list. And yet, to the restaurant's credit, it knows when to use the best of British produce such as cheeses.

In their search for excellence "venue" have achieved great things and where it shows is in the details: Illy coffee for example, easily the best on the market, asking how you want your fish cooked (some restaurants can't even manage that for steak), the amazing paper used for the menus. I could go on but that would leave me no space to tell you that this is one of the few places that is trying to be ethical: wherever possible, organic, or at the very least free-range, produce is used. And, if that weren't enough, there is live music most nights from some of the most talented jazz and classical musicians in the region.

Chili's Texas Bar & Grill
budget, children, veg choice

162-164 East Rd
Cambridge CB1 1DB
Map ref: back D 7
Telephone: 01223 505678
Open Mon-Sat: 10.30am-11pm,
Sun: 11.30am-10pm

Non-smoking area
Children's menu
Wheelchair access inc toilets
Take away
Prices: main dishes
£7.99- £13.99, £5 budget lunch

'Howdy partner, come on right in,' isn't what the nice hostess who seats you at Chili's is wont to say. More likely, it's something commonplace, like 'smoking or non-smoking?' But looking around at the restaurant's interior, with Americana hung all about – saddles, wheel barrow with plaster chilis and working model train – you begin to notice how the staff speak in normal British accents. You've come to a little bit of Texas – the commercial, packaged end anyway – that has been transported to Cambridge, minus the Texas drawl.

> **You've come to a little bit of Texas – the commercial, packaged end anyway – that has been transported to Cambridge, minus the Texas drawl**

This has advantages. Chilis, a big airy modern restaurant serving up to 250 diners, has what people say they want and it draws good crowds. Health conscious? There are 'guiltless' low-fat healthy choices (grilled chicken or pasta). Vegetarian? Chilis outdoes itself, providing seven selections, plus the option to substitute a black bean patty or turkey patty for the 'Texas-sized fresh ground' beef burgers. There's a children's menu, a 'lunch for under a fiver' menu, a bar with big-screen TV for the drinkers and lots of choice for the finicky majority. As one might expect, the food is reliably good, served in largish proportions and flavoured to suit the typical palate (which is to say, with nothing too overpowering). In fact, if you want a lot of spice at Chili's you have to request it specially.

Chili's has the largest choice of Mexican food in Cambridge: enchiladas, nachos, guacamole, quesadilla in all sorts of Texan hybrids, many with cute trademarked names like 'wings over buffalo'. I found the veggie quesadilla – cheese, mushroom and artichoke in flat bread – a treat. Many people go for the sizzling steak 'fajitas', the blackened fish, or ribs with barbeque sauce, which come with potatoes or rice with black beans. These are hearty meals, enough to satisfy anybody with Texas-sized hunger.

Footlights
budget, children (by day), dessert

The Grafton Centre
Fitzroy Street
Cambridge CB1 1ER
Map ref: back D 6
Telephone: 01223 323434
Open daily: noon-11pm

Non-smoking area
Children's menu
Credit cards except
American Express
Wheelchair access via lift
Prices: main courses £ 5.95-£12.95

Over the past couple of decades, Footlights has become part of the Cambridge scenery as a landmark near the main entrance of the only big shopping mall, the Grafton Centre. It has always served food that suits a wide audience – steaks, fish, pasta and a signature smattering of Mexican food. In case the Mexican touch sounds like a threat of hot sauce, the owners have taken care to post a sign on the door saying: 'Our Mexican food is cooked to cater to British- European tastes'.

By day shoppers from the mall – which Footlights overlooks through a huge glass wall – find it just the ticket

The public's taste for Mexican food has waned over the years, so the menu (though still with a good guacamole) has moved more into mainstream English. Food ranges from light snacks for under £4, to T-bone steaks at £12.95 and a 'light' lunch choice for under £5. The children's menu appeals to even the pickiest youngsters.

Footlights is the place for the mall rendezvous. In one room with an arching, wood finish ceiling (it used to be a chapel), the restaurant is a place to see and be seen. The staff are friendly. By day shoppers from the mall – which Footlights overlooks through a huge glass wall – find it just the ticket, as do many office parties, The evening attracts a somewhat younger crowd, more likely to appreciate the beer by the pitcher, bar snacks and saucily named cocktails – Sex on the Beach, Slippery Nipple and (do they dare try it?) the Orgasm.

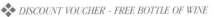

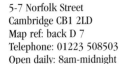

CB2, offspring of the original Cambridge Cyber Café, CB1, refines the cyber café idea with great success. It builds the concept of a lovely student haunt into a splendid free-and-easy café for a broader clientele. This comfortably refurbished old shop also attracts a lot of students but a more mature clientele can feel just as comfortable in its large, two-storey space.

> **If you drop in you too may come back years later to see if it's 'just like it used to be'**

The Varsity

budget, business lunch, children, French, special occasion, veg choice

INSIDER CHOICE

❖ *DISCOUNT VOUCHER - FREE CUP OF COFFEE*

35 St. Andrew's Street	Booking advised
Cambridge CB2 3AR	on weekends
Map ref: back E 4	Prices:
Telephone: 01223 356060	main courses
Open Mon-Fri: noon-2.30pm, 5.30-10.45pm,	£6.50-£9.75
Sat: noon-10:45pm, Sun: noon-10pm	

This restaurant is a Cambridge institution. Established in 1954, by the present owner's father, it has survived the influx of chains and trendy brasseries and now newly-decorated with fresh white walls and blue and white tablecloths it has brought itself up-to-date without losing an ounce of its charm.

> **established in 1954 it has survived the influx of chains and trendy brasseries and now newly-decorated... has brought itself up-to-date without losing an ounce of its charm**

The food is a mix of Cypriot and French with a medley of other influences. It is served in large portions and is very good value. It is also delicious. A moussaka (all of £6.50) comes with a Greek salad (well, Greek-ish, there was only one chunk of feta and the rest was a usual enough mixture) and fills a plate. It is meaty, creamy, and stuffed with aubergines. One of the best choices, unfortunately denied the single diner since a minimum of two people need to order it, is the Cyprus Meze. If you know nothing about this sort of food, this is the perfect introduction. It includes taramasalata, hoummos, tzatiki, Greek salad, halloumi cheese, chillies, Greek mushrooms, olives, calamars, moussaka, whitebait, lamb and a skewered pork kebab. There is also a vegetarian version. All for £9.75 per head.

Wines are available by the glass or carafe (£5.50 for a half-litre) as well as by the bottle (try the Cypriot Othello) and are also reasonable. If you're not drinking alcohol the minerals are a little steep (Perrier £2.50) although this is probably the only place in town to buy Steal water...

The Varsity's windows face onto the street, so it's a good place for people-watching. Don't believe all that you see though... if it looks packed, remember there are two more rooms upstairs.

Central

The Bengal

business lunch, open till late, special occasion

INSIDER CHOICE

❖ *DISCOUNT VOUCHER - FREE CURRY*

4 Fitzroy Street
Cambridge CB1 1EW
Map ref: back D 6
Telephone: 01223 351010
Open daily: noon-2.30pm,
6pm-midnight
including bank holidays

Take away 10% off
Service charge may be levied on
advance bookings
Prices: starters £2.20-£3.35,
breads £0.80-£1.85,
curries £4.10-£8.95,
tandoori £4.95-£9.90

Located at the entrance to the Grafton Centre, the Bengal's exterior reveals little of the open, high-ceilinged, tastefully decorated room inside. Among the Indian restaurants, it has the most modern decor, devoid of excesses of plastic greenery. Around the 15 or so well-spaced tables along either side of the room are comfortable benches and high-backed rattan chairs. Each table has a fresh linen tablecloth – a white one over a pink one – baby blanket-sized serviettes folded hat-like on the plates and fresh flowers. The menu spans the typical range, from biryanis and baltis to tandoori and tikka, with one or two novelties, like Quail Masala.

The Bengal, serving Indian food in Cambridge since 1973 is without a doubt one of the very best Indian restaurants in town

The Bengal's nan (£1.85) was about as perfect as they come, light brown without burns, even and without very thin patches, lightly buttered, fresh and warm. The Okra (Bhindi) Bhajee (£2.20), a side vegetable curry dish, came with a beautiful sprinking of colour made up of red and green peppers, but most of all the vegetable was thoroughly fresh and delicately flavoured. Last, I tried the Fish Ayr-Birian, a thin slice of fried fish covered thickly with spiced tomato sauce. I found it tasty, a bit heavy and bony, but good.

Overall, I was impressed. The food may cost a bit more than it does at some Indian restaurants, but the Bengal, serving Indian food in Cambridge since 1973, is without a doubt one of the very best Indian restaurants in town.

The Cambridge Curry Centre *INSIDER*

**business lunch, open till late,
special occasion**

CHOICE

45-47 Castle Street
Cambridge CB3 OAH
Map ref: back B 1
Telephone: 01223 363666
Open daily: noon-2.30pm, 6-12pm

Take away 10% off
Prices: starters: £2.50-£3.95,
tandoori, £5.75-£7.95, specialities £6.50-£9.50, curries £3.80-
£8.50, breads £0.95-£1.90

As far as decor goes, The Cambridge Curry Centre follows the typical curry house pattern, but is done up to a
higher standard. The two ground floor rooms have a blue
and pink theme, with good traditional Indian paintings on
the wall. There's a fish tank
with carp and a little basement with additional tables.
Each table has a fresh carnation and comfortable
chairs.

**The chicken tandoori
was the best we
tasted... this meal
was a delicious
sample of a very fine
cuisine**

In our quest for the best
in Indian, we ordered familiar items to compare with
the others. At this meal, two items stood out as exceptionally good: the nan (£1.45) and the half tandoori
chicken (£4.50). The nan was properly browned, without burns, light and buttered, which always suggests
that the food is attentively cooked. The chicken tandoori was the best we tasted, thoroughly soft with out
too much chili and well marinated. Fabulous.

Our other dishes were good, but ordinary. The
prawn korma (£4.50), a cream sauce with baby
shrimps, was a bit too sweet and the shrimps slightly
tough, while the Bhindi Bhaji, okra curry, tasted fresh,
but seemed a bit bland. Every meal has highs and lows,
but overall this meal was a delicious sample of a very
fine cuisine.

The Curry Mahal

open till late

3/5 Miller's Yard
Mill Lane
Cambridge CB2 1RQ
Maf ref: back F 2
Telephone: 01223 360409
Open daily: noon-2.30pm,
6pm-midnight

Take away 10% off
10% service charge may be levied
on advance bookings
Prices: breads £1.60-£2.30,
tandoori £6.10-£9.50, specialities
£7.15-£9.95, curries £4-£8.95

Semi-hidden under arched recesses at the back of a
courtyard off Mill Lane, the Curry Mahal has a challenge to attract patrons. But the word gets out and the

Central

waiters work hard to make diners feel at home in the restaurant's two medium-sized rooms, where the mood is like many Indian restaurants – soft lighting, red carpets, pictures of Indian scenes on the walls.

Despite the name, The Curry Mahal has a good range of tandoori as well as curries. We started with a half tandoori chicken (£6.50), which came sizzlingly aromatic with onions. This first success, succulent and spicy, was followed by well-spiced samosas (£2.70), the triangular pockets of potato and vegetable (with meat too if you want) that passed the taste test (but were served without the usual mint sauce). Our lamb bhuna (£4.55), with good chunks of reasonably tender meat, was similarly well satisfying. The dal soup, on the other hand, was bland and the paratha bread, only adequate.

we were impressed by the good cooking and came away well satisfied with the food. The friendly staff added a special warmth to the visit

Overall, we were impressed by the good cooking and came away well satisfied with the food. The friendly staff added a special warmth to the visit.

Curry Queen Tandoori Restaurant
budget, open till late, special occasion

106 Mill Road
Cambridge CB1 2BD
Map ref: back H 8
Telephone: 01223 350407 / 351027
Open daily: noon-2.30pm,
6pm-midnight inc bank holidays

15% take away discount
15% student discount
Prices: starters £1.95-£3.95,
tandoori £5.45-£9.90,
specialities £4.95-£11.45,
curries £3.30-£7.45,
breads £0.65-£1.90

In business since 1972, the Curry Queen is one of the most established and biggest Indian restaurants in Cambridge. It has 10 or so tables on the ground floor and room for another 64 diners upstairs. The dining rooms are decked out in the customary style, with tables lining either side of well-kept, dimly lit rectangular rooms.

the cooking was good, definitely placing the Curry Queen among the better Indian restaurants

I found the service prompt if somewhat indifferent in attitude. But this did not detract from the fine meal. The soft flat nan bread (£1.60) big and evenly cooked, flopped over the edges of the plate. It had a nice sprinkling of sesame seeds. The channa masala (£2.05), chick peas in mixed spices, proved fairly good – well seasoned, if a tad too salty. The two big pieces in my half order of tandoori chicken (£5.45) were the biggest winners, moist and flavourful.

On balance, the cooking was good, definitely placing the Curry Queen among the better Indian restaurants in Cambridge. Its prices are middling and students get a 15% discount.

The Golden Curry

business lunch, open till late, special occasion

INSIDER
CHOICE

111-113 Mill Road
Cambridge CB1 2AZ
Map ref: back H 8
Telephone: 01223 329432 / 467412
Open: daily 12 noon-2:30pm, 6-12pm, including bank holidays

non-smoking area
Take away 10% off
Prices: starters £2.50-£3.15, meat specialities £6.25-£10.95, tandoori £5.50-£6.75, breads £0.80-£1.95, curries £3.85-£6.85

The Golden Curry is spacious and, being on a corner with big windows on two sides, the restaurant is light and airy. The upkeep of the restaurant is head and shoulders above most. No tired wallpaper, peeling paint or musty smells. The large dining area, the bathrooms and the bar all looked new and are kept immaculate.

The attention given to the surroundings carries over to the food. In fragrance, taste and freshness, everything won top ratings, making The Golden Curry our overall favourite Indian restaurant in Cambridge. Our half tandoori chicken (£5.50) came on a

> In fragrance, taste and freshness, everything won top ratings, making The Golden Curry our overall favourite Indian restaurant in Cambridge

sizzling hot tray with onions with a wonderful aroma that whetted our appetites. The spicy and tender pieces, sprinkled with freshly chopped corriander were served on a bed of fresh salad with a lemon ready to squeeze and a light minty sauce. Our vegetable side dish, channa masala (£2.15), chick peas in herb sauce with bits of tomato and green pepper, looked beautiful and tasted just as good. The nan (£1.70) came cooked just right, showing a careful touch.

The Golden Curry has much the same menu range as the ones that call themselves Tandoori restaurants do. So this is a good place for whatever you fancy at a reasonable price, even if, just like virtually all the other Indian restaurants, the people who own and run it happen to be Bangladeshi. I asked my waiter why this is. Bangladeshis, he said, are just the best cooks. In the case of the Golden Curry, I have to say I agree.

Central

The Gulshan Indian Cuisine
business lunch, open till late

106 Regent Street
Cambridge CB2 1DP
Map ref: back F 5
Telephone: 01223 302330 / 301071
Open daily: noon-2.30pm, 6-12pm
including bank holidays

Take away 10% off
Prices: curries £3.95-
£8.25, breads £0.85-£1.95,
half tandoori chicken
£5.25, tandoori dishes
£5.05-£9.25

Behind a lens of coloured glass that is the shop front window, the Gulshan offers a quiet, softly lit private dining room subdivided by half-panels. With a fresh carnation on each table and the tones of Indian film music floating through the restaurant, this sets a calm mood for talking and dining.

I settled on prawn korma (£5.05), nan bread (£1.70) and a vegetable samosa (£2.15). Apart from the samosas, which were just okay, the meal rated a success. The korma, a cream and herbs dish, came on a tiny wok placed on a heating plate. It was excellent, with a rich and spicy taste and lots of tender shrimps. Along with a good nan, it made an excellent meal, one good enough to keep me coming

a quiet, softly lit private dining room... an excellent meal, one good enough to keep me coming back

back. I especially wanted to try dishes recommended by the owner, Ayr Bhuna (£6.95), which is Indian fried fish with onions and coriander, and Chicken Tikka Shaslik Masala (£6.55), marinated meat cooked in the clay tandoori oven with capsicum, onion and tomatoes.

Maharajah Indian Tandoori
business lunch, open till late, special occasion

INSIDER CHOICE

9-13 Castle Street
Cambridge CB3 0AH
Map ref: back B 1
Telephone: 01223 358399
Open daily: noon-2.30pm,
6pm-midnight
Take away

Credit cards except Switch
Prices: starters £1.50-£3.95,
tandoori £5.50-£10.50, specialities
£7.95-£9.85 curries £4.10-£7.95,
breads £0.80-£1.95
10% service charge added to bill

Rather than one big room, the Maharajah has a series of smaller ones, with tables of different shapes and sizes and well-cushioned high back chairs. These spaces create cosy, fairly private nooks with space for some 80 people in the restaurant.

The ground floor has a red and gold theme; upstairs, it's black and silver. Together with the good lighting and pleasing table settings these rooms are the most stylishly and richly decorated of any Indian restaurant in Cambridge. The atmosphere helps, but, of course, is no substitute for cooking well – and in this respect, the Maharajah does exceptionally well, producing excellent dishes with service to match.

A polite waiter in a sort of blue doorman's uniform took my order. The menu has a typical range, with a few imaginative items, such as fruit curries. I tried one of these, a Malayan Lamb with Pineapple (£4.50), curried lamb with a slice of pineapple on top; it had a pleasant rich flavour with an appealing hint of fruitiness. I also had a soft and well-seasoned channa masala, chick pea with mix herbs and spices (£2.50) – a bit soft, but quite good. The tasty triangular vegetable samosa (£2.40) came with a bowl of orange mint yoghurt sauce that was among the lightest and most flavourful I have tasted. This I ate with a tasty, if a touch too crisp, nan bread (£1.95), making for a successful, really good meal. The prices are a bit higher than some Indian places, but the Maharajah makes a meal that is sure to satisfy.

> **most stylishly and richly decorated of any Indian restaurant in Cambridge... the Maharajah does exceptionally well, producing excellent dishes with service to match**

Nirala Tandoori Restaurant

budget, open till late

7 Milton Road
Cambridge CB4 1UY
Map ref: back A 4
Telephone: 01223 360966
Open daily: noon-2.30pm, 6-12pm

Take away
Prices: starters £1.85-£2.95, curries £3.80-£6.75, specialities £4.65-£8.75, tandoori £4.95-£8.10, breads £0.75-£1.70

Looking at it, The Nirala Tandoori is one of those places you might miss. Though plain in exterior with a drab interior, this restaurant makes some of the better Indian food around. It proves that rule that Indian restaurants (in Cambridge at least) are hard to size up by their appearance.

When I ate in the small un-airconditioned dining room, just big enough for a dozen tables, the friendly waiter brought out a soft and spicy chicken tikka

> **he Nirala may look rdinary, but it erves Indian food hat makes the aste buds happy**

Central

(£4.95) that melted in my mouth. It came with really fresh salad. The nan (£1.40) met the highest standards, being not too sweet and evenly cooked. My okra, Bhindhi Bhaji (£2.10) was good, if a bit pale in flavour. Overall, the Nirala may look ordinary, but it serves Indian food that makes the tastes buds happy.

Pipasha Restaurant

INSIDER CHOICE

business lunch, parking, open till late, special occasion

529c Newmarket Road
Cambridge CB5 8LG
Map ref: back C 8 (just beyond)
Telephone: 01223 211459
Open daily: noon-2pm, Mon-Sat:
5.30-11.30pm, Sun: noon-11pm
Take away discount at least 10%
Delivery £1.50 up to 3 mile radius

Parking at the back
Prices: starters £2.30-£3.95,
tandoori £5.50-£9.50,
vegetarian dishes £3.95-
£5.95, specialities £6.95-
£10.95, curries £4.30-
£9.95, breads £0.85-£1.85

Pipasha is brand new, in a newly refurbished former pub on Newmarket Road and with a fresh approach to Indian and Bangladeshi food. Rather than adopting the standard menu, as most do, it has branched out a bit, offering some regional selections, like the very tasty Chicken Sylhet (£5.90), from Bangladesh. It even offers an Indian wine and Bangladeshi beer. But what matters most is that it

it takes great care in preparing the food and in serving it... Pipasha heats the dish at your table to bring it to just the right temperature... delightful

takes great care in preparing the food and in serving it. This is evident from the way the meats and vegetables are prepared – well cut and varied as well as fresh. The flavours come out and just before serving the dishes, the Pipasha heats the dish at your table to bring it to just the right temperature. Our vegetable Balti (£5.95) had a good balance of spices (if perhaps on the oily side), and we had a tasty channa (chick pea) masala (£1.85) side dish. Served in its attractive, if conservatively decorated new dining room by a friendly polite staff, the meal proved altogether delightful.

Standard Tandoori
budget, open till late

52 Mill Road
Cambridge CB1 2AS
Map ref: back F 6
Telephone: 01223 312702 /
322423
Open daily: noon-2.30pm,
6pm-midnight

10% service charge
on reserved tables
Take away/students 15% discount
Prices: starters £2.25-£3.95,
specialities £6.95-10.50, baltis £7.75,
tandoori £6.10-£8.95, curries £4.50-
£7.50, breads £0.80-£2.05

Huge, rather artful bouquets of wall-mounted plastic
greenery decorate this deep shop front restaurant. Rows
of tables run down either side of the long rectangular
room and Indian music softly wails at you over the speakers.

The menu offers a broad selection, from tandoori to
curries, balti dishes (the stir-fried curries) and a considerable wine list. We tried the tandoori chicken starter
(£2.70), which came well
marinated and very ten-
der, though the bed of
salad was slightly wilted.
The channa masala
(£2.05), herbs and chick

**with the 15 percent
discount for students
or take away, it has
some very attractive
prices**

peas came without much gravy but with a nice, gentle
flavour. The nan bread (£1.60), was huge, flopping over
the edge of the plate and brushed with oil– a treat.

The Standard Tandoori makes good food, and with
the 15 percent discount for students or take away, it has
some very attractive prices.

Star of India
business lunch, open till late

71 Castle Street
Cambridge CB3 0AH
Map ref: back B 1
Telephone: 01223 312569 /315834
Open daily: 12-2:30, 6pm-midnight
including bank holidays

Take away 10% discount
Prices: starters: £1.95-
£4.25, tandoori £4.95-
£8.95, specialities £6.95-
£9.95, curries £3.85-£9.50,
breads £0.95-£1.90

Behind a handsome big window just over the crest of
Castle Hill, The Star of India occupies a deep rectangular room with a spacious high ceiling. This place has a
fresh look from a complete refurbishment in mid-1998
and is arranged in the typical way, with rows of tables
and high-backed chairs along the wall. It makes for a
pleasant setting, leaving out some of the fussier elements of Indian restaurant decor – like plastic greenery.

We ordered a few familiar items, which came

Central

promptly. We first tried our nan (£1.50), one of the flat Indian breads, finding it just pretty good, if lacking in softness. The channa Masala (£2.10), chick peas in mixed spices, proved well spiced, chili-hot and of an attractive colour, while our other vegetable dish, the Bhindi Bhaji (£2.10), okra curry, tasted quite good, without the saltiness of some. With these we ordered the lamb tikka (£5.85), one of the dishes cooked in the clay tandoori over. This came sizzlingly fragrant on a hot metal plate and proved well cooked

superior Indian food... a good bet for a good Indian meal and a calm, pleasant environment

and flavourful.

This was superior Indian food, definitely better than most we have had in the Cambridge Indian restaurants. What The Star of India offers may not be adventurous, but is surely a good bet for a good Indian meal and a calm, pleasant environment.

Tandoori Palace

open till late, parking, special occasion

68 Histon Road
Cambridge CB4 3LE
Map ref: back A1 (just above)
Telephone: 01223 506055 / 360817
Open daily: noon-2:30, 6pm-midnight

Take away discount 10%
Parking lot at the back
Non-smoking area
Prices: starters £1.75-£2.95, tandoori £5.50-£8.95, specialities £5.95-£9.95, curries £2.95-£6.95, breads £0.75-£1.40

A Cambridge Evening News restaurant critic recently named the Tandoori Palace the top Indian eatery in Cambridge. It is certainly among the top few. So if you are the sort who always get a second opinion, this is the choice for you.

The Tandoori Palace serves an excellent Indian meal, one of the best in Cambridge and in a fine pleasant atmosphere

In a brick building that was once a pub, the restaurant follows the customary pattern of decor. The well-lit and maintained dining room has tables with good spacing, and each table sports a fresh flower in a vase. The service is polite in a casual, friendly way, making a change from the bored waiters in some establishments. Most unusually, out of more than a score of Indian restaurants in Cambridge, The Tandoori Palace is the only one I have seen with a woman employee.

As for the menu, it follows the usual pattern, with

everything from tandoori to balti and curries on offer. I had a tasty vegetable samosa with a good stuffing (£1.95) and a minty, chili-hot yoghurt sauce and really fresh salad. My half tandoori chicken (£4.50) was tender and flavourful. The waiter thoughtfully asked before he moved the chicken from the hot plate to my plate, as few do. My nan bread (£1.40) was ever so slightly on the over-brown side, but soft and not too sweet. Finally, the channa (chickpea) masala (£1.95) tasted fresh, and although it was without garnish, had a good, mild flavour.

The Tandoori Palace serves an excellent Indian meal, one of the best in Cambridge and in a fine pleasant atmosphere.

The Victoria Tandoori

budget, open till late

INSIDER CHOICE

12b Victoria Avenue
Cambridge CB4 1EH
Map ref: back A 4
Telephone: 01223 313331
Open daily: noon-2pm, Sun-Thu:
6pm-midnight, Fri-Sat 6pm-12.30am

No credit cards
Take away/delivery over
£20 within 5 mile radius
Prices: main courses
£2.80-£8.50

I must confess that my reasons for experiencing the Victoria Tandoori the first time around were of the random sort. I'd moved house, I wanted hot food and I wanted it late at night. It just so happened that the Victoria was round the corner so, without even glancing at the menu, and expecting no more than what I had eaten in several hundred Indian restaurants in the past, I went in.

Beyond the tiny doorway and the predictable hallway decor is a great surprise. Here is an Indian restaurant that produces consistently fresh and tasty dishes at extremely reasonable prices. Two people can easily eat for £15 or less. There are only about ten tables and post-pub closing at weekends it can get quite busy but in general there is little problem getting in. The staff are smart and welcoming, the sort who remember you after just one visit. For my money, Victoria Tandoori is one of the best in Cambridge.

produces consistently fresh and tasty dishes at extremely reasonable prices... for my money one of the best in Cambridge

Central

Bangkok City
business lunch, special occasion

INSIDER CHOICE

24 Green Street
Cambridge CB2 3JX
Map ref: back D 3
Telephone: 01223 354382
Open Mon-Sat: noon-3pm,
6.15-11pm, Sun: 6.15-11pm

10% service charge for
parties of 5 or more
Prices: main dishes
£7-£8.50, noodle/rice dishes
£7-£8.25, set meal £20-£22

Behind its white, flat facade, in a small dining room with Thai statuary and wall hangings, bright flower-pattern tablecloths and soft Asian pop music in the background, Bangkok City serves light and good Thai food. I

light and good Thai food... smooth and tasty, without too much chili... a good meal every time no matter what you order

sampled the two-course set lunch (£7.50). My green bean fish cake starter, consisting of three deep fried patties, came with a dip of fish sauce, chili and slices of cucum-

ber. Delicious. I followed this with green curry, with big pieces of chicken, coconut milk, bamboo shoots, red peppers and peas over steamed white rice. It was smooth and tasty, without too much chili. The lunch was satisfying, well served and relaxed. It was typical of food at Bangkok City. This restaurant does not serve the cheapest of Thai food in the city, but you can pretty much count on having a good meal every time no matter what you order.

Charlie Chan
Chinese Restaurant
business lunch, open till late, special occasion

INSIDER CHOICE

❖ DISCOUNT VOUCHER - 10% OFF SET MEALS

14 Regent Street
Cambridge CB2 1DB
Map ref: back E 4
Telephone: 01223 359336
Open daily: noon-2.15pm,
6-11.15pm

Non-smoking area
Music: Fri-Sat, jazz
10% service on parties of five or more
£15 minimum-Sat evening
Prices: noodle/rice lunch £4.30-
£4.80; main dishes £5.30-£16.50

Charlie Chan's looks a tad fancy, with low lighting, decently spaced tables and service that is friendly but reserved. In fact it is quite casual. That's why on any given day you'll see students dining beside office goers, businessmen and tourists. They come for the tasty, aromatic and well-presented Hong Kong-style Cantonese food and the pleasantly classy, but not formal, atmosphere.

The menu lists a select 80 or so items, like our Sweet and Sour Chicken (£5.30), which came glistening with tangy sauce and adorned with tomatoes and yellow peppers. Sesame seeds sprinkled over the Singapore noodles (£4.30) enriched the fragrance of a well-balanced mix of spring onion and pork flavours. These sorts of dishes put Charlie Chan's in the top class of Chinese restaurants in the area. Prices range from middling to above average, and the portions can be modest (dishes are served on a oval plate about as big as an A5 pad), but you can count on getting good quality food.

pleasantly classy, but not formal, atmosphere... you can count on getting good quality food

Among the favourites, you'll find six versions of set menu. These seven or eight course meals at £14.50-£30.80 per person, incorporate seafood delicacies like lobster and crab at the top end and more common ingredients (prawns, bamboo shoots and beef and egg fried rice) at the low end. We tend prefer the à la carte, but for those who don't these are sumptuous feasts.

In the evenings, the upstairs Blue Lagoon Lounge opens at Charlie Chan's, which is truly more elegant and where live jazz – keyboard, trumpet and sax – is provided on Friday and Saturday nights.

Chato Singapore Restaurant

business lunch, special occasion

2-4 Lensfield Rd
Cambridge CB2 1EG
Map ref: back H 5
Telephone: 01223 364115
Open Tue-Sat: noon-2pm,
6-11pm, Mon: 6-11pm

10% service added to bill
Prices: noodle/rice lunch
£4.65, meat courses:
£4.95-£7.70, set menus £20.30-
£24.20

The large plate glass windows at the Chato Singapore restaurants give passers-by a feeling for the experience inside. In well-lit pastel rooms, rolled pink napkins punctuate the white linen tablecloths. A burst of lilies decorate a focal point bar under a dome of coloured glass. The scene recalls a hotel lobby, stylish, calm and discreet. Once inside, you are shown your seat by one of the team of attentive waiters and waitresses, who complement the atmosphere with good and prompt service.

You feel pampered, even when the restaurant is full, which is quite a feat... the cooking is good

You feel pampered, even when the restaurant is full – which is quite a feat. It is the sort of service that attracts business people at lunch and couples who take

Central

over in the evening. The Chinese/ Malay/ Indonesian food and the atmosphere set the right tone and are accompanied by a good wine list – £9.50 to over £20 a bottle. You can smoke all but cigars.

The à la carte menu is limited, so most opt for the set menus – A through D – for a minimum of two diners. These are minor banquets with lots of food and a price to match £20.30 to £24.20. Satay features on all, and the grilled meat-on-a-stick is always a winner. The peanut sauce is not too thick and offers a hint of chili. This is followed by choices like steamed scallops, stuffed crabs and lemon chicken attractively served on white plates. Though Chato's dishes are not especially adventurous in style, the cooking is good.

Chopsticks

budget, open till late, student

INSIDER CHOICE

22a Magdalene Street
Cambridge CB3 OAF
Map ref: back C2
Telephone: 01223 566510
Open Mon: noon-2.30,
Tue-Sun: 5.30-11.30

No credit cards
B-Y-O bottled alcohol, no corkage charge
Prices: meat courses £5.95-£7.15, vegetable £4.10-£4.30

This tiny Ye Olde England shop front attracts so many people that they line up for a chance to get in on on busy nights. Good and hearty food is the draw. With only a score of seats inside, the restaurant soon fills up with its young and boisterous clientele. Couples, friends, under 40s mostly, bring their own bottles of

people... line up for a chance to get in on busy nights... The food is the kind families in the south of China... eat at home

wine for relaxed and easy meals. Students, who are the biggest fans, come in, throwing their rucksacks against the wall, and make the place home.

The owner, Mrs. Lee, takes it all in her stride. Helped by her 60-year old mother, she cooks the dishes all in the open kitchen at the back – you might as well be in the kitchen the place is so small. You can watch them stir in the woks, chucking in ingredients, ladling in sauces and flipping it all around with practiced flair. The aroma of the kitchen permeates the room.

At lunch, when a £5.95 two-course meal is on offer, the place calms down, but in the evening, the cooks are shouting to the waitress over the hubbub and sounds of cooking. It gives Chopsticks character. The food is the kind families in the south of China, especially Hong Kong and Canton, eat at home – with a lot of seafood choices like the hot Kung-Po King Prawns (£7.15) and popular dishes like Moo-shu vegetarian (stir fry in pancakes) at £4.30. The Singapore Noodles (£5.70) went down a treat, with a good proportion of prawn and red-cooked pork among the noodles.

Dojo Noodle Bar
budget, student, veg choice

INSIDER
CHOICE

Unit 1 &2, Miller's Yard
Mill Lane
Cambridge CB2 1RQ
Map ref: back F 2
Telephone: 01223 363471
Open Mon-Thu: noon-2.30pm,
5.30-11pm,
Fri-Sun: noon-11pm

Credit cards except
American Express
No smoking
Take away
Prices: side dishes £2.45-
£3.70, noodles £4.60-£5.85

To eat at Dojo is to enter modern Asia in a space warp. The aromas hit you first. Hints of tingling sauces, lemon grass, coriander, sizzling meats and steaming noodles tempt the senses at the door. Just inside, the lightness of the rectangular, high-ceilinged room, windowed on three sides, and the cool light pine decor beckons to the phalanx of closely packed back-to-back benches and tables.

noodles are prepared freshly with recipes drawing from Japanese, Chinese, Vietnamese and Thai influences... with some 'fusing' of these traditions

The first problem is which way to face at the table. At Dojo, places are set so that you sit next to dining partners, sharing a wide seat with the next table. This caused us some awkward moments as we sorted ourselves. But then the ambiance took over. Amid the bustle of cooking from the open kitchen and conversations (this being Cambridge, sounding very weighty) the menu demands a close eye. At this pan-Asian restaurant, eight varieties of noodles are prepared freshly with recipes drawing from Japanese, Chinese, Vietnamese and Thai influences, with some 'fusing' of these traditions. The flavours tend to be delicate – gentle rather than powerful – which seems about right for the clientele.

Food comes in ceramic bowls as big as grass sun hats with a bamboo spoon and chopsticks. Along with several fried and steamed rice dishes, there are more than 20 noodle choices, ranging from thick white Japanese Udon to thin rice noodles or ramen, and you can have them in soup, wok-fried or in sauces like oyster or Japanese curry. Each a meal in itself. We found the Thai fusion Hoi Sin Tom Yum (£5.85), delicious. If you

Central

want a tantalizing extra try Yakitori, chargrilled chicken with red pepper and pineapple served piping hot off the grill (£3.55), or another of the varied Asian delicacies that come as side dishes. You'll be transported to pan-Asia.

Hot Pot Chinese Restaurant
budget, children, open till late

66 Chesterton Road
Cambridge CB4 1EP
Map ref: back A 5
Telephone: 01223 366552
Open daily noon-2pm, 6-11pm
(Fri-Sat until 11.30pm)

Credit cards for over £20 only
Take away service/
delivery within 2 miles
10% service charge and
£10 evening minimum
Prices: dishes £2.50-£6

The Hot Pot offers one unusual dish for two or more diners that makes a meal into something like an everybody-dips Swiss fondue feast, but without the cheese: a Chinese hot pot meal. The hot pot, often called Mongolian hot pot for its supposed origins, is a doughnut-shaped tureen with a coal fire underneath and a sort of smoke stack jutting up the middle. The tureen is placed at the centre of the table and filled with boiling soup; you order dishes of thinly sliced pieces of meat, fish and vegetables and dip them into the broth, cooking them at the table. It's fun, delicious and especially good on those cool Cambridge evenings.

> Mongolian hot pot... delicious and especially good on those cool Cambridge evenings.... costs a lot less than in the city centre

The restaurant's droopy lace curtains inside the shop window, the tired-looking awning and plain interior do put some people off. You get few frills, of course, no white linen tablecloths, low lighting or elaborate wall decorations. The quality of the cooking can be hit and miss, but a meal costs less than in the city centre.

Other than serving Hot Pot, the restaurant has a typical Chinese menu of nearly a hundred items: all the usual duck, chicken, beef and pork dishes – the double cooked pork in spicy sauce is a winner (£3.80) along with a prawn with ginger and spring onions dish (£5.50). I found the Singapore noodles plain but tasty.

Hot Pot is worth a try. The restaurant has been attracting a steady clientele from the neighbourhood for 15 years. It gets so busy on some evenings that bookings are recommended.

Peking Restaurant

business lunch, children,
special occasion

INSIDER
CHOICE

21 Burleigh Street
Cambridge CB1 1DG
Map ref: back D 6
Telephone: 01223 354755
Open daily: noon-2.30pm,
6-10.30pm

No credit cards
10% service charge added
Prices: meat/fish main dishes
£10-£17, set meal: £30

The Peking's white facade stands out in a row of non-descript shops along a pedestrianized shopping street, but not in a very distinguished way. Neither are the owners, the Kerrs, from Taiwan, much into advertising. They have relied for many a year on word of mouth and it has served them well. It doesn't take long for any-one seeking a good Chinese meal to find this modest shop front and its pine-panelled, friendly interior.

among the best Chinese food in Cambridge and in good portions... The menu is pages long, listing more than 200 choices

You'll get among the best Chinese food in Cambridge and in good portions though at somewhat higher prices. Moreover, you can have almost any sort you want. The menu is pages long, listing more than 200 choices, with the list seemingly growing all the time and written in between lines of type, with lots of exot-ica rarely seen on Chinese menus (such as deep fried shredded venison). The staff are helpful if this is over-whelming, and a £30 a person set menu provides a ver-itable banquet for four, but you can't go wrong with a few well-chosen dishes.

For starters, try the Mu Shu Pork or vegetables with pancakes (£10) or the deep fried seaweed (£5), which is crunchy and delicious. Hot and sour soups (£4 each) are a pungent follow-up and we liked the Szechuan style Yu-hsiang chicken, pork, prawns or aubergine (£7-£13) with steamed rice. Add a light plate of Chinese vegetables (£7) if very hungry and for a bigger budget, try the sea bass (£17), which can be fried and is deli-cious steamed (but takes a bit longer).

Pho Coffee House

budget, children

32a Regent Street
Cambridge CB2 1DB
Map ref: back F 5
Telephone: 01223 462080
Open Mon-Sat: 8.30am-9pm,
Sun: 10am-9pm

No credit cards
Prices: snacks £1.40-
£1.90, Vietnamese
rice or noodle dishes:
£2.50-£4

The newest addition to Cambridge's East Asian cuisine is Pho, offering Vietnamese food to take away or eat in at the tiny five-table shop front. It is the sort of food that Vietnamese eat at home, requiring only heating up or a minimum of cook-

the sort of food that Vietnamese eat at home... Mine was delicious

ing. The main dishes consist of meats like roast duck (£3.95) or char-grilled chicken with lemon grass over rice (£3.75). You can get Banh Cuon Chay, a vegetarian steamed rice pancake with fish sauce. Mine was delicious.

There are various fried noodles and Vietnamese dishes like spring rolls (£2.50) and Pho Bo – the Vietnamese breakfast of chargrilled beef with onion, chillies, and rice noodles. They also sell, coffee shop things – cakes and tea and such. Pho may be small and unassuming, but the genuine Vietnamese food is a treat.

Sala Thong Thai Restaurant

**budget, children, student
unusual places to eat, veg choice**

INSIDER
CHOICE

❖ *DISCOUNT VOUCHER -£1 OFF A MEAL*

35-37 Newnham Road
(by the Mill Pond)
Cambridge CB3 9EY
Map ref: back H 2
Telephone: 01223 323178
Open Tue-Sun: noon-3pm,
6-10.30pm

No Smoking
Credit cards except
American Express
Prices: starters £2.50-£7.95,
noodles/rice dishes £4.50-£5.95,
main courses £4.95-£10,
set menus £6.50-£15/take away

Behind a door styled and gilded in the Thai fashion, you'll find two small rooms bathed in daylight and peace. This is Sala Thong, which means 'golden pavilion'. Food here is what Thai families eat at home, which is to say the dishes have a clear and uncomplicated flavour. They come on attractive china, often with fresh salad and in reasonable portions. Except for desserts for under £2, most cost £4.95 to £6.95, making this the most economical Thai food around. The set menus offer gradually more elaborate meals ranging from £6.50 to £15.

Sala Thong excels in curries (which simply means 'mixed spices'). Served over a mound of rice with a side dish of tiny dried fish, the lentil, prawn or vegetable curry is worth going out of your way for. Many of the dishes have a fair amount of chili, by the way, so don't hesitate to ask the cook to adjust the hotness. A nice way to balance the spiciness is with a Grass Jelly drink, a cooling mixture of licorice jelly and sweet water.

The dishes have a clear and uncomplicated flavour... the most economical Thai food and ...can also be eaten while punting through the backs... unforgettable

Sala Thong also features a lot of vegetarian choices, satay, stir-fried dishes and Thai desserts, like tapioca pudding with palm seed and lotus nut or steamed banana.

What's most unusual about Sala Thong meals is that they can also be eaten while punting through the backs. Just a few steps from the Mill Pond, Sala Thong's friendly staff will bring out a hot meal in tureens and serve it to you on a double-width punt that seats up to six people. The food costs the same as it does in the restaurant and the punt is from £8 a person per hour. Dining (or lunching) on a punt on a warm day is unforgettable and you can bring your own drinks. (Call Cambridge Chauffeur Punts 01223 354164 for details). The gentle motion of the punt and the beauty of the Backs positively frees the mind from cares. It's one of those things you can only do in Cambridge. But book ahead.

Sushi Express
budget, veg choice

50 Hills Road
Cambridge CB2 1LA
Map ref: back H 5
Telephone: 01223 516016
Open Tue: 11.30am-8pm,
Wed-Sat: 11.30am-9pm

Take away and delivery: (Tue-Fri lunchtime only, orders by 11am, 24 hours notice for large orders, min order for delivery £10)
Prices: rice, fish, noodles or chicken and vegetables lunchbox £4.25-£4.95 noodles under £4, sushi £2.25-£3.95

The sight of sushi shops is now commonplace in London, but out here in the sticks, a real sushi shop is a rarity. Sushi Express is at the forefront of the frontier effort, bringing these

range of pre-prepared ld boxed meals or eshly made hot choices... nuine Japanese food

nutritious, low-fat foods to the people in the provinces. It's popular at lunch – with much of its trade going out via deliveries – but you can walk in to this chic glass-fronted sushi shop and choose your own, either from a range of pre-prepared cold boxed meals or freshly made hot choices from the kitchen. Sushi Express provides stools at countertops along the window and wall if you want to eat in. If the day is sunny, go over to the Botanic Garden on Bateman Street for a completely Japanese effect (and, not incidentally, to avoid the 15% VAT surcharge for eating in the shop.)

The selections include Bento Boxes – traditional Japanese lunchboxes of rice, fish, noodles or chicken and marinated vegetables and Ramen (thin) or Udon (thick) noodles. You can also get Miso (soup) and Japanese curries. But the main show is sushi (typically raw fish, but you can get many toppings, including vegetarian). I tried the bento box and really liked it. This is genuine Japanese food and well made. But I can never remember the differences between the Nigiri, Makisushi, Hosomaki etc. Kudos for anyone who can.

Tai Chuen Restaurant
budget, business lunch, special occasion

12 St John's Street
Cambridge CB2 1TW
Map ref: back D 3
Telephone: 01223 358281
Open daily: noon-10.30pm
Take away

Non-smoking area
10% service charge added
Prices: lunch specials £5.50-
£6.50, starters £3.40-£4.30,
meat/fish dishes £6.50-£9.20,
set meals: £18-£28

Tai Chuen is the up-and-coming Chinese restaurant in Cambridge. With new chefs from London and a menu with a carefully selected Chinese-Asian range of dishes, this is the place to get your tastebuds primed for something tasty. The Hong Kong-ese owner is well attuned to the clientele, which includes students and a lot of international visitors on their way to the sights down the street. They want prompt service and quality. That is what the restaurant provides at a price that is middling to above average.

get your tastebuds primed for something tasty... prompt service and quality

The newly expanded menu, with over 100 items, provides all the favourites, from steamed dim sum to sizzling (and very fragrant) scallops in black bean sauce. The fare is mostly Chinese, but adds several Asian choices, Indonesian satay and Japanese Udon, for example. The speciality of the house is duck, which comes in various permutations (in plum sauce, Szechuan flavouring and with ginger and onion) or as the delicacy aromatic crispy duck, sold as a quarter, half or whole duck (£8-£28). The meat is sliced and you wrap the slices with the crispy skin into a thin pancake with a piece of spring onion, cucumber and dollop of hoi-sin (plum) sauce, for a truly delicious treat.

Don't hesitate to go in if the restaurant looks full from the street. Although the Tai Chuen looks small, its modern, brightly lit interior and upstairs seats 100 diners.

Thai Regent Noodle House & Restaurant
budget

108 Regent Street
Cambridge CB2 1DP
Map ref: back F 5
Telephone: 01223 464355
Open Tue- Sun: noon-2.30,
6-11pm
10% student/take away
discount

No smoking
10% service charge on
parties of 6 or more
Prices: set lunch £4.95,
noodle/rice lunch courses: £5-
£6.25, dinner meat dishes £6.50-
£10, set menus £11.50 to £21.50

Behind the modest frontage, a door leading down to a basement at the busy corner of Regent Street and Lensfield Road, you enter a world of bead string doorways, origami-folded paper napkins neatly set at each table setting and walls bedecked with knick-knacks and posters of emerald Thai beaches. This is the Thai Regent, which serves traditional Thai food in good portions. The staff are

> The Thai Regent... serves traditional Thai food in good portions. The staff are always ready with a smile

always ready with a smile and seem genuinely concerned about whether your food is satisfactory.

The menu, in the middle price range, offers everything from soups, noodle and vegetable dishes to seafood, beef, pork, duck and chicken – making it probably the largest Thai menu around. Everything is freshly prepared, and can be made to order, such as without meat for vegetarians. We had a good Singapore Noodles on our visit, finding it slightly oily, but tasty and plentiful.

Local CAMRA branches listed for this guide the pubs in the area they rank as best for beer. When these were the same as the pubs listed in in the guide, we marked the entry with the CAMRA logo. But many names put forward by CAMRA did not coincide with those listed in this guide, which looked at a broader criteria. For that reason, below we list those CAMRA pubs NOT otherwise listed among regular entries:

<u>Cambridge Branch:</u>
Brandon Creek - Ship
Cambridge - Grapes
Castle Camps - Cock
Fulbourn - Six Bells
Longstowe - Golden Miller
Milton - Waggon & Horses
Six Mile Bottom - Green Man
Teversham - Rose & Crown
Whittlesford - Bees in the Wall

<u>West Suffolk Branch:</u>
Dalham - Affleck Arms
Exning - Rosary Hotel
Exning - Wheatsheaf
Frekenham - Golden Boar
Kentford - Cock
Moulton - King's Head

Newmarket - Bushel
Newmarket - Five Bells
Newmarket - The Yard (Grosvenor)

<u>North Herts Branch:</u>
Royston - Coach and Horses
Royston - White Bear

<u>Northwest Essex Branch:</u>
Arkesden - Axe & Compass
Gt Chesterford - Crown & Thistle
Newport - Coach and Horses
Rickling Green - Cricketers Arms
Saffron Walden - Axe
Wendens Ambo - Bell
Widdington - Fleur de Lys

JOIN CAMRA TODAY

Just fill in the form below and send your remittance (payable to CAMRA) to:
Membership Secretary, CAMRA
230 Hatfield Road
St Albans, Herts AL1 4LW
Rates are: Single - £14, Joint - £17 (at the same address), OAP/Unemployed/Disabled - £8, Joint OAP - £8, under 26 - £8 (date of birth: _____)
For Life/Overseas rates please ask for details.

Name(s)..

Address..

....

....Postcode.........................

I/We wish to join the Campaign for Real Ale, and agree to abide by the Rules.
I enclose a cheque for £...............................
Signature:
....date..............

Central Cambridge
Pubs, Bars
& Night Life

Barstaff Required. Apply With INN.

All Bar One
student, sandwich, wines by the glass

INSIDER CHOICE

36 St Andrews Street
Cambridge CB2 3AR
Map ref: back E 4
Telephone: 01223 371081
Open Mon-Sat: noon-11pm,
Sun: noon-10.30pm

No one under 18 permitted
Prices: big main dishes £6.95-
£9.95, medium £4.95, sandwiches
£.3.95, puddings £3.50, weekend
brunch £5.25-£6.25

Seen from the top down, All Bar One is reminiscent of a huge floor of an ex-factory, with exposed duct, slowly turning fans and a huge clock the shape of a cheese round hung from the cream-yellow ceiling. The walls are half painted in olive green, like in a school or institution.

Seen from floor up, you might think more of a turn-of-the-century working man's bar or maybe a dance studio. Pale golden wood covers the floor and central columns. The same wood forms the solid-looking tables with page-size numbers stencilled on each. The menu is chalked up on two big blackboards, whilst across the room, **drinks flow from a long bar with 24 beer taps and scores of wine bottles geometrically arrayed on the wall. The overall effect is a sort of here-we-are-all-together, one-big-room friendliness** where you can sit with companions on long tables with benches or around square tables.

Bass, the massive brewer that owns the chain makes great efforts (focus groups, surveys, you name it) to make sure they've got the mix right. You've got to give them credit. The feel is altogether appealing. On weekend evenings, the place is packed with a youngish crowd out for the evening or off to a night club. This is in legal terms a pub (hence no kids) and the beers and dozen choices of wines and tequila flow steadily. The evenings buzz with sociability and a hum of voices rather than the music you have to compete with in some of the weekend hot spots.

But the place wouldn't attract a wider clientele by day for long if the food fell short. It doesn't. The food is fresh and rather good. All Bar One offers a slightly off-beat and well-chosen selection of 'big plate' choices like 'Wild game sausages with basil mash, French beans and redcurrant jus' (£7.95) or 'Panfried Swordfish with herb crust, salad and fries' (£8.50). A 'small plate' cousin offers similar fare. There are also sandwiches. Our bagel and smoked salmon was reasonable size, fresh and flavourful. On weekends there is a brunch. All this is served by a crew of white-aproned, and rather gung-ho, youngish staff who seem to like their jobs. You can get games from the bar and a good supply of newspapers is always available.

Bar Coast
sandwich, student, terrace, wines by the glass

345 Quayside
Cambridge CB5 8AB
Map ref: back C 2
Telephone: 01223 556961
Open Mon-Sat:11am-11pm,
Sun: 11am-10.30pm

No one under 18 permitted in the evening
Prices: sandwiches £3.95 to £4.25, burgers/pasta £4.95-£6.25

The 21st-century space is elbow-to-elbow packed with twenty-somethings. You have to angle your way through to get inside beyond the jutting black bar and metallic stools and tables to the lounge seats at the back. Nobody minds. At the back they're eating big plates of bar snacks – nachos and potato skins. Everybody seems to be chatting about something big. And laughing.

> **21st century space is elbow-to-elbow packed with 20 somethings ...Everybody seems to be chatting... And laughing**

Near the bar at front, the men stand around drinking caffeine-buzz drinks and bottled beers. The women, many in strappy dresses, mostly sip from slender glasses, big ones, holding what the wine blurb describes as 'fresh, light, crisp – perfect on its own'. The men are dressed up a bit and generally hold bottles in hand.

Unthinkingly I take out a notebook to scrawl some unnecessary observation, like 'young', which immediately attracts the attention of a group of men standing nearby. What are you writing? Conversation is hard above the decibels of commercial hard house. They and almost everyone else are on their way to the clubs, just having a drink. The dancing clubs get interesting after 10.

I had come to Bar Coast by day and seen a different place, one that does a brisk lunch trade to a much more mixed clientele – and without crowds. The food seems a good deal. There are sandwiches like the tuna melt (£4.25). Until 7 pm there are large plates of burgers, pasta and puddings and ice cream served. After that, well, who wants a big meal when you're heading for the dance floor anyway?

Central-Bars

The Blue Boar

student, wines by the glass

17 Trinity Street
Cambridge CB2 1TB
Map ref: back D 3
Telephone: 01223 506611
Open daily: noon-11pm,
Sun: noon-10.30pm

Food served: noon-4pm
Credit cards except
American Express
Prices: bar food £2-£7

Whether you're a large group going for pre-club cocktails, a Mum or a Dad with a pushchair, or a couple of thirty-somethings looking for somewhere to read newspapers, and drink coffee all afternoon, the Blue Boar can accommodate you. Not only because it's big but also because its style doesn't dictate to a particular customer. This modern, long bar with trendy swirly walls, booths and wooden tables has a jazzy café feel in the afternoons, an office crowd and shoppers at lunchtime and clubbers and drinkers in the evenings. Despite a recent management attempt to turn it more into a club, the Blue Boar is now clawing its way back to its heyday when it was very much a continental bar: selling coffee as well as cocktails, pizza as well as pints. It is a perfect place to escape the rain in the daytime or start an evening's partying with a cocktail (especially on Blue Monday, when £5 buys two). And if you're not a sports fan, this is one of the few larger bars in town that doesn't have TVs.

a jazzy café feel in the afternoons, an office crowd and shoppers at lunchtime and clubbers and drinkers in the evenings

Brown's

business lunch, children (by day),
special occasion, terrace,
wines by the glass

INSIDER
CHOICE

23 Trumpington Street
Cambridge CB2 1QA
Map ref: back F 4
Telephone: 01223 461655
Open Mon-Sat: 11am-11.30pm,
Sun / bank holidays:
noon-11.30pm

Non-smoking area
Wheelchair access inc toilets
Music Mon-Thu: piano 8pm
Prices: starters £2.95-£5.95,
pasta £6.85-£7.75, hot sandwiches
£6.55-£7.95, salads £7.35-£10.95,
main courses £7.35-£14.95

Brown's is the sort of place that everybody knows about, even if they've only been in Cambridge a short while. This is not only a matter of its closeness to the big magnet with columns – Fitzwilliam Museum. Brown's just appeals to a lot of people. Tourists in for a snack, long-time residents meeting friends and quite a few high flyers performing at the Cambridge theatres, all frequent Brown's. People go there not so much to see or be seen, as to enjoy the food and the airy open space of the beige dining room that was in recent memory the outpatient clinic of the Old Addenbrooke's Hospital. It has been done up in a forties style, with potted palms stirred by slowly turning ceiling fans, which is about the right tone for afternoon teas of steaming Earl Grey, liqueur coffees and retro-trendy desserts like Winter/Summer puddings (£3.35).

> **Brown's just appeals to a lot of people... People go... to enjoy the food and the airy open space of the beige dining room**

The menu, though mainly Steak-Mushroom-and-Guinness Pie (£7.95) traditional, is quite varied, increasingly with European choices like our favourite – hot sandwiches, or the aromatic (and vegetarian) char-grilled aubergine, roasted garlic, goat's cheese and rocket in ciabatta bread (£6.55).

If you are more into lounging around with a drink, Brown's long bar is the place. Occupying a large open area near the front (maybe where the patients used to wait), you can now lean up against the bar in continental style, imbibing espressos in all their permutations, good wines and cocktails.

The Bun Shop

budget, business lunch, French, sandwich, Spanish, special occasion student, veg choice, wines by the glass

INSIDER CHOICE

❖ *DISCOUNT VOUCHER -FREE BOTTLE OF WINE*

1 King Street
Cambridge CB1 1LH
Map ref: back D 4
Telephone: 01223 366866
Open daily: main bar 10am-11pm; wine bar noon-11pm, tapas 6pm-midnight (& Sat noon-midnight); French noon-2.30pm & 6-10pm, (& Sun 11am-3.30pm)

Prices: (main bar) food £3.95-£4.95, (wine bar) main dishes £6.45-£10.45, (tapas)£10.95 for 3 dishes, (French) main dishes £7.95-£11.95

If you're unfamiliar with the Bun Shop, it can be a slightly disorienting place. However, you won't get lost because they produce a map to guide you. With a real ale main bar (formerly an Irish theme pub), a wine bar, tapas bar and French brasserie under the same roof, it's rather like a catering version of a multiplex.

> a catering version of a multiplex.... one of the most authentic French restaurants in Cambridge and probably the best value.... Spanish Tapas... wine bar... real ale bar... you won't go wrong no matter what you choose

The brasserie upstairs has recently been relaunched. Though the decor is mostly blue-toned, the restaurant remains warm and inviting. The classically French menu has also been revamped, though I was disappointed, knowing that the chef Franck Parnin comes from Alsace, not to find Baeckofe on offer. It is one of the most authentic French restaurants in Cambridge and probably the best value.

One of the house specialities is fish, with marmite de poissons available on the regular menu and rillettes de saumon on the specials board. Meat main courses include faux-filet and rabbit cooked in a mustard and cream sauce and they are accompanied by imaginative vegetables like globe artichoke filled with pureed carrot and coriander. For those of a dessert persuasion, the chocolate mousse here is better than almost any other on this side of the Channel. If that weren't already enough, the weekly recommended wines are not only very good but reasonably priced (ours was £10.50).

Now the Spanish tapas bar, on the first floor opposite the Brasserie. You get a choice of meat, fish or vegetable tapas, each dish can be ordered individually for £3.95, or less if ordered in multiples of three to 20 for £10.95 to £65.95, giving lots of options for these savoury delights like 'anchovies with olives'. With 30 minutes notice, you can order paellas, ranging from the traditional recipe (chicken, squid, scampi, mussels etc. with garlic, peppers, onions, herbs and rice, simmered and cooked in spiced stock) to a vegetarian paella. These are for groups, with prices ranging from small paellas (£12.95-£29.95) for up to four people to massive for parties of up to 30 people (£53.95-£149.95).

The wine bar downstairs stocks some 50 wines, all served by the glass (£1.80-£3.95) or by the bottle (£7.95-£18.80), plus champagnes. To soak these up, the bar serves a good variety of snacks, including home-made paté in orange sauce and stilton marinated in port – along with baguette sandwiches and more traditional main dishes like Beef and Guinness Pie (£6.95), Fish 'n' Chips (£5.95) and Lamb Cutlet (£10.95). You can also order food from the tapas bar.

The real ale bar, in addition to the two guest beers, serves Greene King, Young's Bitter, Young's Special, Tetley's, and typical pub food like chilli con carne, Beef Burgers and Ploughman sandwiches.

With all these choices, decisions prove difficult. But judging by our experience, you won't go wrong no matter what you choose.

Henry's Café Bar

business lunch, dessert,
children (by day), sandwich, special
occasion, terrace, wines by the glass

Quayside
Cambridge CB5 8AB
Map ref: back C 2
Telephone: 01223 324649
Open Mon-Fri: 9.30am-11pm,
Sat: 9am-11pm, Sun: 9am-10.30pm
Non-smoking area

Wheelchair access inc toilets
Outside table service
Children's menu, children welcome (but not after 7pm unless dining with adult)
Prices: main courses £5.25-£9.75, appetizers £2.75-£4.50, espresso £1.15

Henry's aptly chooses the chameleon as its mascot. This place makes a sort of unexpected Jekyll and Hyde mood transformation as the sun moves across the sky.

*akes an unexpected Jekyll
d Hyde transformation as
e sun moves across the
y... coffee and tea
inkers... power lunching...
e after-work crowd*

From around 10 am come the Jekylls – coffee and tea drinkers, s h o p p e r s, tourists, mums and dads with kids – people with a leisurely space in the day. By noon, the same restaurant attracts the business-types, power lunching either at the tables on the Quay or in the big, living room inside. From their big soft chairs, the diners take in the view of the Magdalene College gardens and punters attempting to navigate the Cam.

That's how things go until the dinner hour, when the Hydes – after-work crowd – begin to filter in. Now and increasingly on weekend evening weekends the day-timers give way to twenty-, thirty and forty-somethings who stand around the curvy dark oak bar at the front. The friendly scene gets more electric as the evening warms (and is not really Hyde-like at all). Piped-in music sets the tone for the elbow-to-elbow drinking crowd, many tanking up for an evening of clubbing down the street. Henry's feels like an entirely different place by 10pm. You can tell because the bouncers wear suits (in contrast with the flak jackets they wear at Bar Coast across the way)

By day of course, the food suits a broad church, offering anything from toasted club sandwich (£5.25) to a 10oz Entrecote steak (£10.95) and Thai crab cakes (£7.95). The big salads – tuna, caesar or oriental – are popular at £6.95-£7.95 as are the ice creams (£3.25-£3.95) and desserts (£3.50) along with the espressos and tea.

But by evening the drinks menus increasingly come out. Henry's offers a score of handy by-the-glass wines and champagne (£2.40-£5.95 per glass or by the bottle). On top of that, its able bartenders stir up some 40 cocktails (£2.50-£4.50) with only a few of the usual embarrassing names like 'Kiss and Tell' or 'Hawaiian Punch'. Thank goodness.

Lawyers Wine and Oyster Bar
garden, open till late, wines by the glass

6 Lensfield Road
Cambridge CB2 1EG
Map ref: back H 5
Telephone: 01223 566887
Open Mon-Sat: noon-12pm

Prices: sandwiches £2.15-£3.35, main courses £5.25-£7.25, 1/2 dozen oysters: £6.95

Taking its name from nearness to the courts on Hills Road, Lawyers makes you feel very legal indeed. Lining the walls are big thick bound books. The Oxford Shorter dictionary is handy in case you urgently need the derivation of zygapophysis or aardvark. And this you can do in style.

Apart from the featured oysters, their slipperiness somehow appropriate for a lawyer's bar (one might add that they are equally popular among lawyers' clients), the menu leans toward seafood with such selections as Prawn Provençal (£6.95) and the Salmon and Spinach Tart (£6.25). The French, continental style in seafood is complemented by hearty meat pies like Steak and

Kidney (£7.25) and salads of beef and smoked salmon (£4.95-£5.75). Along with these menu staples (winter and summer version), there is a daily 'additional' menu that is always full of surprises. On the day I visited, the stuffed pepper with cheese (£5.95) proved light and tasty, and came with a welcome basket of fresh French bread. I ate in the secluded garden courtyard, which, overflowing with geraniums and vines growing over the brick wall, contrasts with the busy restaurant frontage, facing one of the city's busiest intersections. In the garden, the waitress delivers your meal to the sun-shaded table. Delightful! No other restaurant or pub in the centre has a garden to compare. If only Cambridge had a few more warm days to enjoy such places.

Delightful! No other restaurant or pub in the centre has a garden to compare

Lawyers, located on the site of a fabled coaching inn called The Oak, seems just the place for a good glass of wine. In this department the clientele is well looked after by local awarding-winning wine suppliers Noel Young. With 15 reds, 15 whites and ranging from £8.80 for the house wine to £15 for the top of the line, as well as four champagnes, the choice is ample and just the thing for a slippery subject.

Trinity Street Vaults

business lunch, special occasion, wines by the glass

14a Trinity Street
Cambridge CB2 1TB
Map ref: back D 3

Telephone: 01223 506090
Closed July - February 2000
for renovation

As this guide goes to press the Vaults, as The Trinity Vaults is known, is being completely renovated and expanded. The new Vaults, we are told, will have a completely different and larger menu and will accommodate a lot more people – up to 150. We are not at liberty to reveal further information as to what to expect after the big makeover . The old Vaults, had low lighting, wooden tables and comfy chairs amid a room covered with drawings on the light buff walls. The menu was an adventurous range of continental cooking. But that's all history now. If the new Vaults is even grander than the old, this restaurant will be something exceptionally good. Keep this one on your 'try it' list.

If the new Vaults is even grander than the old, this restaurant will be something exceptionally good

Central-Bars

The Anchor
student, terrace

Silver Street
Cambridge CB3 9EL
Map ref: back F 2
Telephone: 01223 353554
Open Mon-Sat: 11am-11pm,
Sun: 11am-10.30pm
Food served Mon-Thu: noon-8pm,
Fri-Sat: noon-3.45pm, Sun: noon-2.30pm

Credit cards except
American Express
Prices: pub food
£1.50-£5, Sunday
roast £5.50, daily
specials lasagne, meat
pie £4.75

The Anchor is a huge, four-levelled pub by the river, popular with students and teenagers and perfect for large groups and warm evenings. There is a suntrap of a terrace, which fills quickly in the summer, as well as a cosier café-bar atmosphere inside. The beer and food range is standard.

popular with students and teenagers and perfect for large groups and warm evenings

It is probably one of the easiest places to find in Cambridge and therefore a good pub to meet in since, unlike many others, it is not hidden away in a back street but sits prominently on a bridge at one end of the Backs. If you're into punting there are rental facilities just outside. If you're not, it's a perfect place to watch others making fools of themselves.

The Bath Ale House
budget, student

3 Bene't Street
Cambridge CB2 3QN
Map ref: back E 3
Telephone: 01223 350969
Open Mon-Sat: 11am-11pm,
Sun: noon-10.30pm

Food served Sun-Thu:
noon-9pm, Fri-Sat: noon-8pm
Credit cards except
American Express
Prices: bar food £1.20-£5.90

You would be forgiven for thinking that this was an original part of Cambridge pub history. It certainly looks like it whereas it is in fact a modern reinvention of such a past. However, it is reputedly built on the site of a fifteenth-century, Augustinian bath house and it is attractive: low ceilinged, timbered and cosy. If you didn't know this was part of the Hogshead chain you probably wouldn't suspect until you saw the standard, printed menus found in all of them.

As in most Hogsheads, there is a wide range of beers and this, it seems to me, is the best reason to visit. The range spans the local (City of Cambridge Atom Splitter and Abbot IPA), the national, (Inch's cider and Brakspear's Bitter) and the international – draught Hoegaarden. Since some are in casks and gravity dispensed, you know that the beer is being well-kept. With the volume of customers they have, it can't be left hanging around for long either.

Food-wise there is a standard bar menu: soup, chilli, pasta, burgers, sandwiches and jacket potatoes. The most interesting choices appear on the blackboard: there is some chance that the daily specials such as sausages with three-mustard sauce and spinach and ricotta cannelloni will be more individual.

reputedly built on the site of a fifteenth-century, Augustinian bath house... there is a wide range of beers and... reasonably priced food deals

Everything is reasonably priced and one of the best food deals in town can be found here in the afternoons: two meals for £5.99 after 2pm until end of food service. That's not only cheaper than many cafés and restaurants, it's also cheaper than fast food.

The Champion of the Thames

68 King Street, Cambridge CB1 1LN
Map ref: back D 4
Telephone: 01223 352043
Open Mon-Sat: 11am-11pm,   No food served
Sun: noon-10.30pm   No credit cards

The Champion of the Thames is a regulars' drinking pub that redefines the term: in similar places you feel uncomfortable breaking the sacred spell that is the 'usual crowd' but not here. No-one looks up and stares at you,

a regulars' drinking pub... that makes no compromises... the beer is excellent

the staff are reasonably friendly and tend to serve you promptly and once you have your drink you are left to your own devices.

It is a pub that makes no compromises: it serves only Greene King beer (reputedly the best pint of Abbot Ale in Cambridge); it has no fruit machines or music; it doesn't serve food (though you can bring your own). As a result the beer is excellent, the pub is always a welcoming spot for a quiet pint and you always know what you'll get. In fact the best way to describe it is: it does what it does and if you don't like it go somewhere else. And considering that it has been here over 140 years and that its longest-serving landlord, Les Carlton, ran it for 28 years, it is obviously a formula that works.

① The Eagle
garden courtyard

INSIDER CHOICE

Bene't St, Cambridge CB2 3QN
Map ref: back E 3
Telephone: 01223 505020
Open Mon-Sat: 11am-11pm,
Sun: noon-10.30pm

Food served: daily
noon-2.30pm, Mon-Thu
5.30-8.45pm
Wheelchair access inc toilets
Prices: pub meals £3-£4.95

The Eagle is a perfect place to take foreign visitors, the only people who still believe in that myth of 'merry old England', but it is not kitsch, quaint or twee. In fact, it is a really good, solid pub which panders to no one and thus pleases everyone, even the locals.

Despite its enormous popularity and the obvious tourist attraction of such a historic building The Eagle still remains a treat

There has been a pub recorded on this site since 1353 and it has been owned by Corpus Christi college since 1488. It is a mix of history, from the fireplaces dating back to 1600, the ceiling which was signed by British and American airmen, à la Zippo, during the last war and the fact that this was the local of Crick and Watson, who discovered the structure of DNA.

Five different rooms, with wooden floors, fireplaces and dark panelling stretch back inside and there is a large cobbled courtyard outside. In winter, there are real fires and in the summer, it is worth fighting for a seat in the courtyard. Despite its enormous popularity and the obvious tourist attraction of such a historic building The Eagle still remains a treat.

Fort St George
garden courtyard

Midsummer Common
Cambridge CB4 1HA
Map ref: back B 5
Telephone: 01223 354327
Open Mon-Sat: noon-11pm,
Sun: noon-10.30pm

Food served Mon-Sat: noon-2.30,
6.30-9pm, Sun: noon-2.30pm
Booking advised for Sun lunch
Prices: bar food £1.95-£11.95,
2-course Sunday lunch £7.95
(main course £5.95)

Technically the Fort St. George doesn't have a garden. But since it looks out over one of the loveliest commons in England, it doesn't really need one. If you're longing for a country pub by the river but can't or won't leave the town, then wander across Midsummer Common to this huge, rambling pub.

The pub gets its name from India, albeit via a rather tortuous route. In 1639 a small fort was erected on the present site of Madras by the East India Company of Armagon and it was named Fort St. George after England's patron saint. Many years later, someone decided that a hostelry on an island in the river Cam bore a resemblance to the fort and the pub became known by its present name. Despite the lack of similarity between the two – for a start the one in India was built

> **if you're longing for a country pub by the river but can't or won't leave the town, then wander across... to this huge, rambling pub**

on a hillside not an island – and a period as a river toll house during the last century when it was known as The Sluice, the name stuck.

No longer on an island, the pub is easily reached by boat or bike. Here you can watch joggers and rowers thirstily plying their way across grass or through water, whilst smugly enjoying a pint of IPA or Abbot. Buy a baguette and a drink and whilst stretched out on the Common you can spirit yourself elsewhere. If you want something to eat, the Fort also offers special barbecue nights, an extensive food menu and a Sunday lunch.

The Fountain Inn
budget, student

12 Regent Street
Cambridge CB2 1DB
Map ref: back E 4
Telephone: 01223 366540

Open: Mon-Sat 11am-11pm,
Sun: noon-10.30pm
Food served Mon-Sun: all day
Prices: bar snacks £0.95-£5.45

The Fountain Inn is, in my opinion, one of the better student pubs, probably because non-students like myself feel quite comfortable drinking in it. Part of the T&J Bernard chain (the real ale and wine part of Scottish and Newcastle) the pub retains its individuality.

> **one of the better student pubs, probably because non-students like myself feel quite comfortable drinking in it**

An intriguing little sign outside, easily missed in the rush to get to one of the best real ale and bottled ale selections available in this part of town, explains that the Fountain was once known as 'one of A Curious Group of Buildings' on St. Andrews Street which depicted differing aspects of Victorian life.' Along the street, there used to be a workhouse, a police station and a church. The pub represented pleasure, the workhouse morality, the station law and order and the church religion. As the sign notes, only the Baptist Church and the Inn still fulfil their original purpose: the workhouse is now Mandela house, the

Central-Pubs

police station a Council building.

Beers on offer may include several different Theakstons, Charles Wells' Bombardier and Batemans' Middle Wicket. Bottled beers on offer include the award-winning St. Peter's range, Leffe Blonde and Brune and Bitburger. Guest beers change weekly and as well as the nine wines always available there is a wine of the month.

Bar snacks, like the beer, are wide-ranging in their appeal – everything from sausage and onion sandwiches to Moroccan curry – and as is the policy with Scottish and Newcastle, always available everyday.

Evidently, in term time, the pub is busy with students especially for sporting events on the big screen. Yet, non-students will still find it pleasant to sneak in here for a beer and a read of the free newspapers.

The Hogshead
budget, student

69-73 Regent Street
Cambridge CB2 1AB
Map ref: back F 5
Telephone: 01223 323405
Open Mon-Sat: 11am-11pm;
Sun: noon-10.30pm

Food served: Fri-Sat noon-8pm, Sun-Thu: noon-9pm
No one under 18 allowed
Prices: bar snacks £1.20-£5.90

The Hogshead chain is probably one of the least offensive modern pub brands. And this particular example is rather attractive. Snugly hidden away off Regent Street, the upper floor commands a fabulous view of Parker's Piece and the huge warehouse windows flood the place

commands a fabulous view of Parker's Piece and the huge warehouse windows flood the place with light... a good place for daytime lounging

with light. With lots of space and plenty of newspapers, it's a good place for daytime lounging, whatever the weather whereas at night,

especially on weekends, it is packed.

Although most of the food, music and style of the place is standardised to fit a corporate model, the range and quality of the beers is not. There are always masses of real ales available, which may include Tanglefoot, Brakspear Bitter and local City of Cambridge brews, and Hoegaarden seems to be a standard option too. The bottled beer selection is also good: Leffe beers are often available. I am also told that Hogshead know how to look after and serve their beers. There are always a couple being served straight from the cask as well as those on gas and hand pumps. So it's not just diversity but quality that they strive for.

The Maypole

terrace, Italian, student, veg choice

Portugal Place,
Cambridge, CB5 8AF
Map ref: back B 3
Telephone: 01223 352999
Open Mon-Sat: 11am-11pm,
Sun: noon-10.30pm

Food served Mon-Fri: noon-2.30,
5-9pm, Sat-Sun: all day
Credit cards except
American Express
Prices: bar food £2.75-£5.95

There are few words that can describe The Maypole:
excellent springs to mind. So does unusual, inimitable
and versatile. Cambridge is very lucky to have such a
pub and I'm just peeved that I never discovered it several
years ago. Secreted away behind one of
Cambridge's less attractive car parks, near the Round Church, it isn't the most obvious hostelry in a town full of riverside terraces and antique courtyards. But it is one of the best, both for the large student population and for those who have long outgrown their youth.

> few words that can describe The Maypole: excellent springs to mind... It is a student pub and yet it's not, it is a cocktail bar and yet not, it is a great place for food but to go there just for the food would be to miss the point

It is a student pub and yet it's not, it is a cocktail bar
and yet not, it is a great place for food but to go there just
for the food would be to miss the point. I thoroughly
enjoyed my Melanzane ai Formaggi, a huge portion of
fresh aubergines cooked with fresh tomatoes and herbs,
thickly covered with various cheeses and served with
crusty bread and I'd certainly return to try the rest of the
(very reasonably-priced) menu. But I'd also go back for a
coffee: they use Illy which is excellent stuff and serve
proper Italian coffees like espressos, cappuccinos and
lattes, none of this filtered rubbish. Then there's the cocktails, made by the landlords Mario and Vincent
Castiglione, who have both won Championships with
their shaking and stirring skills. Reduced to £2.95 for the
whole evening, from an already reasonable £4.25-£4.50,
the list covers classics like bloody marys and margheritas
as well as individual mixes such as the Maypole Leaf and
seasonal ones like Salad Days created to coincide with
the nearby ADC Theatre's production of the same
name. To their credit there are five non-alcoholic
choices, all of which are significantly cheaper.

Nothing is done by halves here. And that, I believe, is
because this is a family business not some corporate
link in a chain. The Castigliones have been behind this

bar for 17 years and their Sicilian roots show through: real Italian food (no pesto ciabatta here, thanks), a real welcome to anyone, with no attempt to pander to any particular clientele (yes, there are a lot of students but you'll still find something to love about this place if you're not) and a real sense of atmosphere, whether it's supporting the football or the theatre.

The Mill

budget, student

The Mill (formerly
The Tap and Spile)
14 Mill Lane
Cambridge CB2 1RX
Map ref: back F 2

Telephone: 01223 357026
Open Mon-Sat: 11.30am-11pm,
Sun: noon-10.30pm
No credit cards

The Mill (formerly The Tap and Spile) is extremely popular with student lager drinkers as well as middle-aged beer fanatics. In the winter its tiny bars are crammed and in the summer the road and bridge just outside are filled with people clasping plastic glasses. It doesn't have a garden but it has lots of overflow space, situated as it is right next to the river and the water-meadows, hence the plastic.

A wooden bar immediately greets you... wooden tables fill the various nooks and crannies. In terms of drinking, this is an aficionado's heaven

The pub is quite small inside. A wooden bar immediately greets you, whichever entrance you use, and wooden tables fill the various nooks and crannies. In terms of drinking, this is an aficionado's heaven. Cask ales abound, with Gales HSB from Hampshire (easily one of the best bitters I have tasted) Fuller's London Pride and Theakston Old Peculier sharing the bar with the more dubious Piddle in the Wind (it tastes like it sounds). One of its other specialities is Lindisfarne fruit wine which at 14.5% proof is not the non-alcoholic alternative I originally thought it might be. Food is not served at the moment though this is likely to change very soon since the pub is changing hands.

The Mitre

budget, student

INSIDER
CHOICE

17 Bridge Street
Cambridge CB2 1UF
Map ref: back C 3
Telephone: 01223 358403

Open daily: 11am-11pm,
Sun: noon-10.30pm
Food served Mon-Thu: 11.30am-
3pm, 6-9pm, Fri-Sun: noon-3pm
Prices: bar food £1.25-£4.95

'We pride ourselves on the excellent quality of our cask conditioned ales. We guarantee if you are not entirely satisfied we will exchange your ale for another AND refund your money!'

This message hangs on several walls in The Mitre and it tells you two things: that they are serious about both their beer and their customers' satisfaction. Apparently, there aren't many takers for the exchange and refund and this isn't surprising since the beers are well-kept. At least four real ales were available on my visit (including Black

> **they are serious about both their beer and their customers' satisfaction...**

Sheep Best, Tanglefoot and Bateman's Jollys D-Day) as well as four regulars (Tetley's Bitter, Marston's Pedigree, Hopback Entire Stout and Morland's Old Speckled Hen) and Addlestone's cask-conditioned cider. The guests change as and when they run out i.e. frequently. If you can drink a pint of each beer in one night you pass the eight-pint challenge for which you'll be given a certificate to commemorate your headache... The pub runs a beer festival in May.

The Mitre first became a pub in 1754, when it used to be a coach house with accommodation. Divided into several different rooms and levels, it has a variety of atmospheres. Classical music is played in the daytime and this is when the quieter, lighter front room, a place for conversation and contemplation, comes into its own. Everything is wooden, tables, chairs, floors, bar and there is a big fire. The huge windows looking out on the road encourage the sort of people-watching usually only found in continental cafés. Further into the pub, and later in the day, the smoke and noise levels increase, pop replaces classical, and the bar becomes busier and more studenty. If I was going to try the pick 'n' mix fish and chips (pay separately for fish £3.40, chips £1.25 and all the trimmings) I'd probably choose to eat it at one of the big wooden tables in the window. But if I wanted a rowdier, smokier pre-club night out I'd head to the back. Whichever area you choose to sit, stand or slouch in, you know you'll be drinking some of the best beer in Cambridge.

The Pickerel Inn

budget, student

30 Magdalene Street
Cambridge CB3 0AF
Map ref: back C 2
Telephone: 01223 355068
Open Mon-Sat: 11am-11pm,
Sun: noon-10.30pm

Food served daily: all day
Credit cards except
American Express
Prices: bar snacks £1.25-4.95

This 600 year-old coaching inn used to be in the centre of town. Here, where only punts float these days, boats used to bring cargo along the river and thus the Pickerel was always busy with sailors and boatmen. Such trade might explain why a brothel and a gin palace made their homes here at different periods. And why a ghost continues, reputedly, to live here. A good spirit, but a spirit nonetheless.

Full of warren-like little rooms which are perfect both for quiet communions with spirits or rowdy rugby sessions

Full of warren-like little rooms which are perfect both for quiet communions with spirits or rowdy rugby sessions, The Pickerel continues to serve many types of punters – circuit drinkers on a Friday, shoppers on a Saturday, tourists on a Sunday, students all year round. It offers real ales (Charles Wells' Summer Solstice, Theakston's Old Peculier, Theakston XB and Abbot Ale for example) and nine wines, served by the bottle or glass. The pub food, which consists of dishes like roast pepper lasagne and Cumberland sausage, is cheap and always available.

The Picture House
Members and Ticket Holders Bar

budget, urban peace

38-39 St Andrews Street
Cambridge CB2 3AR
Map ref: back E 4
Telephone: 01223 504444

Open daily: noon-9pm
Wheelchair access (inc toilets)
Prices: coffee/espressos £1-
£1.20, cakes £0.80-£1

The Picture House is a new cinema above The Regal (see below). The cinema is the successor to the Arts Cinema, formerly in Market Passage, and shows more elevated and arty films than offered at the mulitplex. We list the Picture House (entered by the doors at either side from the front of the Regal) because it has its own bar of the quiet, spacious, stylish type. You have to be a member or have purchased a ticket to use the bar, but anyone can buy a sandwich, quiche or salad and non-alcoholic drink. This is the place for some good food while discussing post-modernism in cinema (or drinking a beer before Godzilla).

Quinn's Irish Pub

Quinn's
Holiday Inn, St. Tibb's Row,
Cambridge CB2 3DT
Map ref: back E 4
Telephone: 01223 556500

Open Mon- Sat: 11am-11pm,
Sun: noon-10.30pm
Food served daily: noon-8pm
Prices: bar snacks £1.50-£4.95

At Christmas, after an evening's late-night shopping loaded down with bags full of presents, I would frequently wander past Quinn's windows on the way to Lion Yard car park and see what the sensible half of the population was doing: singing, revelling and drinking large quantities of Christmas spirit. It looked far more fun than the horrors I had just left behind.

very lively and very friendly... some good draught beers... a stone-flagged floor and bar downstairs... televisions suspended to show sports events upstairs

Quinns is one of a handful of 'Irish' pubs in the city, and most seem to have only one thing in common with pubs in Ireland: they sell beers with the same names. If you can forget what is a very tenuous connection to another country, this place is very lively and very friendly. But if you come expecting a little bit of Dublin, forget it.

The pub is on two levels, a stone-flagged floor and bar downstairs, and a narrow carpeted gallery with televisions suspended to show sports events upstairs. In addition to the Guinness, it is stocked with some good draught beers (Staropramen for example, an excellent Czech lager, and City of Cambridge Hobson's Choice) and there is a food menu which tries to be a little bit Irish, offering soda bread (which turns out to be soda farls...not quite the same thing) with soup. Personally, I'd stick to the more standard options (which bear a striking resemblance to some of those on offer in Bloomsbury's Hotel – the pub is part of it) like hot bap of the day and nachos.

Last, but not least, the loos, at least the womens', deserve a mention...they are completely standard except that the cubicles have saloon doors! Does this mean that somewhere, someone believes that such a detail makes the pub more authentically Irish?!

The Regal

St Andrews Street
Cambridge CB2 3AR
Map ref: back E 4
Telephone: 01223 366459
Open Mon-Sat: 11am-11pm,
Sun: noon-10:30pm

Food served: Mon-Fri 11am-
10pm, Sat: noon-10pm
Wheelchair accessible inc toilets
No one under 18 permitted
Non-smoking area
Prices: from £.1.20

The Regal is a gigantic presence in Cambridge – figura-
tively and literally. It is the largest pub in Britain, covering 11,545 square feet, including the ground and mez-
zanine level, each with a bar, and a balcony and garden.

the largest pub in Britain... The Regal offers a full menu and a good range of real ales

The 340-pub strong JD
Wetherspoon group that
owns the place has named it
after the cinema that once
operated in the building.
(The Beatles performed
there in 1963). The front entrance is 1930s, art deco,
with period colours and sculpted ornamentation like
the cinema used to be.

Like all JD Wetherspoon pubs, music and pool tables
are banned. One third of the area in the Regal is designated as non-smoking. Along with lots of space to
socialise and do pubby things, the Regal offers a full menu
and a good range of real ales. Six beers are served at all
times, including a regular regional beer and others from
breweries across the UK. That sounds pretty regal to me.

The St Radegund

**pets allowed,
student hangout**

CAMRA   INSIDER CHOICE

129 King Street
Cambridge CB1 1LD
Map ref: back C5
Telephone: 01223 311794

No credit cards
Open Mon-Fri: 4.30-11pm,
Sat: noon-11pm, Sun: 6-10.30pm
No food served

The St. Radegund is a TARDIS* of a pub: though the
smallest pub in Cambridge you would be forgiven for
believing it is much bigger. In terms of calculated space,
it would fit into many other pubs twice over, but in terms
of character it is far greater than most of them. Named
after the 6th-century Queen of France who founded a
Priory on the site of present-day Jesus College, the pub is
as individual and renowned as the woman it immortalises.

Eschewing the trappings of fruit machines and pop
music, the St. Radegund concentrates on serving excellent real ales (such as Shepherd Neame's Spitfire and
Fuller's London Pride) and select cocktails (the Bloody

Pubs in the Historic Centre

113

Mary is truly 'poky') in an inimitable atmosphere. Where else can you not only drink great beer, properly chilled Polish vodkas and Red Squirrel cocktails but also discover the true origins of the King Street Run, join the Vera Lynn club or add a leaf to the Raincheck tree? If you can't manage the beer you might find yourself adding to the Wall of Shame. All of these features are explained on the walls around you. For those who run out of vertical things to read, there's always the ceiling, which is covered with

in terms of calculated space, it would fit into many other pubs twice over, but in terms of character it is far greater than most of them... the pub is as individual and renowned as the woman it immortalises

the names of various college societies, burnt on the surface with the aid of a candle. A word of warning: if you're feeling a little under the influence stick to reading the walls, the Visitors' Book and the Round the World Bottle of Beer...those swirly black lines don't go well with a few pints.

Whoever you are, you will find something to amuse your mind or your palate in this wonderful pub. Me, I've joined the Vera Lynn Club. And if you want to know what that is, you'll just have to join yourself...see you on Friday.

(*for those of you who don't know what this means ask a British person aged between 30-40)

The Spread Eagle

budget, terrace, student

67 Lensfield Rd
Cambridge, CB2 1EN
Map ref: back H 4
Open Mon-Sat: 11am-11pm,
Sun: noon-10.30pm

Telephone: 01223 566291
Food served daily: noon-2.30pm,
5.30-8pm except Sun evening
Prices: pub food £2.30-£5.95

I have to say that the Spread Eagle's location has never tempted me, situated as it is on a busy road, but once I'd tried it I dismissed such qualms. This old established coaching inn, which has apparently played host to numerous famous cricket umpires, has been renovated twice and is now a light and polished modern pub. The front wall has been completely replaced with French doors which are

*is old established
coaching inn, which
is apparently
played host to
numerous famous
cricket umpires... is
now a light and
polished modern pub*

Central-Pubs

pulled open in the summer to create a very continental-style atmosphere.

Food and beer are quite varied, Stilton mushrooms and Brie wedges sharing the menu with stalwarts like baguettes and rump steak. As an independent, the pub can offer a good range of beers (there are usually seven real ales available plus Hoegaarden). If you're a regular, or likely to become one, there is a discount scheme which gives you 10% off all food and drink both here and in the Six Bells (a sister pub off Mill Rd), access to promotions, and costs nothing (apart from a £2 refundable fee for the membership card). Such schemes are becoming more and more popular but this is one of the first that gives a blanket discount on both food and drink. That in itself, on a Friday night, is worth an extra round or two in here.

The Town and Gown

gay

Pound Hill	No food served
Cambridge, CB3 OAE	Open Mon-Sat: noon-2pm,
Map ref: back B 2	7-11pm, Sun: all day
Telephone: 01223 353791	

The best known gay pub in the area, long established and the one nearest the main drag, this squat, deceptive little building festooned with hanging baskets rises not a catwalk's length from the bottom of Castle Hill. There are three bars hiding behind the unassertive exterior, a Spartan one at the back and at front two with low ceilings and little nooks and crannies beneath Tudor beams.

The best known gay pub in the area, long established and the one nearest the main drag... not a cruisy place and straights are made perfectly welcome

This is not a cruisy place and straights are made perfectly welcome, though the crush of the Friday night discos, when the place is packed and at its campiest, might bother some; it is often standing room only.

The Town and Gown offers a far better selection of beers than many gay venues and, on the other side of the glazed-in courtyard, where picnic tables and more hanging baskets create a charming daytime atmosphere, the pool table in the stable block is extremely popular, with the girls as much as the guys. Saturdays are paradoxically quiet – presumably because people have parties to go to?

The staff are friendly and the customers will happily chat with strangers. There is a wide age range without it being the least cliquey. The lesbian sorority sometimes congregates in the smaller of the main bars, but as a rule it is fully integrated, and the University manages to mix admirably with the hoi Polloi, as the name suggests it should, though those ubiquitous gowns do tend to come out on carnival nights, the sequinned sort rather than the academic, especially when Dot Cotton is in town (the gay club at the Junction, *not* the soap star, that is).

The Zebra

pizza, student hangout

80 Maids Causeway Cambridge, CB5 8DD Map ref: back C 6 Telephone: 01223 512400 Open daily: (times unavailable) Food served: 6-10.30pm (-9pm Sundays)	Prices: cheese and tomato pizza regular £3.75, large £4.85, toppings 40p (order 4 and get 5th free), other dishes about £4

The Zebra's idea to serve pizza with pints is so simple and effective that it is amazing that others have only just started copying it. This, however, is the original place and you can tell by the hordes of young and old punters who fill the bar in the evenings that I'm not the only one to think so.

The food is good but so is the beer... the landlord and landlady are really friendly and there's a charming Golden Retriever

When I asked Ann Travers why she and her husband had chosen to favour pizza instead of more traditional pub food (some of which is available for anyone who really doesn't like very good pizza) I was expecting to hear of their families' links to Italy or North America, or previous experience in the restaurant business. The reason is much simpler and more laudable. Pizza, Ann stresses, is great with beer; it's snacking food, it's good for groups. 'We wanted to make sure this stayed a pub and didn't turn into a restaurant.'

And it has. The food is good but so is the beer: five real ales are kept on all the time and there are regular guest ales selected from a wide range. Furthermore, the landlord and landlady are really friendly and there's a charming Golden Retriever who will oblige anyone who wants to pet him.

Bar Moosh

INSIDER CHOICE

1-3 Station Road
Cambridge CB1 2JB
Map ref: I 6
Telephone: 01223 360268
Open Mon-Sat: 11am-11pm,
Sun: noon-10.30pm

Food served all day
entertainment: Sat eve
Prices: pasta, salads, meat dishes
£4.95-£7.95, roast duck £5-£10,
bottles of wines £9-£19.95

Bar Moosh is to pubs as John Varnom is to music.

That sums up Bar Moosh, but you won't have the vaguest idea what I mean unless I explain that Bar Moosh is what for two years was Chambers. (The pub owner got a case of wanderlust and sold up). The newcomer announced its arrival in late summer 1999 by painting bright orange over the formerly green facade and, of course, changing the name. (Bar Moosh just rolls off the tongue, the owner says, in explanation).

refined, imaginative cooking that is excellent value at pub prices... What sets the mood and makes Bar Moosh Bar Moosh is the music

The interior has been kept much the same – high-ceilinged rooms featuring big wood tables, bold green walls and a huge mirror at one end. It creates an open, comfortable space. But beyond that the feel of this corner pub is 100% John Varnom – the new owner. Like Varnom, a musician and globe-trotting musical creative spirit (he produced the Sex Pistols), the food is 'spicy eclectic' (his words), capturing influences from North Africa, East Asia, France, England, Italy and more. They come to play in dishes like Fish cakes Rouille (£3.95), Crispy Roast Duck, Merguez sausages and mash (£5.95). The 'Caesar Salad Moosh' (£4.95-£5.95), teams a blackened and peppery rectangle of salmon or chicken over a caesar salad – the way it should be made – with giant croutons. Mine was delightful. This is refined, imaginative cooking that is excellent value at pub prices. It no doubt reflects the Michelin star that Varnom held at one of his London restaurants, Varnom's, in Islington.

But Bar Moosh is not only distinctive for food. What sets the mood and makes Bar Moosh Bar Moosh is the music. Over the speakers come Edith Piaf and Peggy Lee singing blues jazz, followed by select tracks from Groucho Marx for a laugh. Varnom put the tapes together and they have a magic all their own. He too will set the tone for the weekly entertainment, promised to be at a volume you can speak over and featuring anything from rock to jazz and world music.

The Boat House

children, garden, parking

INSIDER CHOICE

14 Chesterton Road
Cambridge CB4 3AX
Map ref: back A 4
Telephone: 01223 460905
Open Mon-Sat: 11am-11pm,
Sun: noon-10.30pm
Food served Mon-Thu: noon-3pm,
6-9pm, Fri-Sat: noon-3pm,
Sun: noon-5pm

Credit cards:
Visa only (for food)
Parking: next to the pub
Prices: pub food, burgers
under £5, meat main
courses £5.96-£6.45,
children's menu £2.45-£2.95

From the vantage point of the spacious, tree-shaded garden at river's edge, life seems much less hurried. That's probably why on warm days big groups of friends get together at the Boat House picnic tables, on the balcony behind the garden or at the tables along the picture windows inside.

the best River Cam-side garden in the centre... a good selection of... beers... cut-above pub food

The Boat House, with the best River Cam-side garden in the centre, is among the more popular drinking holes for the rowers from the boat clubs down the river. A good cross-section of locals and office people, including but not mainly students, make the Boat House an easy for anyone to visit place, even for accompanied children.

Formerly the New Spring and then the Robroy (after a Cambridge rower), this pub has a couple of fruit machines and games, but most come for a good selection of Whitbread Brewery beers – including session beers and guest ales – and the cut-above pub food. The menu includes traditional items for under £5 along with more interesting choices like poached salmon fillet (£5.45) and several vegetarian choices for around £4.

The Burleigh Arms

budget, children

❖ *DISCOUNT VOUCHER - 15% OFF*

9-11 Newmarket Road
Cambridge CB5 8EG
Map ref: back C7
Telephone: 01223 301547
Open Mon-Sat: 11.30am-3pm,
5.30-11pm, Sun: noon-3pm, 6-10.30pm

Food served daily:
noon-2.30, 6-9pm
Prices: steaks £5.95-
£7.95, pizzas £3.75-
£6.55, burgers £2.05-
£2.30, sandwiches £1.40

Under new ownership, renovated and redecorated in late 1998, the Burleigh Arms is a completely different place. Gone is the Mexican restaurant. Instead you find a handsomely wood-panelled interior – fixed up by the new landlords themselves – with all new fittings. The two big rooms, one with a high, arched ceiling, create a well-lit comfortable place for a meal or a drink that is welcoming to everyone – office people, students and, not least, families with children.

a well-lit comfortable place for a meal or a drink that is welcoming to everyone... food is rather tasty... particularly good value

Once a part of a brewery, this family-run pub has a tap and menu to match its style. Along with good beer, including Boddingtons, Guinness and real ales, the menu includes favourites like Shepherds Pie (£2.75) and Pasta Carbonara (£2.95). The service is good and the food is rather tasty, making the prices particularly good value.

The Cambridge Blue
budget, children, garden, pets allowed, veg choice

85-87 Gwydir Street
Cambridge CB1 2LG
Map ref: back E 8
Telephone: 01223 361382
Open Mon-Fri: noon-2.30pm, 6-11pm, Sat: noon-4pm, 6-11pm, Sun: noon-3pm, 7-10.30pm

No credit cards
Non-smoking area
Prices: pub meals under £5

In a long terrace row of brick houses, the Cambridge Blue stands out from the outside for being, naturally, blue. Inside, pub memorabilia cover the walls and a collection of old hats – donated by pub goers – give a comfortable feel to the the two rooms, conservatory and small bar.

Talking and companionship is what the Cambridge Blue is about... The world's only Nethergate-tied pub... is one of the friendliest pubs in the city

Talking and companionship is what the Cambridge Blue is about. The pub has no music, no juke box, no fruit machines, not even a telly. As the world's only Nethergate-tied pub, you get a range of the brewery's best real ales – from IPA to Augustinian – along with an endless parade of guest beers. The pub has stocked upwards of 1,500, after which Nick, the pub landlord, lost count. Apparently his busy political life distracted him from this important accounting task. He ran for national office as a candidate for the Monster Raving Loony Party, along with the late Lord Sutch. So we may never know the real number...

If not knowing the crucial figure bothers you, the

pub offers some stiff rums, including Whole Hog from the Bahamas, Green Island from Mauritius and Bundaberg from Australia. There is an interesting and good range of pub food (The vegetarian chili was super) along with Balti curries on Sunday. The pub offers one of the biggest city pub gardens, stretching back over a space as big as an elongated tennis court and full of picnic tables and shady trees. Pub goers – old and young, with lots of families, kids and pets in tow – enjoy the brief warm periods in a mood of easy relaxation.

The Blue, as it is now affectionately known, was orginally the Dew Drop Inn, and is known to have been a pub as far back as 1874. It has been deservedly listed in the Good Beer Guide for several years and is distinguished as probably the only pub in the world with its own chaplain, Colin Shaw, who was appointed by no less than the Bishop of Huntingdon some years back, and comes around regularly for a pint. If you're in the neighbourhood, we recommend you come by too. This is one of the friendliest pubs in the city.

The Castle Inn

budget, children, student, terrace, veg choice

36 Castle Street
Cambridge CB3 0AJ
Map ref: back B 1
Telephone: 01223 353194
Open daily: 11.30am-3pm, 5-11pm
food served daily: 11.45am-2.15pm, 6-9.15pm

Credit cards except
American Express
Children welcome
Non-smoking area
Prices: pub food under £5

'No teams, no pool tables, no juke box, no fruit machines,' says landlord John Halsey, describing the Castle. Background music it has though, mostly tuned to the radio at lunch, and in the

> **'No teams, no pool tables, no juke box,'**... **a fine, friendly pub**... **where you can enjoy nine Adnams beers**

evenings, 'everybody has to put up with what I like,' which happens to be 'good blues and jazz and NO OASIS.' he says. You would expect a former rock musician to have views on vibes. Halsey belonged to the 70s group, The Rutles, a spoof Beatles, and played with many top singers on tour and in the recording studio.

You may want to pop in to see if you can spot any of the aging hippy stars among Halsey's friends, who occasionally come by. Most people, of course, come to The Castle because it is a fine, friendly pub where you can also enjoy the nine Adnams beers always on tap. On the crest of Castle Hill, next to the ruins of the Roman castle, the three-storey 1748 building retains the nooks and crannies of old. In a complete 1994 renovation by the Adnams Brewery, it gained a quiet picnic-tabled patio as well. The pub serves a good meal for under £5 and is popular with students from the nearby Cambridge colleges and people from the big office complex nearby, as well as tourists, visitors and locals.

The County Arms

43 Castle Street
Cambridge CB3 OAH
Map ref: back B 1
Telephone: 01223 566696
Open Mon-Sat: 11am-3pm, 5-11pm,
Sun: noon-3pm, 7-10.30pm

Food served Mon-Fri:
noon-2pm, 6-9pm,
Sun: noon-2.30pm,
7-9pm
Prices: pub food mostly
under £5

If you follow the logic of the story about the world's oldest axe (the axe head was changed five times and the handle six times, making it the oldest), then The County Arms is ancient indeed. This former hotel is the 1940s successor to a 16th century pub called the Three Tuns that once stood on the flower-filled pocket park next door. A pen drawing of the old pub hangs just inside the County Arms' door.

This former hotel is the 1940s successor to a 16th century pub called the Three Tuns... looking great after a tasteful renovation in 1998

Today, the County Arms is looking great after a tasteful renovation in 1998 gave it a new wooden counter in the middle, dark wood panelling and airy front room. In the back you find a darts board, seating in nooks and a couple of fruit machines. Being across the street from the County Council headquarters and near several Cambridge colleges, a cross-section of people – office workers, neighbourhood regulars and students – come in for food and the wide range of real ales and guest beers. The Tuesday quiz night attracts a crowd and sometimes the publican puts on musical entertainment. This is a friendly pub with fresh premises.

The Cricketers Arms

garden, veg choice

❖❖ *DISCOUNT VOUCHER - BOTTLE OF HOUSE WINE*

18 Melbourne Place
Cambridge CB1 1EQ
Map ref: back D 5
Telephone: 01223 508255
Open daily: noon-11pm
Food served daily: noon-2.30pm,
Tue-Sat: 6-9pm, Sun: noon-2.30pm

No credit cards
Music Wed: 8.30pm jazz,
Sun: 8.30pm Irish folk band
Children welcome when
eating with parents
bed and breakfast upstairs
Prices: pub food under £6

The oldest pub in this part of Cambridge, The Cricketers, takes its name from a stroke of marketing genius in the 19th century. The pub was built in 1838, when housing replaced what had been orchards (hence the local street names – Orchard Street, Adam and Eve etc.). At first, due to the nearness of the local prison (where the Parkside swimming pool is now located), the pub was called The First and The Last. By 1840, apparently wishing to attract a more wholesome crowd, it was changed to The Cricketers, because of the nearness to Parker's Piece where cricket has been played since the 1600s. It must have worked, because the pub is still going, and the clientele looks more likely to be the sort that might play a wicket than spend a tour in the local gaol.

you find a good, varied crowd at this quiet backstreet pub, including a lot of students who come for music and the half price student lunches. On a sunny day, they make good use of the attractive garden

Instead, you find a good, varied crowd at this quiet backstreet pub, including a lot of students who come for music and the half price student lunches. On a sunny day, they make good use of the attractive garden, with its abundant white and purple petunias, the pool table, and not least the good range of beers: real ales like Greene King IPA and Abbot and anything from Carling, Stella and Caffreys to Guinness and Scrumpy Jack on tap. Lunches include the traditional Steak & Kidney Pie (£5) or Spaghetti Bolognese (£5) sort, while the evening meals include B-B-Q chicken (£.6.25), vegetable pancakes (£5.25) and, on Sunday a traditional roast lunch.

Dobblers Inn

children, pets allowed

184 Sturton Street
Cambridge CB1 2QF
Map ref: back D 8
Telephone: 01223 576092
Open Mon-Sat: noon-11pm,
Sun: noon-10.30pm

Food served: daily noon-2pm
Children admitted before 7.30pm
Credit cards except American
Express (purchases over £10
only)
Prices: bar food £3-£5

On the site of an old 'rag and bones' junkyard, so earning the name The Dobblers, this out-of-the-way pub attracts a mix of locals, old and young, and a good number of students. The big square room with high ceilings has a comfortable feel about it, with lots of the old features retained in the 1878 building.

The big square room with high ceilings has a comfortable feel about it, with lots of the old features retained in the 1878 building

There are the usual pubby attractions: pool table, TV projected on a big screen, garden and come-as-you-are atmosphere. Kids and pets are okay (but kids until 7.30pm only. Pets get to stay up late). A big draw is Tuesday quiz night. The pub serves real ales – Bombardier, Speckled Hen, Eagle – and has guest beers, like a recent one, Pedigree. The publican makes good pub lunches for under £5.

This recently refurbished Charles Wells-linked pub has the distinction of being across the road from the site where the first house was levelled by a bomb outside London in World War II. That must have made pub-goers look up from their pints.

The Elm Tree

garden courtyard

42 Orchard Street
Cambridge CB1 1JT
Map ref: back D 5
Telephone: 01223 363005
Open Mon-Sat: noon-2.30pm,
4-11pm, Sun: 1-10.30pm

No credit cards
Entertainment: Sun, Mon &
Thu jazz 8.30pm
No food served

The Elm Tree is the sort of place anybody can walk into and feel welcome. Located on a tree-shaded backstreet, this is a 100-year-old traditional pub – with a few pub stools around the wood bar and lots of red-velvet covered seats around the tables and out in the garden area. People come in for a board game – Scrabble is popular – or for the sports TV or to read the newspapers and magazines. If they are feeling energetic, they might venture a game of bar billiards on the Victorian-style table at the back. Excellent live jazz of the interesting, international variety gives the Elm Tree extra sparkle three evenings a week.

A Charles Wells Pub, The Elm Tree seats about 50 people. It offers real ales like Broadside and, on tap, Bombardier, Eagle IPA and seasonal beers along with a good selection of whiskies.

> the sort of place anybody can walk into and feel welcome... 100-year-old traditional pub... Excellent live jazz

The Empress
children, courtyard, pets allowed

72 Thoday Street
Cambridge CB1 3AX
Map ref: back H 8 (just beyond)
Telephone/fax: 01223 247236
No credit cards

Open Mon-Sat:
11.30am-2.30pm,
Sun: noon-2.30pm
No food served

'We're a nice, steady backstreet pub with courtyard,' says landlord Dave Lewin. That's exactly what is special about The Empress. It is a true community pub. You can join a conversation or sit quietly by yourself. Newcomer or regular, you seem to fit in.

On the intersection of streets of 19th-century terraced houses, the pub dates to 1887 and is probably related in origins to the Jubilee anniversary of Queen Victoria (Empress of India). Flower baskets bedeck the outside, and the interior is bright and simple. Seat areas wrap around the bar and pub goers make good use of the pool, darts, juke box and electronic games. The bar serves a good choice of real ales.

> 'a nice, steady backstreet pub with courtyard'... the interior is bright and simple... The bar serves a good choice of real ales

Rest in Peas

TM-J

Central-Pubs

The Five Bells

gay

❖ *DISCOUNT VOUCHER - FREE PINT*

126-128 Newmarket Road
Cambridge CB4 8HE
Map ref: back C 8
Telephone: 01223 314019
No credit cards

Open Mon-Tue: 7-11pm,
Wed-Sat: noon-3, 7-11pm,
Sun: noon-10.30pm
Entertainment: disco twice a month,
fetish night monthly
No food served

The Five Bells is the easy-going gay pub. It prides itself on being the place in Cambridge where gay men and women can feel at home – whether newly come out or new to town, one of the beautiful people or otherwise. The staff are a friendly lot, enthusiastic about making the Five Bells fun for all.

easy-going gay pub... gay men and women can feel at home... whether newly come out or new to town

As of mid-1999 the Five Bells, gay since early 1998, had been in the process of changing from a brewery-tied pub to a freehouse, which will allow the pub to stock a wider selection of beers and spirits. A major renovation is underway to give the premises a much needed rejuvenation.

The Five Bells does not serve food but has the usual pub features, backgammon, pool table, juke box and beer garden. Twice a month it holds a disco and once every three months, a fetish night.

Fleur de Lys

gay-friendly, parking, pets allowed

73 Humberstone Road
Cambridge CB4 1JD
Map ref: back A 7
Telephone: 01223 356095
No children

Open Mon-Sat: 6.30-11pm,
Sat-Sun: noon-3pm
Entertainment: live bands, discos
No credit cards
Food: Sunday lunch only
Parking at rear

The Fleur de Lys is a gay-friendly pub with the usual quiz nights, darts and pool table. Occasionally it offers live music and discos. Together with its open-minded policies and mixed clientele, the recently refurbished

a gay-friendly pub. friendly and relaxe atmosphere

pub has a friendly and relaxed atmosphere. It is located at the foot of the Elizabeth Way Bridge and across from a petrol station. The pub serves the Pubmaster range of beer, including Carlsberg, Greene King IPA and Boddingtons.

The Flying Pig

INSIDER
CHOICE

106 Hills Road
Cambridge CB2 1LQ
Map ref: back I 6
Telephone: unavailable
Open Mon-Fri: 11.30am-11pm,
Sat: 1-11pm, Sun: noon-3.30pm,
7-10.30pm

Food served Mon-Fri: noon-2pm
No children
Prices: pub food under £4
Music: some Tue & Sun 9pm
jazz, blues, funk etc.

The Flying Pig is the piggiest little pub in the world. Pigs proliferate in every corner. Pig posters and T-shirts look down from the ceiling. Cute piglets, fat ones, standing and sitting pigs, pigs with beatific smiles line the shelves. A full-sized working pig in a flying jacket (like those moving Santas in the shop windows) brings a frothy pint to his piggy lips. This pig no doubt is to remind pub goers of the pub tenant Mick, nicknamed 'the pig', an intrepid traveler who flies planes and for **there is more than Flying Pigs to The Flying Pig (in a pig's eye, you might say if you were Australian): good food, bar billiards, newspapers and magazines, television (thankfully, seldom on, one might add) and at least four real ales** whom the former Crown earned its much more memorable name seven or eight years ago.

And at The Flying Pig, pigs might fly, in fact they do, from all over the world, on postcards from former pub goers who send an unending stream of pigs for posting behind the bar. Of course, there is more than Flying Pigs to The Flying Pig (in a pig's eye, you might say if you were Australian): good food, bar billiards, newspapers and magazines, television (thankfully, seldom on, one might add) and at least four real ales (and no pigwash either) on tap at any time. That's a lot of pig to fit in a poke (I mean pub) where the walls are all black, candles stuck in old Jack Daniel's bottles boost the dim but intimate lighting and the whole place is hardly big enough to park a couple of pig-mobiles side by side. A lot of people come by, office people by day mainly and by evening a good mix of pig lovers – many on the last leg of the pub crawl for pubbers heading toward The Junction for a show or club. Oink!

The Free Press
garden/patio, pets allowed, veg choice

❖❖ *DISCOUNT VOUCHER - FREE PUDDING*

7 Prospect Row
Cambridge CB1 1DU
Map ref: back E 6
Telephone: 01223 368337
Open Mon-Sat: noon-2.30pm,
6-11pm, Sun: noon-3pm,
7-10.30pm

No smoking
Children who behave admitted
with parents
Prices: pub food under £5

On a shaded backstreet, the black and white fronted Free Press looks small, even inconspicuous. But this little pub, inside hardly large enough to park two Fords side by side, has one of the biggest hearts of any in Cambridge. You sense it the moment you walk in. Rowing memorabilia – team pictures, inscribed oars, trophies, odd letters thanking the pub for its hospitality – clutter the walls; postcards from pub friends and paper money

this little pub... has one of the biggest hearts of any in Cambridge... the moment you walk in... the cheer is palpable...

souvenirs creep over onto the ceiling from behind the bar. Flash a smile as you come in and it is returned as both staff and regulars seem happy to receive new-comers. Young and old, locals and office workers mix easily, and the cheer is palpable at meal times. On cool evenings, the warmth gets really warm when a wood fire burns in the open hearth.

The food here is particularly good. Nothing is deep fried. There are lots of salads and interesting simple foods like chicken or vegetable burritos. Vegetarians are especially well-catered for, with imaginative, tasty foods cooked for good eating. There are excellent patés and unusual desserts like a beautifully purple mulled wine pudding. And it is all still pub food – with everything for under £5.

Run by the pub licensee and his wife for more than 21 years, the Free Press is a place for a chat, to play pub games like cribbage or dominos or stroke the cat and rabbits out in the flowered garden. In the 70s and 80s students used to amuse themselves by seeing how many people they could pack into a phone-booth sized 'secret' room of the pub called a snug. The record is an incredible 61. This was no easy record to set, requiring medics on hand to revive the semi-smothered. When the pub literally started bursting at the seams the record setting days had to be called to a halt.

There may be no more stuffing, but there is still a lot

of huffing and puffing – The Free Press hosts its own rowing teams – 18 of them – for the annual May Bumps competitions, and last year its women's team led the pack and the men came in eighth. And when it is all over the rowers come by for the best part. This Greene King-linked pub offers several real ales, including Abbot, IPA and Mild XX and two lagers, along with Guinness on tap (which they take the time to pour properly). It specialises in malt whiskies, stocking brands such as Glenmorangie, Highland Park and Talisker. While drinking the rowers can admire the 10-foot hull section of the University of Cambridge rowing shell salvaged from a 1984 race mishap and perhaps think that, no matter how the race went, it could have been worse.

Fresher & Firkin

student, wines by the glass

16 Chesterton Road
Cambridge CB4 3AX
Map ref: back B 4
Telephone: 01223 324325
Open Mon-Fri: noon-11pm,
Sun: noon-10.30pm

No one under 18 admitted
food served: daily noon-7pm
Credit cards except
American Express

For the most part, students find The Fresher & Firkin congenial, with its big spaces and room for all. On any evening students come in droves, including a lot of foreign students, fanning out over the spacious ground floor. The big room, once a fitness centre and before that one of the seven cinemas that once operated in Cambridge, has all the attractions – fruit machines, electronic games and full-size pool table. It even has pub games like Giant Connect 4. It has a long, long wood and brass bar, serving the range of Firkin brews, ales and session beers.

> **students come in droves, including a lot of foreign students... The big room... has all the attractions – fruit machines, electronic games and full-size pool table...**

Opened in 1995, Fresher & Firkin has its own microbrewery, though now idle. But microbrewery beer is delivered to the Cambridge pub from the Fresher & Firkin branch in Watford. There is also a function room upstairs used by private groups and, if planning permission is forthcoming, this will be where bands play in future.

Central Pubs

The Granta

garden courtyard

14 Newnham Road
Cambridge CB3 9EX
Map ref: back F 2
Telephone: 01223 505016
Open Mon-Sat: noon-11pm,
Sun: noon-10.30pm

Food served Mon-Fri:
noon-2.30pm, 6-8pm,
Sat-Sun: noon-4pm
Prices: pub food £3-£6

It's 1970s inside and picture perfect outside. That's the Granta, a converted mid-19th century watermill overlooking the weeping willow-edged mill pond at the southern end of the Backs. Inside, the pub is the result of a 1975 remodeling of an area that had once been a garage into a knotty pine room with fruit machines and juke box – nice enough, but nothing to write home about. Usually you find a good mix of people – students, locals, visitors – drinking the Greene King brews and eating the food on any day of the week.

a converted mid-19th century watermill overlooking the weeping willow-edged mill pond... looks a picture... If you feel like taking in a punt ride, the Granta is also the best place to do so

What distinguishes the Granta is the outside and what you can see there. The listed, three-storey building made of grey Gault brick itself looks a picture. Petunias spill from huge baskets hung from the walls and a cosy courtyard paved with the same old brick opens to the street. Behind the pub, a broad wooden deck overlooks the pond. You can see the water from inside but on warm days the deck is the ideal place to take in the tranquillity of ducks paddling around and punts gliding. It takes away worldly cares.

If you feel like taking in a punt ride, the Granta is also, in our view, the best place to do so. Most people see the punts at the Quay first, so they tend go there, but the Granta punts are less expensive and a punt ride takes you though a green and calm end of the river as well as the (often) bumper-car crowded historic end. Self-hire punts go for £7 an hour on weekdays and £8 on weekends or £5.50 per person for chauffered rides. For information call Granta Punt Hire Co at 01223 301845 (granta.boats@lineone.net).

The Green Dragon
**children, dessert, garden,
pets allowed, veg choice**

*INSIDER
CHOICE*

The Green Dragon
5 Water Street, Chesterton
Cambridge CB4 1NZ
Map ref: back A7 (just beyond)
Telephone: 01223 505035
Open Mon-Sat: 11am-11pm,
Sun: noon-4pm, 7-10.30pm

Food served Mon-Sat: noon-
2.30pm, 6-9pm, Sun: noon-2pm
Children not allowed after 7pm
Entertainment: Wed quiz night
9pm, occasional music
Prices: bar food £1.10-£7.95,
Sunday roast £4.95

The Green Dragon is really two pubs: the sunny, outside garden pub with a view over the river to Stourbridge Common, weeping willows and grazing cows and the smoky, antique building full of TVs, newspapers, banter and beer. Conveniently for my description but not so convenient for the punters a road divides one from the other. Luckily it is a pretty quiet road. There is more danger from the cyclists careering headlong over the bridge into the beer garden than there is from cars.

> two pubs... sunny, outside garden pub with a view over the river... and the smoky, antique building full of TVs, newspapers, banter and beer

Perfect for a sunny day or evening but also perfect for the not-so-sunny seasons with its low ceilings, timbered nooks and (by winter) huge open log fire, the Green Dragon is apparently one of the oldest pubs in the town if not the oldest (it's a close-run contest with The Pickerel). It has had its spirits license since 1630 but is reputed to have been trading as a beer house since at least 1550. Oliver Cromwell is known to have stayed here. As a Greene King pub it offers IPA and Abbot plus the much rarer Mild (said to be the best pint of Mild in town) and a weekly guest ale like Marston's Pedigree. The pub food, which ranges from sandwiches and ploughmans to daily specials and Sunday lunch, is traditional and good value.

If you arrive on a hot Friday evening, expect the garden to be busy but not overcrowded, with a mixed and cheerful crowd of punters enjoying the sunshine and atmosphere.

The Live and Let Live

40 Mawson Road
Cambridge CB1 2EA
Map ref: back H 7
Telephone: 01223 460261
Open Mon-Fri: 11.30am-2.30pm,
Sat: 12.30-2.30pm,
Sun: noon-2.30pm, 7-10.30pm

Non-smoking area
Children allowed when
eating with adults
Prices: pub meal under £5

The story goes that the owner of the pub on Mawson road was fuming. Parliament had passed a law allowing anybody to sell beer. Everywhere people were selling pints out of their living rooms, cutting into his pub business. He plastered the outsides of the pub with posters protesting the act, demanding that Parliament get off his back. 'Live and Let Live' the posters said. The name stuck, and so today we have a Live and Let Live that has been a pub continuously since the middle 1800s.

Nothing fancy here. No pub games or fruit machines. Just nice people, locals and quite a few visitors... The pub is distinguished for its good beer...

The Live and Let Live has somehow lived up to its name. Nothing fancy here. No pub games or fruit machines. Just nice people, locals and quite a few visitors. These are people at ease, feeling open and friendly. They sit around wooden tables and talk animatedly over drinks and good quality pub food. Gas lights, a rarity these days, cast a particularly warm glow over the low, wood-panelled room and music plays in the background. As a visitor, I felt right at home. It was easy to join in bar conversations or just sit back.

The pub is distinguished for its good beer. This includes cask conditioned real ales – Adnams, Everards, Tiger and the like – and one that is brewed expressly for the Live and Let Live: Bruno's Bitter. You can get it only at this pub. The beer won the Live and Let Live the area chapter of the Campaign for Real Ale's pub of the year award. It's a remarkable pub and well deserves the honour.

Panton Arms

budget, garden courtyard

INSIDER
CHOICE

Panton Street
Cambridge CB1 1HL
Map ref: back H 4
Telephone: 01223 355733
Open Mon-Sat: 11am-11pm,
Sun: noon-10.30pm

Food served Mon-Sun: noon-2pm,
Mon-Sat: snacks only 6-8pm
No children
Prices: pub food £3-£5

Possibly the loveliest backstreet pub in Cambridge, the Panton Arms looks a picture. It rises on the corner of two streets of 19th-century terraced houses. The cream-yellow walls bedecked with overflowing baskets of petunias beckon you in. Around one side, a listed wrought iron gate opens into the paved pub garden, with more flowers and rows of picnic tables. Like many Cambridge pubs, the Panton Arms was once the front of a brewery. The gate, wide enough for a big horse-drawn wagon, was the entrance to Bailey and Tibbet, a brewery later purchased by 'Greene King & Sons Ltd', whose name the gate now bears in big gold letters.

possibly the loveliest backstreet pub in Cambridge... walls bedecked with overflowing baskets of petunias beckon you in... reputed to have the best beer in Cambridge... we tend to agree

The pub has two rooms, a back room of more recent vintage where food is served, and a smaller front room that was the original pub. In the small room with the pool table and fruit machines and juke box, you'll find pictures of the old brewery and a rare cast iron plaque celebrating the 1897 Diamond Jubilee (60th) anniversary of Queen Victoria as ruler of 'Great Britain and Ireland, Empress of India' and all the colonies. You can still drink a toast to her here, as they did over 100 years ago, and join the broad mix of people who frequent this well-run pub.

The Panton Arms has a good pub menu, real ales and is reputed to have the best beer in Cambridge. We tend to agree. Publican J K John has been running the pub for eight years and in the business for 30 years and knows how to keep a keg.

The Portland Arms

budget, student

129 Chesterton Rd
Mitcham's Corner
Cambridge CB4 3BA
Map ref: back A 4
Telephone: 01223 357268
Open Mon-Fri: 11am-3pm, 6-11pm,
Sun: noon-2.30pm, 7-10.30pm

Food served: daily noon-2pm,
Wed-Sat 6-10pm
No credit cards
Music: nightly live folk, rock
(cost: free to £7)
Prices: pub food under £5

The Portland Arms is three pubs in one. In the comfy, sofa-filled main room with a nautical theme (after the pub's namesake, the Earl of Portland), you find all sorts – people from local offices, locals, regulars – and when the music starts rolling, a still mixed but youngish crowd. Over in the saloon bar, the cribbage tournament gets heated along with darts and bar billiards.

an open, 'come join us' feel... folk music reigns supreme... If you have but one night to spend to get to know Cambridge and its music, this is an excellent choice

Neighbourhood people and regulars seem to be most numerous, but with an open, 'come join us' feel. In the back room, almost nightly, you hear fine folk music along with a range of popular music.

Music reigns because four music impresario organisations make the pub home. The Monkey House and Wild Strawberry Music bring bands and DJs with anything from indie to funk and beyond. But folk music reigns supreme here because both the Cambridge Folk Club and the Mayflower Folk Club, the city's two big folk organisers, strut their stuff at the Portland Arms. Only here in Cambridge do you hear the grass roots traditions and modern permutations of folk music. In a typical month, they bring in vocals on diatonic accordian, jazz and swing bands, French traditional dance musicians, pianists with vocal accompaniment, many performing original compositions. Though small, this venue is a favourite among some of the nation's leading folk musicians, but at the same time there is an open stage for all comers.

The Portland Arms, built in stages from 1932 to replace what had been the Scales Hotel, has undergone a renaissance in the past few years. The management has brought the music clubs back where they had once been in the 1960s, and generally given the pub a new energy. The good range of beer, mainly the Greene King range, with a few guest beers, is supplemented by a food of mostly traditional pie-and-mash choices on the under £5 menu. It's a lovely pub with a bright spirit. If you have but one night to spend to get to know Cambridge and its music, this is an excellent choice.

The Rock

200 Cherry Hinton Road
Cambridge CB1 4AW
Map ref: back I 6 (just beyond)
Telephone: 01223 505005
Open Mon-Sat: 11am-11pm,
Sun: noon-10.30pm
Parking at back

Food served Mon-Sun:
noon-2pm, 6-9pm
Music: weekends
Outdoor picnic tables in front
Credit cards except American
Express (food only)
Prices: pub food under £5

The Rock is a big pub dedicated to sports. If a big match is on TV or cable – racing, cricket, football, rugby, golf, pool, you name it – the four 24-inch TVs and big screen will be tuned in. Sports memorabilia in the form of autographed photographs of sports heros adorn the walls and outside the Union Jack and St George's flags proudly fly. On Saturdays, the pub throws in live music as well.

a big pub dedicated to sports. If a big match is on TV or cable... the four 24-inch TVs and big screen will be tuned in... welcoming, friendly

Believed to have been named after a man called Rockingdale who once owned a lot of property in the area, the Rock has lots of electronic games and fruit machines, the Greene King range of ales and a welcoming, friendly face.

The Salisbury Arms
budget, children, pets allowed, student, veg choice

76 Tenison Road
Cambridge CB1 2DW
Map ref: back I 7
Telephone: 01223 576363
Open Mon-Thu: noon-2.30pm,
6-11pm, Fri-Sun: all day

Food served daily: noon-2pm,
Mon-Fri: 6-8pm
Non-smoking area
Prices: pub food £3-£5
Children welcome until 8pm

Among the handsomest pubs in Cambridge, The Salisbury Arms looks small from the outside but grand inside. Once a hotel, the 1886 building was renovated in the 1970s by the Campaign for Real Ale, turning it into the vision of a real ale drinker's pub. It maintains that feeling today, and a dedication to good beer, stocking at any one time up to eight well-kept real ales and also guest and session beers.

Central-Pubs

The airy, wood-panelled rooms are big enough to give everyone space. You can drink in peace amid the beer festival posters at one end, oblivious to the multi-channel TV in the two-storey high bar area toward the back or have a meal in the non-smoking dining room. The menu ranges from salads to vegetarian choices and a good value Sunday roast lunch.

Among the handsomest pubs in Cambridge... the vision of a real ale drinker's pub... big enough to give everyone space... cheery atmosphere

Not surprisingly, the pub attracts a good cross-section of people, with a lot of students among the locals and, as the publican likes to call them, the 'young at heart'. The pub is also a first stop on the stag party circuit.

The staff – a friendly lot – foster the cheery atmosphere at this Charles Wells-linked pub as do light Cambridge-y touches like the cyclist – a mannequin on a bike anyway – suspended from the vaulted ceiling.

The Wrestlers

Thai, veg choice

337 Newmarket Road
Cambridge CB5 8JE
Map ref: back C8 (just beyond)
Telephone: 01223 566554
Open: Mon-Sat: noon-3pm,
5-11pm

Food served Mon-Sat:
noon-3pm, 5-9pm
No credit cards
Prices: main course £6-£7

Ten years ago Cambridge had no Thai food (in a pub or restaurant at least). The Wrestlers was the first to introduce Thai and it was an instant success. A decade later, the Wrestlers is full of office goers and locals who come in for a curry and a pint. The pub, an unelaborate green-walled, wood-floored room with a bar at centre, is particularly popular among the techies from the science parks not far away.

The food matches the decor – simple and hearty. I tucked into green chicken curry (£6.10) one lunch that had a good balance of coconut on chili, big pieces of chicken, red bell pepper and peas. The menu posted on a blackboard lists a score of unfancy curries, fried rice and noodles that are served in good-sized portions. You can wash down the meal with the Charles Welles range of beer and then play a game at the pool table or fruit machine.

The pub itself is a handsome 1920s building on an unhandsome commercial street. It is a successor to other pubs on the site, apparently dating back hundreds of years to the medieval Stourbridge Fair, which took place behind the pub on Stourbridge Common. The pub name is believed to come from the wrestlers and other side shows at the fair, where Isaac Newton bought Venetian crystal that he used in his experiments with optics. One wonders

first to introduce Thai and it was an instant success.... an unelaborate green-walled, wood-floored room with a bar... The food matches the decor – simple and hearty....

what Isaac would have discovered if he could have had a good green curry with his apple?

The Boat Race

170 East Road
Cambridge CB1 1DB
Map ref: back D 6-7
Telephone: 01223 508533

Open daily: from 8pm
Entry fee: free to £6
No one under 18 admitted
Bar service, no food served

On 11 May 1994, a previously little known band hit town for a one-night only performance. It began in obscurity, but by the time the booking at the Boat Race came up, its reputation had outgrown its engagements. Nonetheless, they turned up, acted like a bunch of prima donnas and played what by all accounts was a blister-ing half-hour set.

willing to take a chance on unknowns, it has been able to snap up top acts before others knew they existed... rock, folk, celtic, blues, indie, pop and even a smattering of comedy...

The band's name was Oasis. The rest, as they say, is history. The episode says a lot about the Boat Race. Since the mid-1990s, it has been book-ing up-and-coming bands from all corners of Britain and abroad. Because it has been willing to take a chance on unknowns, it has been able to snap up top acts before others knew they existed.

Its stage at the front of a squash court-sized room presents a stream of live music with an excellent sound system. Up to 200 people at a time can hear the daily pro-gramme of rock, folk, celtic, blues, indie, pop and even a smattering of comedy. In the recent past, it has present-ed acts like Midge Ure, Boo Hewerdine, Ezio and more.

No fancy packaging here. The Boat Race, with its pub-type bar serving beer, wine and spirits, is as basic, wood-panelled and unpretentious as it is relaxed. It attracts a cross-section of people, from students to an older set interested in the music and home-grown talent.

Central-Pubs

Chicago Rock Café

22 Sydney Street
Cambridge CB2 3HG
Map ref: back D 4
Telephone: (01223) 324600
Open: Mon (international language
students only) 8pm-1am, Tue (Anglia
Polytechnic students only) and Wed
(Cambridge University students only)
and other nights 9pm-2am

Entry fee £4-£5
No one under 18 Mon-Thu,
No one under 21 Fri-Sat
Dress: smart casual – no
blue jeans, no trainers no
heavy boots,
Prices (typical): bottles
£2.70, pints £2.40, soft
drinks £1-£1.50

The Chicago Rock Café, tucked in an alley off Sydney
Street, has undergone a bit of an evolution, becoming
more and more nightclub and less and less bar café. By
early 2000 it is scheduled
for a full makeover, moving
it upmarket and making it
bigger and more attractive
to the more mature (read
21-35) age group. In its old
persona, it used to play 50s
and 60s music and serve a
limited menu, but more
recently it has grown out of solid foods and joined the
mainstream (night) club crowd. The drinks are the main
feature and music-wise it does all sorts of music, from r
'n'b and dance to the new chart stuff.

used to play 50s and 60s music and serve a limited menu, but more recently it has grown out of solid foods and joined the mainstream (night) club crowd

What the refit will bring has at the time of writing
not been announced, but for now it is has an Americana
theme. The place is adorned with half of a Cadillac, pictures of baseball players and similar paraphernalia, creating character for the up to 520 clubbers who crowd
in on a typical night.

Fez Club

15 Market Passage
Cambridge CB2 3HX
Map ref: back D 3
Telephone: 01223 519224
Open daily: from 8pm or
8.30pm-2am

Entry fee: free to £8 depending on
day and time
No one under 18 admitted
Bar service, no food served
Prices (typical): beer £2, spirits
£2.50

Grotto-like, dark and pulsating, classy and funky come
to mind in describing the Fez Club. The club itself has
its own list: no attitude, no drunks, no guest lists, no
dress code. Behind a door that looks a bit like an
entrance to a castle dungeon, you pass a youthful
bouncer, with red jumper, and then fee takers at the
bottom of the stairs. Up one flight and the music beats

into your body as you choose between a lounge at the tables or the long bar or a foray into the coloured lights over the dance floor. The space has been fashioned into stony, cave-like rooms with low lighting.

A good part of the mostly well under-30 clientele come in with friends, ready to party. The men dress down often and the women

fashioned into stony, cave-like rooms with low lighting... the funky alternative... neither mainstream nor rebel

dress up, but not too much, and they all seem to have a bit of Saturday Night Fever, even if it's a weekday. This is the funky alternative on the Cambridge night club scene, neither mainstream nor rebel.

A typical rota begins on 'Magic Monday' – student night – with music 'spanning the decades' (free before 10pm, £2 with NUS, otherwise £3.50 after 9pm); on Tuesdays Espiritu takes over and it is international student night (free before 9pm, £4 before 10pm, £5 after). These bring in the younger clubbers, mostly in the 18-20 range.

The rest of the week it gets a bit older, averaging around 24. On Wednesdays DJ plays sounds 'only for funksters' (free before 9pm, £3 before 11pm, £5 after); Thursday there are street beats and R 'n' B night (free before 9pm £3 before 11pm, £5 after); on Friday House music (£3 before 9pm £5 from 9-10pm, £8 after); Saturday features Ministry of Sound with 'wicked garage' (£5 before 10pm, £8 after; Sunday brings 'spiritual'vibes – gospel garage (free, last drinks 10.30pm).

The Fez Club is relatively small, with a capacity for just 300, and seems to maintain an adequate level of security.

Fifth Avenue

Heidelburg Gardens, Lion Yard
Cambridge CB2 3NA
Map ref: back D 4
Telephone: 01223 364222
Open: Mon-Sat 9pm-2am
Entry fee: £0.90 - £6.50, discount for groups

No one under 18 admitted
dress code: Fri-Sat no jeans, no trainers, shirts with collars required
Prices: (typical) beer £2, spirits £2.60

In a long, low room with walls, floor and ceiling all painted black, coloured lights flash and mix with body-penetrating vibrations of dance music. Clubbers girate to the pulsations or, in the

owy and fashionable... celebrates mainstream uth culture

low light off the dance floor, gather in small groups –

looking around, drinking, smoking, chatting. Some stand by the bar or outside on the patio where, on warm days, a barbeque is on offer. Others lounge in the soft chairs. Dress is neat and often showy and fashionable – some of the women sport strappy evening wear.

Just beyond, a line of after-pubbers waiting to enter is being vetted by the nattily suited, ear-phone wearing phalanx of bouncers. Occasionally, one of the burly security men moves through the throng to discreetly eject an unwelcome patron, but no one seems bothered. Security appears to be well in hand and the mood is light.

Located above a row of shops in the Petty Cury Shopping Street, Fifth Avenue celebrates mainstream youth culture for a mainly 18-25 year-old clientele. The programme suits their tastes. A typical rota is as follows: 'Hustle' Mondays for 70s and 80s music (£3.50 before 10.30, £4 after); 'Big Holy Noise' Tuesdays for students with student IDs only (£3.50 before 10.30, £4 after); 'Pure FM' Wednesdays features a mix of R 'n' B and soul (£2 before 10:30, £3 after); 'Hey You' Thursdays, with music from around the world, is for foreign students (£5 all night); 'A Kick Up the 90s' Fridays is a retrospective of 90s and top chart music (90p entry before 10:30, £6.50 after); 'Definitive' Saturday offers the best of the charts and dance floor music (£5.50 before 10:30, £6.50 after).

This is a middle-sized club with a capacity of 635, although plans are afoot to expand.

The Junction

Clifton Road
Cambridge CB1 7GX
Map ref: back I 5 (just beyond)
Telephone: 01223 511511
Booking hotline: (0115) 9129000
(booking fee charged)
Box office hours Mon-Sat: noon to 6pm,
Additional hours on club, performance nights

Club night entrance fee: £3-£12
Large parking lot
Wheelchair accessible inc toilets
Prices: café food under £5, pints £2.30, wine £1.70

Although The Junction, strictly speaking, is more entertainment venue than night club, its regular club evenings form a big part of the Cambridge scene. In fact, The Junction club nights can be huge, bringing up to 1,050 jiggling, jiving, jumping clubbers together at a time in its skating rink-like auditorium venue outside the city centre.

The clubs alternate with live music performances of anything from blues to music of the Cameroonian Baka

Pygmies, but a typical month includes a few clubs for over 16s and over 18s. The Dot Cotton Club is Lesbigay, while the Havana nights feature Salsa music. Music ranges across the club spectrum – Reggae, House, Soul, Swing, R 'n' B, Jungle and Speed Garage. Hours also vary, with some running from 7pm to midnight and most from 10pm to 2am or all night, with late admission at midnight or 1am. The DJs pour on the music, with the usual rainbow of lighting effects and smoke.

> club nights can be huge, bringing up to 1,050 jiggling, jiving, jumping clubbers together... Music ranges across the club spectrum – Reggae, House, Soul, Swing, R 'n' B, Jungle and Speed Garage

Being so varied, it is a bit hard to pigeonhole The Junction, which was established as a charity in 1990 as a result of a campaign by young people for an entertainment venue in the city. A £5 million lottery grant recently won to extend and improve its facilities should add a lot to its attractiveness. At present, the Junction holds some 85 live music, theatre, dance, and comedy events a year in addition to clubs.

These appeal to a wide range of people – in fact the Junction has made its name by its creative programmes that bring in the community. But some late-night clubs can be a bit rough-edged with such big, well-oiled crowds. Clubbers may be searched at the door and drinks are served in plastic cups rather than bottles. More than a dozen burly bouncers keep an eye on the crowd in case of an incident. Security is a concern at all nightclubs, but the size of The Junction and its expanse of hard-to-police parking lot can magnify the problem. Even so, the security seems reasonably good.

Kambar

1 Wheeler Street
Cambridge CB2 3QB
Map ref: back E 3
Telephone: 01223 357503

Open: 10pm-3am
Entry fee: £2-£5
No one under 18 admitted
Bar service, no food served

You can tell a lot about a night spot by sizing up the bouncers. At the upmarket 5th Avenue, they wear suits with red ties. At the more traditional Henry's Café Bar they wear black night jackets, while across the Quay at the metallic Bar Coast, the fashion dictates black flak jack-

> casual, come as you [ar]e, no pretensions [ve]nue with a capacity [of] just 200... a little [rou]gh and ready and a [bit] rebellious in feel

ets. At Kambar, a somewhat foreboding black shop front between a tea shop and a low-cost long distance calls outlet, the bouncer wore a grey sweat suit top with a floppy hood. He chatted with some under 18s masquerading as over 18s who wanted to be let in, suggesting they try another venue.

When I approached, looking obviously over 18, he bid me a cheery, 'Go right in,' and resumed his discussion with the teenagers. I paid my fiver at the counter and went upstairs to find dimly-lit, Tudor-style rooms, the first a bar with some high round tables and stools. From the next, a dance floor with DJ overlooking what at 10.30pm was filling up. He poured out a jarring stream of Drum and Bass music, a descendant of Jungle, which if you've never heard it sounds like a slightly musical version of gears grinding. In the other two rooms, the early clubbers sat around at tables and chairs on the perimeter, sucking on beers and chatting in what at that point was not excessively loud music.

This is a casual, come as you are, no pretensions venue with a capacity of just 200. It is a a little rough and ready and a bit rebellious in feel, but that's the way the 18-25s who make up the majority of clubbers here like it.

Po Na Na

7a Jesus Lane
Cambridge CB5 8BA
Map ref: back C4
Telephone: 01223 323880
Open Mon: 7pm-midnight, Tue: 8.30pm-midnight, Fri-Sat: 8-midnight
Entry fee: £1.50-£3, no fee for members (£50 a year, 50% off for students)

Credit cards for over £10
No one under 18 admitted
over 21s only on weekends except for members
Prices (typical): £2.20 lagers, cocktails £4-£5 (£3-£4 in happy hours - all night Mon-Tue, Wed-Thu till 10.30, Fri-Sat till 9.30)

Underneath the monument-like facade of Pizza Express, the earth rumbles by night with the pulsations of Po Na Na, a youthful late night cocktail bar with a dance floor.

To dive in, walk past the lolling group of 20-somethings who have come up for air or a natter on their cellular phones, dodge the scrutiny of the fat red bouncer and head down the steps. As soon as you've paid the entrance fee to the coat room lady, you're in. Now prepare to enter a world dolled up for intrigue, Casa Blanca and Bogart slumped over the bar.

The ceiling of the main room is hung with bedouin tents and red pepper-shaped lanterns, and in the corners, potted palms stand out against sand-coloured walls. Groups of 18-25-ish clientele laze round on the big C-shaped, leopard-skin patterned couches around low tables with candles in coloured glass. Punters mostly sip from glasses served up on the bar decorated with zebra skin-design panels. This is beer and cocktail territory. Beers, any of 10 lagers, go for £2.20. For 50cc shot cocktails, you pay £3 for a shooter and £4 for a martini. Music not

a youthful late night cocktail bar with a dance floor... prepare to enter a world dolled up for intrigue, Casablanca and Bogart slumped over the bar...

being overly loud, the couples and groups chat and mix. T-shirts and jeans are okay.

Po Na Na is the come as you are, everyday night club. It feels okay to come alone.

Over on one side, there is dancing. Hot bodies pound and sway to the disco sounds pouring through the red and green lighting. DJs in a little control room overlooking the floor serve up the disco beat – underground, freestyle, house, garage, bathroom... you name it, but it's all chilled cool and not too heavy... and Monday is Latin night with salsa lessons.

Q Club

3 Station Road
Cambridge CB1 2JB
Map ref: back I 6
Telephone: 01223 315466
Open (schedule varies), usually
9pm-2am

Entry fee: £1-£2
No one under 18 admitted
No credit cards
Bar service only

The smallest of the Cambridge nightclubs, the Q-club fosters an image of exclusivity. It virtually disguises its presence. The entrance to the basement nightclub is marked with a Q and nothing else. The basement itself, painted

an image of exclusivity offers a range of the more anarchic music – rock, metal, alternative

wildly in jungle colours, has a small bar and a dance floor about as big as a parking space. It offers a range of the more anarchic music – rock, metal, alternative – and is sometimes closed to outsiders for groups who reserve the whole place for parties.

Central-Clubs

Red TV Café Bar

desserts, parking, sandwich, student

Sturton Street
Cambridge CB1 2QF
Map ref: back D 8
Telephone: 01223 716309
Open Mon-Fri: 10am-11pm,
Sat-Sun: 9am-11pm

Credit cards except
American Express
Car parking free to patrons
Prices: main courses £3-£10,
fancy burger £5, fresh salads £4

In a black glass box of a former community centre along a tree-shaded local park are housed Red TV– a local-access cable TV station – Red Radio, an associated local radio station, and not least, Red Café Bar. These are part of an experiment in local media that is the brainchild of a Cambridge entrepreneur. This preface is necessary in describing Red Café, which

> **escapes the usual pigeon holing... by also serving as eatery... sometime nightlife hot spot and a broadcasting studio open to the public... you get to sit in director's chairs with 'STAR' stencilled on the back**

rather misses the usual pigeon holing by also serving as eatery, lobby to this mini-empire, sometime nightlife hot spot and a broadcasting studio open to the public.

On Thursday nights from 7-11pm for example, the café hosts Cambridge's own version of Top-of-the-Pops. In an evening broadcast live over Red TV (channel 8), anyone who sings (or who thinks they can) steps up to the karaoke mike under the hostsmanship of the over-active, crewcutted Red TV presenter. Re-runs of this evening, video with fancy lighting and cameraman moving around for odd-angle shots play in the café on big monitors by day, but mercifully, with Red Radio's popular music (on 107.9 FM) rather than the original soundtrack. Getting in front of the camera looks like fun, and it is surely everyman's opportunity for those precious minutes of TV fame Andy Warhol warned us about.

From 7-11pm on Fridays and Saturdays, Red Café turns into disco nightclub, with DJs for the dancing pleasure of the younger set – and no entry fee.

Red Café is not least an eatery where you get to sit in director's chairs with 'STAR' stencilled on the back and partake of some trendy grub in a casual setting. The bar does the usual – with wine, cocktails and beer – while the food menu ranges from the 'pre-production burger' (£3) to the 'Bay Watch' salad with prawns and avocado. They also have quite a good selection of desserts and coffee – including things like espresso laced with grappa – and mango tea. What we tried was good, in good portions and reasonably priced.

Close to Cambridge

Cafés, Restaurants & Pubs

the game is...... a foot.

The Barn Tea Rooms

children, garden, rural peace

Burwash Manor Farms
New Road, Barton
CB3 7BD
Map ref: front F 3
Telephone: 01223 264821

Open Mon-Sat: 10.30-4.30pm,
Sun 11am-5pm
No credit cards
Hot food served daily: noon-2.30pm
Prices: meals about £5

If while roaming the countryside around Cambridge you come across small signs along the verge inviting you in for fresh asparagus, toys and tea you have reached Burwash Manor Farms. These one-storey wooden buildings – former pig yards – were transformed five years ago into shops and a tea room. The farm outlet sells its own produce, especially asparagus, sweetcorn and pumpkins, and the others sell children's software, acupuncture and aromatherapy products, baby clothes, lamps, curtains – all somewhat unusual stuff. This little shopping area is in fact, one of the success stories of farm diversification.

a little magnet for rurally deprived city folk... pause amid your meanderings among the shops for a nice cuppa and a snack

The shops look out on the 15th-century moated manor of the Radford family, who have made the farm a home for four generations. When their prize-winning pigs would no longer sell, they could have sold the property for housing. But someone had the bright idea of turning the area into a little magnet for rurally deprived city folk. This suited the village of Barton, which didn't want an estate, and has provided locals with employment.

And so we have the Barn tea rooms, where you can pause amid your meanderings among the shops for a nice cuppa and a snack. Cakes and scones are served all day and at noon you can buy simple hot meals. The fare is fine, nothing special mind you, but then you don't come out here just for the tea.

death by chocolate

Coton Orchard and Vineyard

children, desserts, garden, rural peace

Cambridge Road
Coton CB3 7PJ
Map ref: front E 3
Telephone: 01954 210234
Open Mon-Wed, Sat: 9am-5.30pm,
Thu-Fri: 9am-8pm, Sun: 10.30am-4.30pm

Wheelchair accessible
Prices: hot lunches
£4.50, Sunday roast
£5.95, tea from £1.80

Spacious, modern and surrounded by greenery, this coffee shop is far removed from its counterparts in Cambridge. Not only is it one of the most verdant places for tea it is also one of the cheapest with a pot of tea, scone and cream (£1.80) costing less than half that charged elsewhere. Lunch is also available everyday including Sunday, when a three-course roast will cost you all of £5.95. The organic apple juice, made from the orchard's apples, is renowned and with a full license you can also try some of the Vineyard's wine. Somehow, from one acre of vines, they manage to produce around 7,000 bottles per year.

> **Spacious, modern and surrounded by greenery, this coffee shop is far removed from its counterparts in Cambridge**

When you've finished your lunch or tea take a turn in the shop. For under those stands of candles, cards and cookery books lies the best dance floor in town. Once a darts hall, this huge space has also served for line dancing and even marriages: the Orchard was once registered to perform the ceremonies. And if you feel guilty about what you've just eaten, there is plenty here to inspire calorie-burning activity, whether it's gardening or strawberry-picking.

death by chocolate

The Orchard Tea Rooms

children, desserts, garden, pets (outside only), rural peace, unusual places to eat

Mill Way
Grantchester CB3 9ND
Map ref: front F 3
Telephone: 01223 845788
Opening hours vary by season
(approximately 10am-7pm in
summer, 10.30am-5.30pm in winter)
Credit cards except Switch but only
for bills of £10 or more

Wheelchair access all outside
areas, not toilets and
restricted in pavilion
Expect crowds and queues
on summer weekends
Entertainment: outdoor
theatre in summer
Prices: tea £1, cakes from
£1.25, lunches £3.25-£5.50

For a long time, I couldn't understood the attractions of afternoon tea. Obsolete for most Brits, observed by tourists, it was a tradition that seemed out of place and out of time. But, having sat in a deckchair in the Orchard gardens sipping Darjeeling and eating sultana scones with jam and cream, I now realise that its out-of-synchness is precisely the point. Whether enjoying the fabulous apple orchards that give this historical spot its name or cosying up inside the original nineteenth-century pavilion, you will understand very quickly why some of the most famous and brilliant names in British history felt comfortable here. The worries of work, routine, money and study seem years away.

some of the most famous and brilliant names in British history felt comfortable here. The worries of work, routine, money and study seem years away

Exclusive, pompous, middle-class? Maybe. But at £2.75 for a pot of tea, a scone with butter, jam and cream, and a deckchair in the sun, the pleasures of the Orchard are within the reach of most people's budgets. You can linger in the gardens for as long as you like and the calm of the trees and birds attracts students, pensioners, families and tourists. If lounging isn't your thing, pick up a free copy of the History of the Orchard and discover the illustrious company that precedes you. Immortalised in the poem 'The Old Vicarage, Grantchester' by Rupert Brooke, who in 1912 wondered from the Café des Westens in Berlin whether there was 'honey still for tea?', the Orchard is renowned for its Bloomsbury Group associations. Along with Brooke, Bertrand Russell, E.M. Forster and Virginia Woolf all enjoyed tea in the Orchard. But like Cambridge, a short walk across the meadows or a punt ride away, the Tea Rooms have had many famous visitors, from Crick and Watson to Stephen Hawking, Sylvia Plath to Germaine Greer. And if that sounds too high-brow, remember that John Cleese and Emma Thompson have also enjoyed these deckchairs.

Cambridge Quy Mill Hotel

business lunches, rural peace, special occasion, terrace, wines by the glass

Newmarket Rd
Stow-cum-Quy CB5 9AG
Map ref: front E 5
Telephone: 01223 293383
Open Mon-Fri (breakfast): 7-9:30am,
Sat-Sun: 8-10am, Mon-Sun: (lunch) noon-2:30pm, (dinner) 7-9:45pm, snacks all day

Prices: bar snacks and sandwiches £3.75-£11.50, speciality à la carte main courses £10.95-£17.50, Sunday lunch £7.50 (1 course) – £15 (for 3)

Quy Mill is a hotel-restaurant situated just north-east of Cambridge and, with its ample gardens and car parking, it is a perfect place to retreat to without driving for miles. Rebuilt in 1830 it was a working water mill until 1948. Under the current ownership it has been transformed into a country house hotel with plenty of room for individual diners and corporate events (a speciality). The original water wheel can still be seen both inside and outside the restaurant.

> a perfect place to retreat to without driving for miles... a country house hotel with plenty of room for individual diners and corporate events

If you want a pub feel there's a pubby bar with a tiled floor and several real ales including London Pride, Hobson's Choice and Bass. Just down the steps is the Celtic room, with tartan carpet, a stag head on the wall and a huge array of malt whiskies. Next door a massive vaulted room full of sofas and armchairs tempts lounging. There is also a large outside terrace.

Food is available all day (mostly teas and sandwiches in the afternoon). The menu, which has been designed to offer something for every pocket and taste, ranges from typical bar snacks such as steak and Guinness pudding and sandwiches to an à la carte menu with specialities like roasted Barbary duck breast on an Apple and Celeriac Rösti served with Muscadet and ginger sauce. The wine list is wide-ranging and good value with many bottles under £16 and five whites and five reds served by the glass.

Close to

The Coach & Horses
business lunch, children, garden, special occasion

18 High Street
Trumpington CB2 2LP
Map ref: front F 4
Telephone: 01223 506248
Open Mon-Sat: 11am-3pm,
5.30-11pm, Sun: 2-4pm, 7-10:30pm

Food served: noon-2:30,
7-9:30
Prices: starters £2.50-£4.95,
main course £7.95-£14.85,
wines £7-£20

After eight years as a boarded-up, unloved building along the busy A10, the Coach & Horses is back. Completely renovated a couple of years ago, the 18th-century coaching house has been reborn as a restaurant-pub. The white two-story Tudor style building with big baskets of flowers looks out across the old London road onto the Post Office and the heart (such as it is) of Trumpington.

interconnecting rooms with their exposed old beams set the tone for the traditional and European fare... earning the Coach & Horses a reputation for refined dining

The seven or eight interconnecting rooms with their exposed old beams set the tone for the traditional and European fare, exemplified by main courses like Chicken Chablis, Springtime Duck, and Wild Boar Sausages with Horseradish Mash Potatoes. Dishes like these are earning the Coach & Horses a reputation for refined dining. Part of the Old English Inns group, the Coach & Horses serves a range of real ales and has a considerable New World and French wine list.

The Coach & Horses is said to have a ghost, a Roman soldier, who apparently gave the building's former squatters a start. Lately he demonstrates his good manners by rearranging the crockery by night – or so suspects the waitress.

The Crown and Punchbowl

INSIDER CHOICE

children, business lunch, garden, special occasion, rural peace

High Street
Horningsea CB5 9JG
Map ref: front E 5
Telephone: 01223 860643
Open daily: noon-2:30, 6-10pm
(bar till 11:15pm)

Prices: bar snacks and light lunches: £5-£10, three courses, à la carte or specials: £20-25, reduced rate portions for children

The Crown and Punchbowl is a 17th-century Inn, reserving all the character of its history but making sure that its hospitality is very up-to-date. The food, the attitude and the service are all wonderfully unstuffy and whether you stop off alone for a quick bar snack or reserve yourself a table for Sunday lunch with all the family, the experience will not disappoint you.

> **all the character of its history but... its hospitality is very up-to-date... Real fires, cushioned settles and sweet-smelling wood smoke offer a welcome retreat... I came away determined to return**

The original inn has been extended several times, absorbing cottages and adding conservatories in the process. The result is a series of different rooms, each with a particular character, which somehow manage to be both snug and airy. Real fires, cushioned settles and sweet-smelling wood smoke offer a welcome retreat from damp Fen weather and the conservatories and garden make the most of limited sunshine. What with a deer head on the wall, piles of logs in the fireplace and soft Cole Porter-esque music playing, you could easily imagine yourself in another time, or at least on the set for *Four Weddings and a Funeral*. I half expected Hugh Grant to saunter in and start playing with his fringe.

Just as the rooms follow no set, neat layout neither does the food and drink. Chalkboards are used to advertise bar snacks, wines, desserts and fish specialities so none of the choices available are ever, as it were, fixed in stone. An ambitious à la carte menu, offering starters such as Sweet Pickled Herrings with fanned avocado pear and fresh potato salad (£4.95) and main courses like Roast Guinea Fowl with cranberry and whisky sauce (£13.25), would be more than enough to tempt most palates. But the bar snack list, which may include Gnocchi with sun-dried tomatoes, peppers and olives in chilli olive oil (£7.95) and the fresh fish board, with choices like Monkfish tails in a cream thermidor sauce (£11.45), make decisions difficult.

Close to

The food is modern but substantial. My warm black pudding and apple salad (£4.25) was listed as a starter but was large enough, with the soft brown bread, to be lunch. Desserts came highly recommended and the mint chocolate cheesecake, with its soft mousse filling containing tiny pieces of fresh mint leaf, was both inventive and gorgeous, a rare combination.

A freehouse, the Crown offers a variety of beers which are changed as and when each barrel runs out (on my trip the City of Cambridge Hobson's Choice was on offer, along with Ruddles County Ale and Courage Directors). Wine choices are also changed regularly.

I came away determined to return which is the best compliment for any restaurant.

 # The Phoenix Restaurant

business lunch, Chinese, rural peace, special occasion

INSIDER CHOICE

20 The Green
Histon, CB4 4JA
Map ref: front D 4

Telephone: 01223 233766
Open daily: noon-2pm, 6-10.30pm
Prices: set meal £14.50

Histon is one of those lovely Cambridgeshire villages that still has a focal point, in this case a lush green that dips slightly down to the river. It is no surprise to discover that a Michelin-rated restaurant like The Phoenix occupies a prime spot, looking directly out over this rare vision of pastoral harmony.

an exceptional Chinese restaurant, highly regarded by the local and not-so-local population... portions are not big... this is a place to go out of your way for

At first glance, The Phoenix looks like a pub. Indeed when I first saw it I didn't notice the lions sitting either side of the front door. Nor did I spot that the pub sign had Chinese characters on it not some witty little painting. But a closer look reveals an impressively well-kept frontage, far too tidy to be a pub (especially as its lovely position is somewhat compromised by the extraordinarily busy crossroads nearby). The windows reveal large round tables, neatly laid out with fanned napkins. No, this is no boozer.

It is, in fact, an exceptional Chinese restaurant, highly regarded by the local and the not-so-local population. Inside the decor is elegant and airy, whatever the season (they have air-conditioning) and the welcome is gracious and professional. The menu offers many standard dishes and a lot more special ones, such as Szechuan Mussels and Chilli and Garlic Prawns. For somewhere of this standard The Phoenix is not particularly expensive, even though portions are not big. Like all good Chinese restaurants, at least in my opinion, it serves banana and apple balls fried in batter, a dessert that everyone should try once in a lifetime.

This is a place to go out of your way for, a place for special occasions. Indeed, unlike some Chinese restaurants, The Phoenix is somewhere to spend, rather than end an evening.

Sycamore House

special occasion, rural peace

INSIDER CHOICE

1 Church Street
Little Shelford CB2 5HG
Map ref: front F 4
Telephone: 01223 843396
Open Tue-Sat: from 7.30pm,
last booking 9pm

No smoking
Children over 12 welcome
Credit cards except
American Express
Booking advised, especially Fri-Sat
Prices: 3-course dinner £22.50

Cambridgeshire is full of small, country restaurants but few are as admirable and accomplished as Sycamore House. Michael and Susan Sharpe, who previously owned the equally highly respected Restaurant 22, converted this 300-year old building from a wreck of a pub to an attractive and elegant cream house. Inside the dining room is just as refined without being too formal.

The three course fixed-price menu is short, changes monthly, and includes a salad course. Cooking relies on excellent ingredients and intensity of flavour so there is no over-complication of the classic and no watering-down of the essentials.

admirable and accomplished... refined without being too formal... original and memorable food... calm and knowledgeable service and an easy atmosphere

Unusual starters like escolar fritters with a lightly curried sauce sit side by side with a more classic broad bean soup with truffle oil. The escolar (a meaty white fish from the South China Seas) was moist and crisply complemented by the light batter and the spice of the sauce. Salad follows, a fresh combination of the usual (lettuce) with the unusual (shredded French beans and pumpkin seeds) and then the truly wonderful main courses arrive.

My rack of lamb with creamed onions and puy lentils sounded simple, tasted complex and was a sheer delight. Rarely do three ingredients really mesh as these did. A crispy duck leg on rösti with apple sauce was equally intense and perfectly balanced. Homemade praline ice-cream in a brandysnap basket and chocolate

Close to

nemesis were as beautifully presented and executed as the previous courses.

Combined with this original and memorable food is calm and knowledgeable service and an easy atmosphere. Here, flavour and quality take precedence over gimmickry or garnish. Sycamore House is a restaurant that really focuses on the food served without forgetting the customers who eat it.

Ancient Shepherds

business lunch, garden, special occasion

INSIDER
CHOICE

High Street
Fen Ditton CB5 8ST
Map ref: front E 4
Telephone: 01223 293280
Open Mon-Sat: noon-2.30pm, 6.30-11pm,
Sun: noon-3.30pm

Food served Mon-Sat: noon-2.15pm,
Tue-Sat: 6.30-9.30pm,
Sun: noon-3.15pm
Non-smoking area
Credit cards except American Express
Prices: main courses £5.95-£12.50

The Ancient Shepherds has always been renowned for good food and this tradition should continue as a result of the recent arrival of new tenants. The landlord, Vic Firth, is a chef who has worked in several 5-star hotels and he plans to ensure that the menu reflects a wide range of different tastes: everything from Fen Ditton sausages and mash to breast of duck with honey and lavender. The menu changes three or four times a year and there are always seasonal specialities chalked up on the blackboards. Sausages with onion gravy at £6.95 is a real bargain considering the quality of the sausages and size of the portion. Further along the menu, dishes like pork with mustard sauce are, again, served in large portions with gratin dauphinois, courgettes, carrots and broccoli (this is not a chips pub).

> **renowned for good food and this tradition should continue... a listed building and has an extremely inviting lounge... the garden at the back is secluded**

The pub is a listed building and has an extremely inviting lounge with leather Chesterfields and low tables. There are three real ales, like Flowers IPA and Benskins available, plus guests. The garden at the back is secluded and shady. One of the dining areas is no smoking.

The Barley Mow

garden, children, Thai

7 High Street
Histon CB4 4JD
Map ref: front D 4
Telephone: 01223 234071
Booking advised on weekends

Open daily: 11am-11pm,
noon-10.30pm
Food served Mon-Fri: noon-2pm,
6-10pm, Sat: 6-10pm, Sun: 7-
10pm
Prices: main course £4-£5.50

This is not only a Greene King pub but also an extremely good Thai restaurant and takeaway. What's more the prices are pub not restaurant prices. £5 will buy you a main course and fried rice or noodles. The maximum you will pay for such a combination is £6.50 and for that you'll be eating Hot Mixed Seafood or Tom Yum Ku. The starters are reasonably priced

> **an extremely good Thai restaurant and take away... the prices are pub not restaurant prices**

too, two gorgeous chicken satay sticks for £2.50. The chicken green curry (£4.50) was spicy (not for the faint-hearted) and beautifully smooth and the seafood tom yum (£5.50) was an immoderately large portion and full of mussels, prawns and plenty of lemongrass. The Thai fried noodles (£1) were a tad mealy for our taste but that is a tiny criticism in such a sea of compliments.

The pub has an enclosed garden with swings, and a pool table in the rather soulless mass of the public bar. The lounge bar is smaller and more comfortable.

If you don't live in Histon, or don't fancy eating out, there is also a take away service. Call ahead and it will be ready and waiting. Just don't order the seafood tom yum to go... it doesn't like corners.

"frying saucer"

The Blue Ball Inn
budget, garden, rural peace

57 Broadway
Grantchester CB3 9NQ
Map ref: front F 3
Telephone: 01223 840679
Open Mon-Sat: 11.30am-2.30pm,
Mon-Fri: 5.30-11pm, Sat: 6-11pm,
Sun: noon-3pm, 7-10.30pm

Food served Tue-Sun:
noon-2pm and most evenings
No credit cards
Music: Jazz and Blues duos
Bed and breakfast
Prices: pub food £2.50-£6.95

Out of all the pubs in Grantchester this is the most original, in that it hasn't been tarted up in any way and still has a tiny bar, a log fire and wooden floors. If you look at some of the black and white photographs around the room, you will see the pub at various times over the last 100 years (it dates from 1767). Compared to what has happened to some pubs in the county, it seems like a relic from those pictures now. And for that reason alone it is a treasure.

a treasure...This is a place that concentrates on being a pub, not a restaurant, but it still has an excellent, individual bar food menu...

There are only a couple of pumps, serving Greene King Abbot Ale and IPA as well as 1664 and Carling so you are not confronted with a battery of choice and flashing lights as you walk in. Instead, you'll find properly pulled pints. It is obvious that this is a place that concentrates on being a pub, not a restaurant, but it still has an excellent, individual bar food menu. Everything is made from fresh ingredients and the choices change regularly. Likely dishes include lentil, coriander and tomato soup, hommos with pitta and tabbouleh and bobotie with baked potato. For dessert try Athol Brose...something you won't find on a menu anywhere else in Cambridgeshire.

On a table a pile of newspapers and board games sit waiting for readers and players to use them in the garden or in front of the fire, and live music, usually jazz or blues duos, is played a couple of times a week. But this is a pub where no entertainment is really necessary. Merely sitting and sipping here is a pleasure.

The Blue Lion

budget, garden, special occasion

74 Main Street
Hardwick CB3 7QU
Map ref: front E 2
Telephone: 01954 210328
Open Mon- Sat: noon-2.30(Sat till 3pm), 5.30-11pm,
Sun: noon-3pm, 7-10.30pm

Food served daily except Sun eve
Min bill £10 for credit card
Booking advised weekends
Prices: fish and chips (Monday only) £3.95, main courses £5.95-£11.95, Sunday roast £10.95

At about 7pm on a Monday night in Hardwick in the Blue Lion, you can be spirited away to the seaside. Here, they serve fish and chips on a Monday, and only fish and chips, and it is, give or take a sea spray or two, some of the best I've tasted inland. Huge pieces of haddock and homemade chips with side orders of mushy peas and bread and butter, all for £3.95. Take away is also possible but that seems to defeat the object since here it is possible to eat out and go home to no washing-up for less than £10 for two people. And I know that, however much I love cooking, I'm not about to start preparing homemade tartare sauce to rival the delicious one they make here.

> be spirited away to the seaside... They serve fish and chips on a Monday... and it is some of the best I've tasted inland.. the portions are huge

It is the perfect start to the week. For those who can't face the above delights, the Blue Lion also offers a comprehensive bar meals menu at all other times: boards in the fireplace detail what is available, which usually includes daily chicken, fish, steak and vegetarian options. Desserts include caramelised lemon tart, which resembles a lemon crème brûlée in a pastry shell. You can eat in the garden or the conservatory, but whatever you choose, make sure you're hungry: the portions are huge.

The George Inn

budget, garden, sandwich

71 High Street
Girton CB2 OQD
Map ref: front E 3
Telephone: 01223 519342
Open Mon-Sat: noon-11pm,
Sun: noon-10.30pm

Food served: noon-10pm
Credit cards except American Express, Diners Club
Prices: pub food £1.90-£5.99

The sandwiches here are huge. I mean massive and they're ridiculously cheap. A double-decker BLT sandwich will cost you less than £3 and it's a lot bigger than anything you will get for that money in the centre of

Cambridge. If you live in Girton then this is a local find for you. if you don't then it might be worth the trek. Heidi and Eddie have been tenants behind this particular bar since April 1999, but

If you live in Girton then this is a local find for you. if you don't then it might be worth the trek

they've managed several others. Their attitude is friendly, welcoming and completely un-Cambridge: that is they want customers to come in and enjoy themselves but they are not trying to curry favour with any particular group. Thus, here you will find locals as well as the neighbours, the neighbours in this case being students from the Cambridge Academy of English just down the road.

Heidi has become involved with running charity events and now every Sunday a fund raising car boot sale takes place in the small car park behind the pub. There is a garden, a large pool room and eventually, the pub will have its own pool and crib team.

The pub is, as I write, very much in its infancy but, if its first steps are anything to be relied on, it should become an asset to Girton.

The Green Man
budget, garden, Indian, Mexican

59 High Street
Grantchester CB3 9NF
Map ref: front F 3
Telephone: 01223 841178
Open Mon-Thu: 11am-3pm,
5-11pm, Fri-Sat: 11am-11pm,
Sun: noon-10:30pm

Food served Mon-Thu:
noon-2pm, 6-9pm, Fri-Sat:
noon-9.30pm, Sun: noon-9pm
Credit cards except
American Express
Prices: £3.50-£15.75 (chicken
fajitas for two)

Grantchester is somewhere I associate with riverside walks and afternoon tea. It is a quintessentially English

they serve a few English dishes but most of the food on offer is of a spicy variety... no one will be able to complain about lack of choice

village which is why it is always a surprise to go to The Green Man for lunch. Here, they serve a few English dishes but most of the food on offer is of a

spicy variety. The menu is mostly Mexican with a few additional Indian dishes so it is ideal for those evenings when no one can decide what they want to eat or where. Chicken jalfrezi, cheese quesadillas or a simple sandwich... all of these options are available at the same time so no one will be able to complain about lack of choice. Beer-wise there are usually at least two real ales (Adnams, Hookey or Abbot) and a guest.

The pub gets busy at lunchtime, especially in the summer when there are often barbecues and buffets in the garden. You might wonder, as I did, where exactly the garden is, since out front there are a few tables but not much grass and the back of the pub looks onto its car park. However, across the car park and down an alleyway is a long garden which leads right down to the riverside meadows. As a result of its position it is very much a weather-oriented pub: if the sun's out it will be packed; if it's grey you'll have more chance of getting a table.

The Hoops

budget, business lunch, children,

1 School Lane
Barton CB3 7BD
Map ref: front F 3
Telephone: 01223 262230
Open Tue-Sun: noon-11pm

Food served Tue-Sun:
noon-2.30pm, 6.30-9pm
No credit cards
Prices: bar food £1.50-£4.50,
Sunday roast £5.50

The Hoops is one of those pubs that is rapidly becoming obsolete. A Grade 2 listed building, it is smack in the middle of a village, close to the post office, church and shop; it has two separate bars, each with a different character, and it serves cheap pub food without frills.

The garden is populated by some very friendly ducks... a perfect example of a proper village pub

Inside, there is a public bar with a tiled floor and a darts board on one side and a carpeted lounge with flowers on the tables on the other. Outside, hanging baskets add to the attractiveness of this red-roofed cottage. There is plenty of space for children to play outside (although there are two roads to watch out for) and a log-climbing frame for the adventurous.

The garden is surrounded by chestnut trees and populated by some very friendly ducks, who will be glad to help you finish your lunch. At the prices charged here, you could afford to buy them a sandwich each. Scampi and chips, for example, costs only £4.50 and it comes in a basket. Egg and chips is only £1.50 (cheaper than fast food and served in nicer surroundings) and sandwiches start at £1.60. Greene King own the pub so you'll find Abbot and IPA. The Hoops is a perfect example of a proper village pub.

Jolly Brewers

business lunch, garden, special occasion

INSIDER CHOICE

❖ *DISCOUNT VOUCHER - £5 OFF RESTAURANT MEALS*

5 Fen Rd
Milton CB4 6AD
Map ref: front D 4
Telephone: 01223 860585
Open daily: 11.30am-3pm,
6-11pm
Food served daily: noon-2pm,
Tue-Sat 7-9pm,
restaurant: Thu-Sat 7-9 pm

Non-smoking area
Credit cards except American
Express
No children except in restaurant
Prices: bar snacks £3-£7,
restaurant main courses £9.75-
£11.55, Sunday lunch 3 course
(inc. coffee) £10.50, 4 course
(inc. coffee) £12·75

Though owned by the Pubmaster group, this double-fronted, white-painted pub has an individual quality, developed by the family that run it. Pam and Mick Sparham took over this former brewery in July 1998 and the pub already has its own character. The staff are professional and friendly, the atmosphere is calm and welcoming and the beers are well-

professional and friendly, the atmosphere is calm and welcoming and the beers are well-kept... The food ... is of the same high standard...

kept and served properly. The food on offer, both in the bar and the restaurant, is of the same high standard as everything else.

Bar snacks include the everyday like ham and brie baguettes (from £3) and the unusual such as venison sausages with claret and juniper berry gravy, served with bubble and squeak (£6.25). The restaurant menu is ambitious. Having discovered that the hare on the menu (served as honey roast fillet with a blackcurrant and rosemary jus £11.55) had been shot and caught by one of the barmen, I had to try it. But Sea bass with bacon, pernod and fennel and Roasted Magret of duck with Pesto and Calvados jus sounded equally tempting. To start, the terrine of salmon with horseradish and lime sounded fabulous and was, (although I'd like to be served bread with my starter next time, please!). A good summer pudding with cream finished the meal.

With food of this calibre, it might help if the serving staff were a little more knowledgeable about the food and wine available but other than that my only complaint was that it wasn't warm enough to sit outside in the Pollyanna-pretty front garden for a cup of coffee.

Family pubs that offer friendly and professional service, well-kept beers and interesting food, the sort of place that appeals for dinner or a bar snack, a quick pint or a game of darts, where you feel both at home and a sense of occasion are rare: this is one of them.

Plough and Fleece

business lunch, gardens,
sandwiches, special occasion

INSIDER
CHOICE

High Street
Horningsea CB5 9JG
Map ref: front E 5
Telephone: 01223 860795

Open Tue-Sat: 11.30am-2.30pm,
7-11pm, Sun: noon-2pm, 7-10.30pm
Prices: bar food £1.90-£10

The Plough and Fleece is the sort of pub that can turn a business lunch into a trip to your local, along with requisite friendly bar staff, recognisable faces and redoubtable fare. Situated about 5 minutes' drive from the A10/A14 Milton roundabout, it would appeal to anyone who loves real pubs.

The public bar, with its red-tiled floor and red-painted ceiling, is both a relic from the days before machines and music ruined most pubs' character and a reminder of what is still possible, even in an age of pub chains.

> **Food straddles every price bracket and purpose... Whether you're a local or a stranger, a business person or a tourist, you will feel at home here**

The bar in the middle of the building is flanked by a sit-down-and-be-served restaurant on one side and a public bar, with a real fire and high-backed settles on the other. In the latter there is plenty of room for quiet reflection by the fireside as well as bar-room bores. Though there is no music, and tables are relatively close together, other conversations do not seem intrusive.

Food straddles every price bracket and purpose. If you want a snack or a light lunch try a toasted sandwich (£2.10), made with thick slices of fresh bread instead of the thin ready-sliced muck, some hot garlic cockles (£3.75) or home-cooked ham, eggs and fried potatoes (£4.75). For more substantial appetites or dinner, Welsh fish pie (£6.75), Rabbit with bacon (£7.50) and Barbary duck (£9.50) could easily be followed by Norfolk Treacle Tart, Cherry Cobbler or Home-made Ginger and Brandy ice cream (£3).

Whether you're a local or a stranger, a business person or a tourist, you will feel at home here because the Plough and Fleece is the sort of pub that every foreigner romanticises and every native regrets.

Close to

The Red Lion – Grantchester

budget, children, garden

33 The High Street
Grantchester CB3 9NF
Map ref: front F 3
Telephone: 01223 847210

Open: Mon-Sat 11-11pm, Sun
noon-10.30pm
Food served: Mon-Sat noon-9pm,
Sun noon-8pm
Prices: bar food £2.10-£10.25

For those who have children, The Red Lion could be a dream. This is a family pub with high chairs, a children's menu and dedicated fun and games for the younger generation. It has a children's playroom called Bumpy's (£1 per child) which could easily occupy little ones for hours. Birthday parties are frequently held here and

a family pub with high chairs, a children's menu and dedicated fun and games for the younger generation

children obviously love it, if the high-pitched screaming is anything to go by. If they get bored with the indoor fun there is also an outdoor play

area to keep them going for a bit longer. For once the hard part isn't getting them in, it's getting them out...

The pub is massive (the garden alone seats 86) so if kids aren't your thing, there is space to avoid them. Pub food is served all day, with a special reduced price menu between 3-7pm. The menu is standard pub grub such as jacket potatoes, sandwiches, steaks and salads. Greene King ales like Abbot and IPA are complemented by several lagers.

One little afterthought: unlike a famous Swedish furniture store with a similar facility, children must be supervised.

The Red Lion – Histon

children, garden

27 High Street
Histon, CB4 9JD
Map ref : front D 4
Telephone: 01223 564437
Open Mon-Thu: 11.30am-3pm, 5-11pm,
Fri: 11.30am-3pm, 4-11pm, Sat:
11.30am-11pm, Sun: noon-6pm, 7-10.30pm

Food served Mon-
Sat: 11.30am-2pm
No credit cards
Price: bar food
£1-£4.75

The Red Lion freehouse is very much a beer pub, but it isn't just attractive to those in search of real ale. It has a big enclosed garden, with swings, slides and a pond, a very comfortable lounge, as well as a really nice public bar, full of light wood and high settles. There's lots of space, which is useful because this pub always seems busy.

Built in 1836 it is the youngest pub in the village and was created as a result of the 1835 Beer Act. It has continued true to its beer-championing origins and now runs an annual beer festival every year during the first week of July as part of the Histon Feast Week.

Throughout the rest of the year there are always at least six cask ales available at any one time. Regulars include Bateman's Mild, Tiger Best Bitter

very much a beer pub... a big enclosed garden, with swings, slides and a pond, a very comfortable lounge, as well as a really nice public bar

and Nethergate's Augustinian Ale but the choices change constantly. In addition, there is a menu for Belgian beers such as Leffe and Duval. Food is served lunch times only with specials such as Spicy Italian Meatballs and Lamb Pepperpot, all priced under £5. The pub recently had new pétanque courts built for its two teams and there are also crib and darts teams.

The Rupert Brooke

budget, business lunch, desserts, garden, sandwich, special occasion, veg choices, wines by the glass

❖ *DISCOUNT VOUCHER - £5 OFF RESTAURANT MEALS*

2 The Broadway
Grantchester CB3 9NQ
Map ref: front F 3
Telephone: 01223 840295
Open Mon-Fri: 11am-3pm,
6-11pm, Sat: 11am-11pm,
Sun: noon-10.30pm

Food served Mon-Sat:
noon-2pm, 6-9pm,
Sun: noon-2.30pm, 6-9pm
non-smoking area
Credit cards except American
Express and Diners Club
Prices: bar food £5.50-£11.95

The history of the Rupert Brooke is a little hazy. A fire in 1867 is known to have destroyed some of the building and a maidservant, convinced she'd started the fire, ran into the river to put herself out and died. It has been rebuilt and

a cosy and welcoming pub... the perfect place for anyone who wants good food in an adult environment... The food is varied and imaginative...

extended since then, of course, but its true origins remain a mystery. Now a cosy and welcoming pub, which combines the modern (carpet) with the less so (wooden floors), it somehow manages to have character without kitsch.

Named after the early twentieth-century poet who immortalised this pretty village in 'The Old Vicarage', the Rupert Brooke is the perfect place for anyone who wants good food in an adult environment – children are only allowed in the garden.

The food is varied and imaginative. The pub's speciality is vegetarian and fish dishes although meat dishes are also available. There are seven different vegetarian options everyday – and I'm talking Provençale Nut Wellington or Parsnip and Chestnut Bake not boring pasta bakes – as well as nine fish dishes. Geoff, the chef and landlord, used to teach catering and now he not only cooks but trains his staff as well.

Even though it considers itself more of a food than beer pub, there are still three real ales plus guests as well as lots of wines to choose from.

Like many a good pub, the Rupert Brooke is learning how to make its customers happier. The Dead Poets' Society, a loyalty scheme set up by the landlady, gives its members the chance to win tickets to the Arts Theatre (which is sponsored by the pub), get discounts off dinner and receive a newsletter of special events.

Tally Ho

children, garden

77 High Street
Trumpington CB2 2HZ
Map ref: front F 4
Open Mon-Fri: 11am-3.30pm, 6-11pm,
Sat: 11am-11pm, Sun noon-10.30pm

Food served daily: noon-
2.30pm
pub garden
Prices: pub food under
£4.50

The Tally Ho is the local's local, remarkable for the abundance of activities. Darts League? That's Wednesday and Friday, and, yes, ladies darts is Tuesday. Pétanque? Cribbage? Billiards? All have regular leagues, plus two football teams and a cricket team. This is the centre of the Trumpington village community, welcoming to newcomers, and also a place that a lot of passers-by on the A10 find friendly.

the local's local, remarkable for the abundance of activities... this is the centre of the... community

Along the old London Road, The Tally Ho is an 18th-century coaching house featuring selections from the Greene King range of beers and some 30 different malt whiskies. In one room there is a bar, with walls full of sports trophies and a big hearth where a real fire burns on cool days.

The Three Horseshoes

business lunch, garden,
rural peace, special occasion
wines by the glass

INSIDER
CHOICE

High Street
Madingley CB3 8AB
Map ref: front E 3
Telephone: 01954 210221
Prices: restaurant main courses
£7.95-£16.95

Open: restaurant noon-2pm,
7.30-9.30pm (closed Sun eves).
bar open daily 11.30am-2pm,
Mon-Sat: 6-11pm, Sun:
6-10.30pm. Bar food served:
daily noon-2pm, 6.30-9.30pm

On the outside this pub looks much like any other: a thatched white cottage with a garden and a car park. Inside, however, you immediately recognise a difference. In the bar, lighting flush with the ceiling illuminates a shiny blond wood bar, with nothing on the surface like towels and ashtrays. Light wooden tables, mirrors and white crockery all establish a refreshing environment. The restaurant is equally appealing, with wicker, white tablecloths and a conservatory creating a summery open feel.

> Everything about the Three Horseshoes has been carefully thought out... If you're looking for a gastro-pub, look no further

Once you stop admiring your surroundings you can concentrate on the food. The main menu offered in the bar and restaurant changes monthly. It is innovative and enticing, if a little wordy ... most of the descriptions of main courses take up at least two lines of an A4 page. There is also a daily bar-grill menu (only available in the bar) which is more concise in every respect. Everything is beautifully presented but the portions are definitely on the small side. One table next to me hadn't quite realised that the long list of vegetables and ingredients per dish was all they were getting and that starches and green vegetables were extra. My salad of cold poached salmon trout was quite lovely to look at, and the fish was delicious, but the promised strong flavours of fennel, radish failed to come through. The horseradish aioli was brightly coloured but blandly flavoured.

Since I was driving, I couldn't take advantage of the Three Horseshoes's other great trump card: one of the most highly regarded wine lists in the country. And for once the single diner or light drinker is not punished: the Huntsbridge Group who own the restaurant has also been awarded the Mondavi/Decanter award for best UK wines by the glass list. So whether you want to spend a couple of pounds or a couple of hundred, you will find something to suit palate and purse. For the non-wine drinker there are three real ales and the

Close to

chance to try a rarity: Freedom Pilsner, a British-brewed lager.

Everything about the Three Horseshoes has been carefully thought out: cane sugar cubes; tiny glass dishes of black pepper and sea salt on each table; proper wine glasses that enhance the taste. If you're looking for a gastro-pub, look no further.

The Unicorn
children, garden, sandwiches

Church Lane
Trumpington CB2 2LA
Map ref: front F 4
Telephone: 01223 845102
Open Mon-Sat: 11am-11pm,
Sun: noon-10.30pm

Food served Mon-Sat: noon-2.30pm, 6-9pm, Sun: noon-9pm
Credit cards except American Express
Prices: bar snacks £3-£8, dinner £5.75-£9.95

This white cottage pub is set in a big garden. The site, if not the building, has been in existence since 1620 and a beer house recorded here since 1858. The inside is all wooden chairs and tables complemented by a wooden spoon when you order food. The garden has a big children's playground, and there are fruit machines and music. Staff are young, friendly and helpful and the service is fast.

big children's playground... staff are young, friendly and helpful and the service is fast... What is special, for me, is the sandwiches.

What is special, for me, is the sandwiches. My £2.95 pork and apple daily special was served in chunks of granary bread with thick slices of roast pork and apple, a larger than average salad garnish and a pile of crisps. If this was the size of a light lunch I'd hate to attempt a larger one, like one of the sausage and mash combinations. Six different types of sausage are available and you can have four of the same or four different with mash and onion gravy for £4.95 or one of each type (i.e. six altogether) for £6.95. I think, having seen the sandwich, that you might need to share...

The Volunteer

business lunch, special occasion

60 Trumpington Street
Cambridge CB2 2EX
Map ref: front F 4
Open: Mon-Sat 11am-3pm,
6-11pm, Sun noon-3pm,
6-10.30pm

No children
Food served Mon-Sat:
noon-2.30, Sun noon-3pm
Prices: starters £3.50-£4.25,
main courses £7.95-£13,
desserts £3.50-£3.75

We arrived at The Volunteer just as the kitchen was closing, and were not able, for the purpose of this edition
to revisit. But we can report good signs. This is a food
pub. On a weekday night the moderately sized pub was
full, with what looked
like a clientele well satisfied by their food
(every plate picked
clean). There are no
games, no teams, no
fruit machines, no pool tables, just a big, unfancy well-
lit room around the pub bar where the Savoy Hotel-
trained chef serves gourmet fare. The kitchen serves up
dishes like Breast of Guinea Fowl or Roast Blue-eyed
Cod with Fennel & Butter Beans with a finale of Fresh
Lemon Syllabub (a light mousse with white wine).

> **on a weekday night the moderately sized pub was full... the Savoy Hotel-trained chef serves gourmet fare**

The clientele is of the mature sort, ranging from
locals from the affluent community nearby to businessmen and A10 passers-by. They wash down victuals with
Whitbread real ales amid the company of memorabilia
and posters about military volunteers and campaigns.

The White Hart

budget, business lunch, children,
dessert, opens early, rural peace,
sandwich, special occasion, veg choice

❖ *DISCOUNT VOUCHER - FREE DESSERT*

1 Balsham Road
Fulbourn CB1 5BZ
Map ref: front E 5
Telephone: 01223 880264
Open Mon-Sat: 11am-11pm,
Sun: noon-10.30pm
Food served from 8am,
noon-3pm, 7-9.30pm and as
called for between these times

Bed and breakfast
Booking advised weekends
Music: folk, seasonal events
Non-smoking area
Prices: main courses £1.70-
£12.95, carvery main course
£5.95 (Sun lunch), £7.95 (Fri
evening), senior citizen's
lunch £4 (Mon-Sat)

Despite the fact that it is mid-afternoon, a notoriously
quiet time in rural pubs, the White Hart is very much
open for business. Three different people greet me

Close to

cheerily in the space of a few minutes. Though massive, this pub knows how to create an intimate friendly environment.

The building dates from 1867 and if you look on one of the central pillars, just beside the fruit machine, you can see a photograph depicting soldiers celebrating peace in 1918. On close inspection you will notice that one of the horses has only three legs... The pub's modern incarnation has a real fire, lots of exposed brick walls decorated with farm implements and a large heated beer garden.

intimate friendly environment... a real fire, lots of exposed brick walls... beer garden... Food is both traditional and European

At weekends the White Hart is an extremely busy food pub, with the attitude that as long as customers want food, they will be served. Food is both traditional and European (everything from roasts to Stincotto, pork shank with aromatic herbs, and, occasionally, wild boar) and there is a grown-up 'young diners' menu which includes fillet steak as well as more run of the mill options. As a Greene King tenancy it serves IPA, Abbot and regular guests and for the non-beer drinker there is a reasonably priced wine list and a good selection of different coffees (I recommend the iced café frappé on hot sunny days). If you can't face the drive home after dinner, they even do bed and breakfast.

The White Horse
budget, garden, Mexican

INSIDER CHOICE

Longstanton Road
Oakington CB4 5BB
Map ref: front D 3
Telephone: 01223 232417
Open Mon-Fri: noon-3pm, 6pm-11pm, Sat-Sun: all day

Food served Mon-Fri:
noon- 2pm, 6-10pm; Sat: all day;
Sun: noon-10pm
Credit cards except American Express
Booking advised
Prices: £4-£9.15

The White Horse in Oakington is a strange phenomenon: a country pub, packed on a Wednesday evening, where a visitor will feel as welcome as a local. It struck me as the most lively village pub in the whole area. This might have something to do with the sizzling fajitas and spicy food on offer (mostly Mexican) or the jazz-funk music they were playing. But whatever the reason, this place is worth a drive.

The lounge bar walls are decorated with blackboard menus and Mexican-esque wall hangings. Nachos, quesadillas and fajitas predominate at reasonable prices but there are other options like pints of prawns (£4.25) and sizzling squid with green onions (£4.25). For children there are mini fajitas and little dillas. Everything is well-presented, extremely delicious and served in large portions. As a Greene King tenancy it serves IPA and Abbot and one guest ale but more importantly, considering the food, they also have Mexican bottled beers like Tecate, Sol, Dos Equis and Corona. Service is generally friendly and prompt.

> lively village pub... with spicy food on offer... served in large portions... a pub that welcomes and appeals to everyone

The cheerful and busy atmosphere is evident inside and out. Pétanque is actually a game that is played here (they have two pub teams), not just a label on the door, and the garden is full of the teams as well as couples, teenagers and a group having a late business meeting. There is a small patio, lots of children's climbing equipment plus a couple of tyre swings over grass, and a small bricked-off pond with a mini waterfall. It is truly a pub that welcomes and appeals to everyone, whether planning business or playing boules.

The White Swan
budget, rural peace, special occasion

CAMRA

Main Street
Stow-cum-Quy CB5 9AB
Map ref: front E 5
Telephone: 01223 811821
Open Mon: 5.30-11pm, Tue-Sat: 11am-2.30pm, 5.30-11pm, Sun noon-2.30, 7-10.30pm

Food served Tue-Sun: lunch and evenings
Prices: bar food £1.50-£6

The village of Stow-cum-Quy (pronounced like 'why' not 'we' as one local archly pointed out) has a real gem of a pub in the White Swan, perfect for those looking for a regular drinking pub with real ales and real food

> a real gem of a pub... perfect for those looking for... real ales and real food...

Busy yet friendly, the tiny public bar has an array of pumps worthy of somewhere much bigger with lots of names unheard of locally. Mauldon Mouse Trap, Woodforde's Wherry and Beamish Black were all on tap, as were Adnams, Theakston's Best Bitter and Shepherd Neame Spitfire. This is also a good place for a quick pub lunch or a more leisurely dinner. Hot baguettes with interesting fillings like mushroom provençale as well as standards like bacon, cheese and tomato cost from £2.95 and there are lots of daily specials, like homemade chicken, ham and leek pie, Stilton and bacon tart and venison sausages.

Around Cambridge

Cafés, Restaurants, Pubs & Night Life

Roast Tomatoes with Basil and Olive dressing.

The Almonry Restaurant & Tea Rooms

budget, garden, sandwich

The College, High Street
Ely CB7 4JU
Map ref: front B 5
Telephone: 01353 666360
Open Mon-Sat: 10am-5pm, Sun:
11am-5pm, lunch specials noon-2pm

No credit cards
Prices: lunch: £1.95-
£6.95, tea: £0.90 (for a
pot) - £2.25 (pot of tea
plus scone, cream and
jam)

If you're in Ely for the Cathedral then there is no better place to have lunch, tea or morning coffee than the Almonry. The tables in the beautiful walled gardens are the only place in the city to combine tea and a view of this magnificent building. Even if it's raining you'll be able to soak up a local architectural glory by sitting in the 12th-century vaulted undercroft. Views and vaults aside, the Almonry is great for feasting the stomach as well as the eyes. At lunchtime there is a wide range of sandwiches, jacket potatoes and salads available as well as a blackboard of daily specials, including quiches and fresh fish, all served with full salad, side salad and fries or new potatoes and vegetables. Later on in the day, try huge sultana scones with butter, or jam and cream, some Cathedral teabread or lemon meringue pie. Everything is made on the premises, the portions are generous and, even when busy, the service is prompt and polite.

> **The tables in the beautiful walled gardens are the only place in the city to combine tea and a view of this magnificent building**

Waterside Tea Rooms

budget, children, desserts, sandwiches, veg choice

❖ *DISCOUNT VOUCHER - £2 OFF MEAL FOR TWO*

52 Waterside
Ely CB7 4AZ
Map ref: front B 5
Telephone: 01353 667570
Open Weds-Sun:
11am- 5.30pm
(till 6pm weekends)

No smoking
No credit cards
bed and breakfast from late 1999
£2 minimum for adults after
12.30pm weekends & bank holidays
Prices: lunch £2.20-£4.50, tea from
£1, cakes from £0.95

I'm not sure what is more tempting about the Waterside tea rooms, the cakes or the array of books and games made available to the customer. The coffee and walnut cake was quite gorgeous and obviously homemade but I was so engrossed in flicking through some of the tomes I'd amassed from the window ledges that I was in danger of missing it. This is obviously a place where you can feel very comfortable, very quickly.

The Latimers, who have been running the tea rooms for just over a year, obviously know how to create a homely, family environment. And I don't mean the Addams family. The Waterside looks like a private house, both inside and out. This impression is compounded by the fireplace, the piano and the canaries singing in the hall. And the bathrooms are so lovely and well-thought out that I wanted to ask if they wanted a lodger. However, since the chance to move in and settle down by the fire was not on offer (at least until late 1999, when bed and breakfast accommodation will be provided), I had to content myself with tea. The menu is both surprising – toast with gentlemen's relish is rarely found elsewhere – and standard – sandwiches, jacket potatoes and salads at lunch, crumpets, cakes and scones at tea. But small touches make it stand out. I have never, for example, seen chocolate zucchini cake on offer in Britain. And why has nobody else thought how sensible it is to offer reasonably-priced children's sandwiches, with spreads like Marmite, mashed banana and honey, rather than expecting parents to order something large and expensive for a child who probably won't eat anyway?

> **The coffee and walnut cake was quite gorgeous... a homely, family environment... looks like a private house... reasonably-priced children's sandwiches**

Child-awareness is extremely high on the agenda here: though only a small place, they have made room for baby-changing facilities and have secured breast-feeding friendly status from the National Childbirth Trust. Such forward thinking, so rare in merry old England, makes it possible for everyone to enjoy the Waterside, whatever their age...

Dominique's
business lunch, special occasion

INSIDER CHOICE

8 St. Mary's Street
Ely CB7 4ES
Map ref: front B 5
Telephone: 01353 665011
Open Wed-Fri: 11am-3pm,
7-9pm, Sat: 10.30am-3.30pm,
7-9pm; Sun: 10.30am-5pm

Credit cards except
American Express, Diners
Booking advised, especially at
weekends
No smoking anywhere
Wheelchair access except toilets
Prices: £2.50-£7.25 lunch,
£19.25 three-course dinner

There is a small wedding party arriving at Dominique's so I'm lucky to get a table reservation for noon. Within minutes of my order being taken, the rest of the tables are full and two couples have already learnt that not booking, even at lunchtime, is somewhat unwise. I'm intrigued. The restaurant doesn't look much from the outside and even inside, at least in the front room, the layout is no more special than that of any other small town café. It certainly doesn't look like somewhere for dinner. Only the specials menu, which has 23 choices and is far removed from standard lunch offerings and the wooden hearts on the wall, symbol of the Vendée region of France, tell me that Dominique's is unlike any other Ely lunch spot.

When my particular choice arrives, Confit of Duck Leg on a bed of salad it is evident why this place is packed to the gunnels... In fact, it's ideal for any kind of lunch or dinner

Vendée is a region of salt marsh and sea, home to some of the best beaches and seafood in France. Dominique's lunch menu, which includes Warm Pigeon Breast Salad, Rabbit, Prune and Armagnac Terrine and Baked Ratatouille reminds me more of rich Gascon food than of that found near the Atlantic. But that isn't a complaint. When my particular choice arrives, Confit of Duck Leg on a bed of salad it is evident why this place is packed to the gunnels on a Friday. The duck is cooked perfectly, the skin crisp, the meat moist and not dried out and I swear that the little roast potatoes surrounding it have been cooked in duck fat which is why they too taste out of the ordinary. I'm a little disappointed by my very un-French salad, which contains radish, shredded carrot and iceberg lettuce, but the dressing is so good that I still devour the lot. Having tasted this and seen the 3-course evening menu, I can see why this would be ideal for a wedding breakfast. In fact, it's ideal for any kind of lunch or dinner.

ⓘ **The Fen House Restaurant**

INSIDER
CHOICE

rural peace, special occasion

2 Lynn Road
Littleport. Ely CB6 1QG
Map ref: front A 6
Telephone: 01353
860645
Non-smoking area

Open Fri-Sat: from 7:30pm
(some Wed eves, lunches and dinners on
request at other times. Call to discuss.)
Credit cards except American Express
Booking advised
Prices: Four-course dinner: £28

There are some local restaurants that are constantly
shouted about, appearing in Guides and national newspapers. Others, like the Fen House, hardly make any noise
at all. Instead, they slowly sneak up on you, like the truth.
Once you have visited them, everywhere else is reduced
to a fable: existing in your mind but not really there.

Situated in
Littleport, at the north-
ern reaches of this flat
county, the Fen House
is aptly named. From
Cambridge you must
skim across the fens,
circumvent Ely and

**a restaurant like no
other... incredible food
and professional service
with an atmosphere and
environment that
immediately puts the
customer at ease**

most of Littleport before sidling into the town at its lim-
its. On the left is a white cottage, the word restaurant
picked out in black across the side.

Here, in a cosy yet elegant interior David and Gaynor
Warne have created a restaurant like no other in the area.
The trick, it seems to me, is to combine incredible food
and professional service with an atmosphere and environment that immediately puts the customer at ease. You
can't feel out of place here, whatever you're wearing or
whoever you are. Energy isn't spent on empty protocol
and elite practice. It's saved for the food.

A four-course meal here is an experience. French-
inspired and certainly not nouvelle in size, each course
draws a little gasp from the satisfied eater. Canapés
such as sweetcorn wrapped in bacon, which were
brought out as we lounged on comfy sofas sipping a
fantastic 1995 Brouilly, were a tiny and tasty hint of
what was to follow.

In the calm of the dining room, the quiet only dis-
turbed by the rustle of the willow leaves through the
open French doors, we enjoyed a meal that sang. To
start with, homemade rolls (on this occasion basil and
olive oil) were brought out... I ate only a little, fearful of
filling up precious stomach space. My smoked trout
salad with a herb vinaigrette (crystal clear and yet full
of taste) and my partner's braised calves' livers with a
curried sauce were exceptional. The main courses,
stuffed quail with creamy risotto and fillet of beef with
wild mushroom and red wine sauce served on crispy

Around North

noodles, accompanied by sugar snap peas, horseradish mash, new potatoes and french beans, were both substantial portions but with none of the loss of quality usually associated with quantity. The beef was finely textured and richly flavoured, the quail delicate and perfectly complemented by the risotto sitting in a neat circle underneath it. We welcomed a respite before an excellent selection of British and Irish cheeses (Carrigbyrne, Cashel Blue and Ribbledale smoked goats cheese) and desserts. The sharp and fresh flavours of lemon parfait with caramel and strawberry fromage frais with strawberries and shortbread were a fitting finale, light and summery.

After such a meal, who can bear to leave? Especially when the coffee comes in silver pots with petit fours and the sofas are so inviting. Sliding out into the night the restaurant once again becomes the little house on the fen, quietly guarding a secret worth discovering.

Indian Garden
business lunch, special occasion, open till late

❖ *DISCOUNT VOUCHER - FREE STARTER*

13 Victoria Street
Littleport CB6 1LU
Map ref: front A 6
Telephone: 01353 863642
Open daily: noon-2.30pm,
6-11pm (Fri-Sat until 12pm)

Credit cards except
American Express
Non-smoking area
Booking advised at weekends
Prices: main courses: £3.50-£9.95

Littleport isn't the first place one thinks of when looking for a great Indian restaurant but it should be. The Indian Garden, an unassuming low white building in the centre of the town, offers some of the most innovative and interesting Indian and Bangladeshi cuisine in Cambridgeshire. You might not have tried Amina Chicken or Reshmee Kebab but once you have it will be difficult to revert to the standard offerings available in most Indian restaurants. Everything is of the highest quality, from the poppadums, served with the usual sundries as well as a rarely-found red onion chutney, to the main courses, which all zing with the taste of fresh herbs such as coriander and fenugreek.

some of the most innovative and interesting Indian... cuisine... Everything is of the highest quality... Service is gracious and prompt and the prices reasonable

The restaurant, which offers a blend of Bangladeshi and Indian cuisine, wants to develop new twists to established favourites, and there are several options on the menu with an asterisk or a hash sign, signifying a new or experimental dish. One is Amina Chicken which is, if you're wondering, chicken cooked with a garlic, ginger, coriander, green pepper and spring onion sauce, served sizzling. It is excellent. If you don't want to stray from more usual choices, they are all available and the chef will happily make any dish that is not listed. Both draught Kingfisher and Cobra in bottles are on offer as is a rather good house red wine (a mere £3.95 for half a litre) which goes unexpectedly well with curry. Service is gracious and prompt, and the prices reasonable.

Needhams Farm Restaurant
children, desserts, business lunch, special occasion, rural peace, veg choices

❖ *DISCOUNT VOUCHER - FREE BOTTLE OF WINE*

Main Street
Witchford, Ely CB6 2HT
Map ref: front B 5
Telephone: 01353 661405
Open Tue-Sun: noon-2pm, 7-9pm

Credit cards except American Express and Diners Club
Wheelchair access inc toilets
Booking advised on weekends
Prices: main courses £11.50-£12.95

Needhams isn't listed in many of the mainstream food guides, but it should be. When I first read the name I thought that this must be one of those rural restaurants used to showcase and sell the produce of a farm. How wrong I was.

What I found was an incredibly civilised and sophisticated restaurant, beautifully organised and executed on every level.

The ingredients and the owners are English, the style of cooking is very French, the combination is gorgeous.

> *an incredibly civilised and sophisticated restaurant, beautifully organised and executed on every level... the owners are English, the style of cooking is very French, the combination is gorgeous*

Menus are changed seasonally, thus the summer menu offers lots of fresh salmon, local asparagus and strawberries, all cooked to show off not squander their qualities. With the first taste of my lemon sole served with butter sauce, I was transported back to Nantes, land of beurre blanc and white fish. A delicate and perfect balance between the richness of the sauce and the lightness of the fish. Fillet of beef with Roquefort butter sauce was equally wonderful, cooked uncompromisingly blue as requested, the sauce unmistakably sharp and salty. With the main courses came superb fresh local vegetables: whole carrots and new potatoes; run-

Around-North

ner beans and broccoli.

Nothing could really fail to please after such a wonderful dinner but the lemon tart exceeded expectations. Slightly warm, with a raspberry sauce it was both delicate and tart. My only disappointment was the coffee: it was good but it was filter and I'm a stickler for espresso after a meal. However, that is the tiniest, idiosyncratic criticism. It certainly isn't enough to make this place anything less than one of my personal favourites.

And I haven't even mentioned the wine list yet which is nothing short of a miracle: affordable (I counted 17 bottles under £10) and accessible. The wines are described by the owner as 'ready-to-drink', the sort of wines that are recognisable and quaffable, yet not run of the mill. The last time I saw a 1995 Crianza on a restaurant menu it was double the price we paid here.

If this place was in France it would be lauded, if it was in the centre of Cambridge or Ely it would be inaccessible, both in terms of price and volume of customers. However, for the moment, it is both affordable and accessible. A restaurant worthy of such a name.

The Old Fire Engine House

business lunch, children, garden, special occasion, urban peace

INSIDER CHOICE

25 St Mary's Street
Ely CB7 4ER
Map ref: front B 5
Telephone: 01353 662582
Open Mon-Sat: coffee 10.30-11:30am, lunch 12.30-2.00pm, tea 3.30-5.30pm, dinner: 7.30-9pm, Sun: 12.30pm-2pm, 4-5:30pm.
Booking advised

Closed: bank holidays and for two weeks at Christmas
Children welcome (half-price half portions at lunch and dinner)
Non-smoking area
Credit cards except American Express
Prices: tea £3-£4, dinner main courses from £11.50-£14.80, desserts from £3.70-£5

The Old Fire Engine House has an enviable and deserved reputation. A gallery and restaurant for 31 years it has been in the Which Good Food Guide for 27 of them, one of the longest running recommended entries. Situated just beside Ely Cathedral, almost directly opposite the Tourist Information office in Oliver Cromwell's House, it is easy to miss since, existing as it does so close to the Cathedral, it is not allowed to advertise itself beyond a demure slate nameplate beside the front door and a painted arch over the car park entrance.

Even stepping through the front door, you might still ask yourself if this is indeed the right place. A superb gallery to the right of the front door and a tiny snug of a bar to the left, an inviting hall and no sign of menus do nothing to dispel the immediate impression that this is someone's house. Eventually, at the end of the hall, next to a door into a Burnett-esque secret garden, you find the kitchen with the dining room beyond. Tea, morning coffee, lunch and dinner are all served in this room, which is a cross between an 18th-century morning room (or, at least how I imagine such a place to be: light, airy and

A gallery and restaurant for 31 years it has been in the Which Good Food Guide for 27 of them... The fabulous walled garden... has a daisy-spotted lawn, masses of trees and just as much charm as the restaurant itself

with a pleasant view) and a scullery, with its uneven tiled floor, sprigged curtains, scrubbed pine kitchen tables and comfy cushioned settles. Jane Austen would feel quite at home here. The fabulous walled garden, which, weather permitting, is also used for service, has a daisy-spotted lawn, masses of trees and just as much charm as the restaurant itself.

The location itself merits a visit just for tea or coffee. But having tried afternoon tea, (£4.80 for a generous pot of tea, home-made scones, jam and cream and a sky-high piece of cake: all available individually – £1.20 for tea, £1.35 for cake and £2.30 for scones) I was tempted to jog round the Cathedral for a few hours to work up an appetite for dinner. The menu is described as traditional English which, in most places, tends to mean scampi and chips or microwaved steak and kidney pie: here they know what they're talking about. Seasonal and regional ingredients feature heavily: starters include locally smoked eel and local asparagus; main courses on offer include Braised beef and mushrooms in Guinness and port and Spiced pigeon breast with fennel and a vegetarian Red Dragon pie with mushroom stroganoff. Every detail of the Old Fire Engine House from service, taste and style, appeals.

The Anchor Inn
business lunch, garden (riverside), rural peace, special occasion

❖ *DISCOUNT VOUCHER - £5 OFF A MEAL FOR TWO*

Sutton Gault, near Ely
Cambridgeshire CB6 2BD
Map ref: front B 4
Telephone: 01353 778537
Open daily: noon-3pm,
Sun-Fri: 7-11pm,
Sat: 6.30-11pm

Food served daily: noon-2pm,
Sun-Fri: 7-9pm, Sat: 6.30-9.30pm
Booking advised
Non-smoking areas
Prices: two-course lunch Mon-Fri
£7.50 (not bank holidays), main
courses £9.95-£14.95

The Anchor Inn dates back to 1650, when it was built to provide accommodation and food for the workers who were digging the new rivers in the Fens. It is right next to 'The Hundred Foot Drain' or New Bedford River and has a riverside terrace to take advantage of its position. A beautiful white and green cottage on the outside, inside there is a warren of small rooms, wonky floors and scrubbed pine tables. It has a big bar and, as a freehouse, a good real ale, but what it is renowned for is food. Which is good, although the special two-course lunch menu is nowhere near as interesting or groundbreaking as the à la carte option. The set lunch offers soup, salads, seafood pie and sausages and mash, whereas the more extensive (and expensive) menu may list quail with satay sauce, wild pigeon supremes and 'Denham Estate' venison steaks. One of the best desserts on offer, if you can call it that, is the British cheese selection which is an education to anyone who thinks that Cheddar and Stilton are all this country can muster. They even serve them at the right temperature, that is if you are prescient enough to order them at the start of the meal.

> **A beautiful white and green cottage... Lots of real ales but what it is renowned for is food... this is a pub worth the journey**

There are a some minor oddities – a charge for bread on the set lunch menu – but the overall impression is that this is a pub well worth the journey.

The Cutter Inn

children, garden (riverside), rural peace

Annesdale
Ely CB7 4BN
Map ref: front B 5
Telephone: 01353 662713
Open daily: noon-2.30pm, 7-11pm
(longer hours in summer)

Food served daily: noon-2:30,
7-9pm
Children welcome
Prices: bar snacks £2.25-
£13.95 (children's menu
£2.95)

Named after the peat cutters who used to drop in the
pub after a long day on the Fens, The Cutter Inn makes
the most of Ely's other main attraction: the River Great
Ouse. Huge and sprawling this is a place for boat-watch-
ing and Sunday afternoon
idling by the water. Tables on
the riverside terrace and those
in the large open bay windows
are always busy, especially in
the summer, so arrive early if you want a view. Inside,
this is a Noah's Ark of a pub, all wood and creaky floors.
The bar is stocked with Old Speckled Hen, Directors,
John Smith's and 1664 and a bar snacks menu is on offer
everyday. Don't expect fancy food: this is solid, pub grub
including everything from potato skins and homemade
pies to trout and fillet steak. What I like about this pub
is its attitude: flexible, friendly and family-oriented. A
good mooring for landlubbers and seafarers alike.

> A place for boat-
> watching and
> Sunday afternoon
> idling by the water

Fish and Duck

children, garden (riverside), pets
allowed, rural peace

Holt Fen
Little Thetford CB6 3HR
Map ref: front B 5
Telephone: 01353 649580
Open year-round Sat-Sun: 11am-
11pm, from July to Sept weekdays:
11am-11pm, October-June weekdays:
11am-3pm, 5.30-11pm

Food served Mon–Fri:
noon-2pm, 5.30-9pm, Sat,
Sun & bank holidays: all
day
Credit cards except
American Express
Prices: £1.50-£11.50,
daily specials around £6.75

You have to drive through a lot of salad and know
where you're going in order to reach the Fish and
Duck. Field after field of black peat and green leaves sit
between the road and this pub and as you drive along
a mile or two of narrow tarmac track, in between the
railway and the planted furrows, you need faith to
reach the jackpot. But it's worth it to arrive at this rustic building, perched on the confluence of the rivers
Cam, Old West and the Great Ouse. Its very location

makes you feel like a born adventurer, ready to jump into one of the many boats moored in the pub's marina.

It's not a journey I would wish to venture on at night, especially if I hadn't experienced it in daylight. Though listed as being in Little Thetford, what that actually means is that you can reach it from said village but only on foot. Because although there is a road in the village called Holt Fen the pub is actually slap bang on the fen, far from the likes of roads and street signs. Take with a pinch of salt its signs which state very clearly that it is open all day: I arrived at 2.55pm and it was very, very closed. Not a place to be stuck at 3pm in the afternoon when you're desperate for the loo and a quiet sandwich, in that order, and miles from anywhere. The next time I arrived at 5pm on a Friday and it still wasn't open, despite protestations that in the summer (and this was mid-June) all day meant precisely that.

Perches on the confluences of the Rivers Cam, Old West and Great Ouse. Its very location makes you feel like a born adventurer

So why recommend it? Because of the location. Because of its refreshingly unrestricted attitude towards all the usual pub bugbears, like smoking, dogs and children. Because when I finally got in I found a 550-year-old pub is beautiful inside, with a huge conservatory and lots of country collectibles, artworks and 400 books (for your reading pleasure) on the walls. Because the friendly owners seem to know what a pub is for, even if they don't always open when they say they will. (If they are out, wait a bit, the owner later told me. Chances are they've just popped out and will be right back). Because the Fish and Duck has a good reputation for food and five real ales. It's worth driving through salad for all that.

To get there: don't go to the effort of driving to Little Thetford. Leave the A10 at Stretham, either exit, and head through the village, following the (one) sign for Wicken. Drive out of the village to a railway crossing: immediately on your left there is a sign for the Fish and Duck next to a track edging the fields. (If you find yourself crossing a mini Tyne bridge and seeing signs for Upware and Swaffham Bulbeck, you know you've gone too far.) Turn onto the road and follow the signs.

The Five Miles from Anywhere No Hurry Inn

children, open till late, rural peace

Upware, Ely
Cambridgeshire CB7 5YQ
Map ref: front C 5
Telephone: 01353 721654
Open Sat: 11am-2am,
Sun: noon-10.30pm, Mon-
Thu: 11am-3pm, 7-11pm,
Fri: 7pm-2am
Booking advised, evening

Food served daily (except Fri): 11am-
2.30pm, Mon-Fri: 7-9.30pm, Sat-Sun:
7-10.30pm (bar snacks after)
Music: karaoke 12.30pm every Wed,
with live entertainment until 2pm,
Fri 7pm-2am
Prices: bar snack £2.25-£5.75, à la
carte £4.50-£14 (available from Dec
1999)

Unlike some pubs, the Five Miles from Anywhere No Hurry Inn has an apt name. It might take you a while to find it but you won't be in a rush to leave. Down a leafy lane leading from the main road out of Stretham village, then a little further down a dead end, sits this riverside pub. The site has been occupied by an inn for over 400 years but the original burnt down in 1956 and has now been replaced by a modern brick building. In the past it was known for having the sign of the broadsword which meant it was a safe haven for highwaymen.

> this is a good place to hide out even now, especially since it has an entertainment license and late hours... The pub's position is lovely: right on the Cam with a large garden, prize-winning hanging baskets, a riverside terrace and children's playground

Whether you arrive by boat or road this is a good place to hide out even now, especially since it has an entertainment license and late hours. One of the nicest live acts is the jazz every third Sunday. When it's warm, the band plays outside and punters sit and sprawl on the grass, on the river jetty, where ever there's space. It's like a mini outdoor festival.

A freehouse, the pub offers five different real ales at any time and the selection changes twice a week (i.e. you can thus sample ten different brews in 7 days). You might find Hobson's Choice or Bass, or if you're lucky Fox's Knob or Vi-ale-gra. Food-wise, the à la carte restaurant is closed for refurbishment until December 1999 (estimated). But bar snacks are still served, even after 10.30pm at weekends. On Sundays there is an all-you-can eat carvery, priced per course (£6.50 for 1, £8.50 for 2 and £9.99 for 3) but no bar snacks.

The pub's position is lovely: right on the Cam with a large garden, prize-winning hanging baskets, a riverside terrace and children's playground, including a bouncy castle. With a full chidren's license and plenty of space The Five Miles is good for families, large groups and anyone stuck out in the Fens in need of a drink...

 ## The Fountain

pets allowed, garden patio

1 Silver Street
Ely CB7 4JF
Map ref: front B 5
Telephone: 01353 663122

No food served
Open Mon-Fri: 5-11pm, Sat: noon-2pm, 6-11pm, Sun and bank holidays: noon-2pm, 7-10.30pm

Entering the Fountain you are greeted by a shining bar and a smiling welcome. This recently renovated pub is a haven for tourists and locals, anyone in fact who enjoys properly kept beers and a real pub atmosphere.

Built in 1830 and lovingly restored by the current landlord, there is no end to the delights on offer both in terms of beer and atmosphere. It is one of the few pubs in the whole region which not only offers Czech Budvar and Belgian Hoegaarden on draught but also serves them in proper glasses. Regional real ales are also well-represented: Nethergate Swift, Adnams Broadside and Southwold are all served together with other regularly changing guest ales. Non-beer drinkers will find plenty to keep their palates happy, with an excellent selection of Australian wines and non-alcoholic beers.

> a haven for tourists and locals, anyone in fact who enjoys properly kept beers and a real pub atmosphere... Without piped music, fruit machines and television, the pub successfully revives that antiquated habit: conversation

If this wasn't already enough, the Fountain is also attractive and cosy, with tiled floors, cosy leather settles and none of the dubious accoutrements found in other pubs. Without piped music, fruit machines and televisions, the pub successfully revives that antiquated habit: conversation. You can't help but feel at home when everyone is so friendly.

As a traditional wet pub, there is no food served, but the peckish will find Kettle Chips and Pringles adequate ballast before trying yet another lovely pint. It is no surprise that the Fountain won CAMRA Cambridgeshire pub of the year in 1997: it has all the hallmarks of quality.

The Hop Bind

pizza, garden patio

212 High Street
Cottenham CB4 4RZ
Map ref: front D 4
Telephone: 01954 200701
Open Mon-Thu: noon-3pm, 5-11pm,
Fri-Sun: noon-11pm (until 10.30pm Sun)

Food served: Mon &
Wed-Sun: noon-2pm,
5-8pm
Prices: pub food
£1.70-£4.50

The Hop Bind is a young, bright Greene King pub which looks very up-to-date considering it was built in 1851 as a brewery and pub. The interior is painted in a trendy orange, which contrasts with the more traditional frontage, but both are cheerful and well looked after. A long, polished bar runs the length of

cheerful and well looked after... pop music, even on a Sunday lunchtime, keeps the atmosphere lively...

the pub, with traditional tables in the front, high bar tables and stools in the middle and a small patio.

The clientele tend to be young, but not too young and mixed-age groups predominate. Loud pop music, even on a Sunday lunchtime, keeps the atmosphere lively as do the darts, bar billiards and fruit machine at the back. There is a small television at the front of the pub and a 6-7ft large screen for showing sporting events. Standard Greene King ales are available, IPA and Abbot as well as a guest ale like Marston's Pedigree, which changes frequently. Food is of the bar snack variety, such as burgers, scampis and chips served in baskets, and there are also pizzas which are slightly more expensive. The staff are friendly and affable.

The Maid's Head

children, garden, veg choice

12 High Street
Wicken CB7 5XR
Map ref: front C 6
Telephone: 01353 720727
Open daily: 11.30am-3pm,
6.30-11pm (till 10.30pm Sun)

Food served daily: 11.30am-2pm,
6.30-9pm
Booking advised Fri-Sun
Prices: £2.80-£12.95

Beer has been served at this site on the village green since 1579, though the original pub unfortunately burned down in 1983. Its attractive replacement, built in 1985, has a big public bar, with a pool table and fruit

range of beers... Food available all week... interesting à la carte... friendly and welcoming

machine, and an equally large lounge bar opening onto the green, which serves as the garden. In the winter the lounge is warmed by a central brick fireplace whereas in the summer it is flooded by sunshine.

As a freehouse, the Maid's Head offers a range of beers. There are four real ales, including Greene King IPA and Worthington as well as guests like Smiles Maiden Leg Over. Food is available all week, lunch times and evenings and as well as standard pub grub like baguettes (from £2.80) and scampi (£6.75 with chips and salad) there is also an interesting à la carte.

Start with local Fenland mushrooms, panfried with Stilton, wine and cream (£3.45), continue with medallions of beef in a garlic and shallot sauce (£12.95) and conclude, if you have room, with an orange and brandy pudding (£3.25). The menu offers vegetarian options and there are daily blackboard specials. The three-course Sunday roast (£8.95, including a starter, choice of four roast meats plus a vegetarian option, dessert and coffee) is popular and it is advisable to book. Service is friendly and welcoming to everyone, without any local preference.

The Maid's Head is family-run and children-friendly, with two high chairs available for customers' use. As well as the garden on the green, there is also a children's play area behind the pub.

The Plough
budget, garden patio, rural peace

INSIDER CHOICE

106 Main Street
Little Downham CB6 2SX
Map ref: front A 5
Telephone: 01353 698297
Open daily: noon-3pm, 7-11pm
(Sun: till 10.30pm)

Food served Tue-Sat:
noon-2pm, 7-9pm
No credit cards
Wheelchair access
Prices: £1.50-£10.99

This tiny cottage, with two rooms and a stable door entrance, is welcoming and warm for regulars and visitors. Physical dimensions are in inverse proportion to the friendliness displayed: within minutes of sitting at the bar I had been engaged in conversation. Instead of feeling like an interloper, I felt very much at home.

Considering the Plough was on the verge of closing down for good in 1998, having been up for sale for one year, Rose and Roy Goldsmith have done a remarkable job of turning it into a success. Two fires, and settles add to the cosiness but the main reason this pub is so likeable is that the people behind the bar make it so. Rather than disinterested teenagers, there are two engaged and experienced pub managers (Rose has been in the business since she was 15; the couple used to run the

Chestnut Tree in West Wratting) who make it their business to see that you enjoy yourself. It is no surprise then that 3 couples have met and married as a result of meeting in the bar.

It is not only the welcome that draws the customers. This Greene King pub (IPA and Abbot but possible guests in the future) has a good selection of bar food, ranging from sandwiches

This tiny cottage... welcoming and warm... the main reason this pub is so likeable is that the people behind the bar make it so...

(lots of thick-sliced bread and meat) to steaks. Specials may include Half Guinea Fowl in Onion Gravy or Beef in Ale. On Sundays there is no food but snacks of roast potatoes, cheese and biscuits and cockles are put out for the punters, free of charge.

Prince Albert

budget, children (garden only), garden, pets allowed

62 Silver Street
Ely CB7 4JB
Map ref: front B 5
01353 663494
Open Mon-Thu: 11.30am-3.30pm, 6.30-11pm, Fri-Sat: 11am-3.30pm, 6.30-11pm, Sun: noon-3pm, 7-10pm

Food served Mon-Sat: noon-2pm
No credit cards
No children under 14 allowed in bar (children permitted in garden)
Prices: bar food £1.90-£5

The Prince Albert is a good example of why first impressions are not always to be trusted. The pub's frontage isn't particularly special and as the first place you see when you leave the Cathedral car park on Barton Road the temptation is to overlook it in the search for other delights in the centre of Ely. But if you want to sit in the best pub garden in the

if you want to sit in the best pub garden in the city and have some real pub food it's worth stopping here

city and have some real pub food it's worth stopping here.

The walled gardens won the Brewery Garden of the Year award from 1991-1999 and it is easy to see why. Geraniums spill from chimney stacks on the patio and several aviaries run the (considerable) length of the garden. Sitting in the sun here is a good way to escape the crowds closer to the Cathedral. Inside isn't bad either: snug without being stuffy. At lunchtime try some bacon lattice flan with salad, liver and sausage and onion in Yorkshire pudding with gravy or a homemade pie. And if you're one of those organised souls who has brought a packed lunch, the Prince Albert will happily let you eat it in the garden as long as you buy a drink.

Mocha Café and Diner

budget, children, desserts, opens early, sandwich

11 Central Arcade
Saffron Walden CB10 1ER
Map ref: front H 5
Telephone: 01799 523695
Open Mon-Sat: 8.30-5pm,
Sun: 10am-4pm

Credit cards except
American Express
Wheelchair access inc toilets
Prices: food £0.80-£6.50

When you first approach the Mocha you see an Italian café, with steel and raffia chairs and galvanised aluminium tabletops. When you enter you see a mix of plastic dinettes and tapestry booths. Finally, when you head upstairs to the loos, you find pinball machines and pool tables. Depending on where you're sitting or standing, you could imagine yourself in the fifties, seventies or nineties.

one of those places where you can have what you want when you want... The whole place combines the no-nonsense approach of a short-order diner with the charm of an Italian café

It is not surprising, then, to discover that this café-diner has been here for over 30 years. Despite its longevity it is certainly not stale, even if going back through the various parts of the building feels like going back in time. You can have a cup of tea but you can also have cappuccino, you can have a burger or an all-day breakfast. Without stealing the words of a rather more famous slogan, this is one of those places where you can have what you want when you want.

Staff are friendly and everything is served efficiently and quickly. The whole place somehow combines the no-nonsense approach of a short-order diner with the charm of an Italian café. It lives up to the coffee it is named after: sweet but with a kick.

Le Paradis Restaurant

**children, business lunch,
special occasion, veg choices**

Duxford Lodge Hotel
Ickleton Road
Duxford, CB2 4RU
Map ref: front G 4
Telephone: 01223 836444
Food served daily: noon-2pm,
7-9.30pm (no Sat lunch)

Non-smoking area
Booking advised
Prices: fixed price lunch 2-course
£9.99, 3-course £13.99, fixed-price
dinner 3-course £20.50, 3-course
Sunday lunch £16.95, à la carte
also available

Flying is usually high on the agenda for any visitor to
Duxford, since the airshows and the Imperial War
Museum are such draws. Duxford Lodge Hotel makes
the most of this in its decoration, with paintings and
drawings of aircraft in the bar and of birds of paradise
in the restaurant. The
atmosphere is relaxed,
comfortable and profes-
sional, ideal for business
lunches as well as less
formal occasions.

In the half-panelled
restaurant, plain white
linen tablecloths and
napkins contrast with

**The atmosphere is
relaxed, comfortable
and professional, ideal
for business lunches
as well as less formal
occasions... Le
Paradis offers high
class wines and foods
at high street prices**

the bright wallpaper and carpets. Piped music and well-
spaced tables keep conversations private. The fixed-
price lunch is good value. Typical starters include
chilled melon cocktail with raspberry sorbet, soup and
prawn and smoked salmon cocktail. Main courses will
include a fish, vegetarian and meat option, all beautifully presented and obviously freshly prepared from
prime ingredients. French-inspired, the timings are perfect, the sauces accomplished and the vegetables treat-
ed with as much respect as the meat or fish. The wine
list is one of the most intelligent I have seen, listing bottles by type (Chardonnay, Pinot Noir, Shiraz/Syrah). It is
also reasonable. There are five £10 house wines but,
admirably, each section of the list includes a £11-£13
bottle. Service is friendly, albeit a touch leisurely for
those in a great hurry.

Le Paradis offers high class wines and food at high
street prices.

The Old Hoops

business lunch, open till late, special occasion, veg choice

INSIDER CHOICE

15 King Street
Saffron Walden CB10 1HE
Map ref: front H 5
Telephone: 01799 522813
Open Tue-Sat: noon-2.15pm
and from 7pm-midnight

Booking advised
Prices: two-course set lunch
£8.95, two course set dinner
£13.95 (available Tue-Fri), à la
carte starters around £4.50,
main courses from £7.50

Situated on the first floor of a building just off the market square, there is no chance to see inside The Old Hoops. Only a discreet box beside the door shows you the daily set lunch and the à la carte menu. But venture upstairs and you find a room where the darkness of the green ceiling and the wooden bar are happily offset by white tablecloths and lots of windows.

The Old Hoop's menu is short and classic which is, in my opinion, a good sign. Long menus generally speak volumes (and not particularly good ones) about the quality and freshness of ingredients. I choose the vegetarian option, potato and onion cakes with ratatouille, because it is the only one that also features on the à la carte, followed by the profiteroles with chocolate sauce. The potato cakes are a revelation: three propped up on a bed of thickly chopped peppers and courgettes. Not only are they freshly-made but also, considering the simplicity of the ingredients, incredibly tasty. The Old Hoops obviously likes the number three since there are also three profiteroles, large and a perfect balance of crisp choux and soft cream.

if you want an excellent balance of flavour and service with finesse, The Old Hoops is the place to provide it

The usual trade-off between large portions and taste is overcome by the Hoops: they do large (the grilled lemon soles whizzing past me were enormous) without stinting on taste. And with ingredients of this quality there is no resorting to finicky sauces or superfluous garnish.

If you consider masses of choice an advantage this isn't the place for you. But if you want an excellent balance of flavour and service with finesse, The Old Hoops is the place to provide it.

Il Piccolo Mondo
**children, business lunch,
special occasion, veg choices**

*INSIDER
CHOICE*

14-16 Hill Street,
Saffron Walden
CB10 1JD
Map ref: front H 5
Telephone: 01799 506096

Non-smoking area
Open Mon-Sat: noon-2pm,
6.30-10.30pm
Booking advised at weekends
Prices: main courses £4.95-£15

The colour scheme and decor at Il Piccolo Mondo tell you a great deal about what to expect from the food and the service: blues, creams and whites create a composed and graceful atmosphere and although only air-conditioning and pretty white curtains separate the interior from the exterior, the environment is calm and soothing, far removed from daily realities.

Both food and service are equally composed. Even when very busy, the staff remain efficient, professional and gracious. The food and everything that accompanies it are of the same high standard. Croutons and bread sticks sit on every table, and

Il Piccolo Mondo has only been open since mid-1999... Yet it has the poise and style of a long-established operation. This Italian restaurant is a rare treat: elegant but affordable

once orders have been taken a selection of olives and fresh bread arrives. The standard menu is difficult to choose from with its reasonably priced gnocchetti, tagliatelle and other pasta dishes, as well as meat main courses, but Il Piccolo Mondo also specialises in fish. Staff explain the catch of the day, which might include sardines, sea bass, monkfish and halibut, when distributing menus.

My potato gnochetti with a cheese sauce, accompanied by a side salad, were perfect: not too rich yet very filling. The pasta is fresh and, though served and priced as a first course, the portions resemble main courses, leaving little room for vanilla pannacotta or tiramisu. Coffee, however, comes with some amaretti biscuits, which help to end the meal on a sweet note.

Il Piccolo Mondo has only been open since mid-1999, though the owners ran a similar restaurant in Newmarket for five years. Yet it has the poise and style of a long-established operation. This Italian restaurant is a rare treat: elegant but affordable.

The Pink Geranium
business lunch, special occasion

INSIDER CHOICE

25 Station Rd
Melbourn SG8 6DX
Map ref: front G 3
Telephone: 01763 260215
Open Tue-Sat: noon-2pm, 7-10pm
Booking advised

Prices: set lunch £14 (2 courses), £18 (3 courses), à la carte £20-£28 main courses, 3-course set lunch/dinner £30 and 5-course fixed tasting menu (only per table) £50

The Pink Geranium is well-known for its famous television chef, Steven Saunders, and for its food. Saunders has made a name for himself both locally and nationally with cookery programmes like Ready Steady Cook, books and, of course his restaurants. I was a little apprehensive about my visit, worrying about dress codes and price, which are usually rather over the top in renowned eateries. But my fears were calmed when I arrived. A rosy thatched cottage decked out in wicker and floral chintz can't intimidate anyone for long and once you spot that the lunch menu is only £14 for two courses you start feeling very comfortable indeed.

well-known for its famous television chef... The food here is more than accomplished and upbeat, with stacks and sauces very much the signatures

The food here is more than accomplished and upbeat, with stacks and sauces very much the signatures. The reworking of simple classics (serving smoked salmon as a pavé layered with lemon and coriander butter rather than the usual thin sheets on a plate) tends to be much more successful than the classics themselves (an uninteresting gazpacho) but star quality shines through in unexpected places. The asparagus and wild mushroom millefeuille, a vegetarian option, was beautifully presented and cooked. Descriptions err on the wordy side which can at times be perfectly accurate and at others, a little confusing (guinea fowl was served with a café crème sauce, which refers to the colour not the ingredients).

The head waiter's choice of wines was infallible and in general service is faultless which considering the physical environment and the signature characteristic of each dish is quite remarkable: the beams are cottage low, the meals skyscraper high... how would you fancy balancing the latter whilst dodging the former and walking down a step from the kitchen? Not funny, if you're rather tall as our waiter was. His forehead, he said, knew the beams intimately.

Steven Saunders might not always be cooking at

lunchtime (it is best to ring and check) but he plans and tests every menu and the dishes on them as well as cooking either here or at Sheene Mill most evenings. Overall, the Pink Geranium is excellent at presenting the whole picture, a little less concerned with the details. Lunch is incredible value but I have a feeling that dinner might be a more worthwhile and gastronomic occasion.

The restaurant

business lunch, special occasion, wines by the glass

Victoria House, 2 Church Street
Saffron Walden CB10 1JW
Map ref: front H 5
Telephone: 01799 526444
Open Tue-Sat: 7.30pm,
last booking 9.30pm

Credit cards except
American Express
Booking advised at weekends
Prices: main courses £9-£16,
starters £4-£7, wine list £9-
£120, wines by glass £2.50

A new addition on the food circuit, the restaurant is discreetly announced by a black and white banner hanging outside. A bit too discreetly actually since I had to rely on the help of a local to find out that it was down the steep stairs in an old cellar bar.

Once Porter's wine bar, it has now been revamped in a Habitat-inspired style. Husband and wife owners, Karen and Christopher Williams wanted to create the sort of atmosphere that they would look for when going out. Brick walls and blue tablecloths dominate creating a modern atmosphere that manages to avoid being cold. Only open since summer 1999, tables are already becoming difficult to book at weekends.

an old cellarbar... revamped in a Habitat-inspired style... Brick walls and blue tablecloths dominate creating a modern atmosphere... food is fusion influenced...

The food is fusion influenced, which signifies bold combinations of colour and taste and long menu descriptions. A typical starter might be chargrilled scallops with orange slices and watercress whereas ambitious main courses include roast guinea fowl breast filled with garlic, herb and pancetta stuffing and chargrilled fillet of Scottish beef. Generally, everything is beautifully presented and well served, although sometimes elaborate garnishes and sauces (and their descriptions!) overshadow the ingredients.

The wine list is very new worldy, with a few nods to the classic. There are no house wines but it is possible to have just a glass. Service and welcome are eager and attentive.

Around-South

Sheene Mill

business lunch, garden, special occasion

INSIDER CHOICE

Station Road
Melbourn SG8 6DX
Map ref: front G3
Telephone: 01763 261393
Open daily noon-2pm,
7-10pm

Credit cards except Diners Club
Booking advised
Prices: 2-course lunch £10, 3-course
Sunday lunch £18.50, à la carte
3-course dinner £25 (add 15% auto-
matic service charge to all prices)

Sheene Mill hotel and brasserie is a 17th-century water mill situated in the village of Melbourn. Along with its sister restaurant The Pink Geranium (literally just down the road), it has put this village on the foodie map. It helps that both are owned by a television personality,

Service is friendly and professional and the combination of rural idyll and metropolitan restaurant works well

Steven Saunders, who has made a name for himself on programmes like Ready Steady Cook. Saunders's busy lifestyle (TV, books and a cooking school to name a few) makes it difficult to be in the kitchen all the time (though he is involved on a daily basis) so he sometimes delegates the cooking, but staff informed me that you could be in luck on a weekday evening.

The mill has several different characters: a lovely riverside conservatory and lush green gardens, a bar with orange walls and a funky, bright blue and yellow dining room. Lunch here is a reasonable £10 for two courses or £14 for three (plus the 15% service charge).

I began lunch with by looking over the menu in the sunny bar with a bowl of olives for company. For starters I chose the seared rare tuna with mizuno salad and pimento oils (mizuno, I was informed, is a Japanese leaf) though the tian of crab with smoked salmon and garden pea risotto were equally tempting. The tuna was a wise choice, crisply char-grilled on the outside and perfectly rare inside. It was followed by a sizeable braised shank of lamb, with garlic mash, port wine jus and fresh vegetables. The meat and its sauce were rich yet not over-whelming and the side dish of broccoli, radish, mange tout and carrots were good on their own, as well as a fresh accompaniment for the main course. The iced white chocolate and ginger parfait was, like the preceding courses, a balanced contrast of flavour and texture, the firm parfait and crunchy brandy snap tuile comple-mented by chocolate sauce and slivers of strawberry. All for £15 plus the 15% service charge. No wonder it's packed every day, even on a Monday lunchtime.

Service is friendly and professional and the combi-nation of rural idyll and metropolitan restaurant works well. And if you want to take away a souvenir of your visit there are plenty to choose from: the pictures in the dining room are for sale as are Steven Saunders's cookery books, photographs and pasta sauces.

The Chequers

budget, desserts, garden, special occasion, wines by the glass

INSIDER CHOICE

High Street,	Food served: noon-
Fowlmere SG8 7SR	2pm, 7-10pm
Map ref: front G 3	Non-smoking area
Telephone: 01763 208369	Booking advised
Open Mon-Sat: 11.30am-2.30pm, 6-11pm,	Prices: food £3-£18,
Sun: 11.30am-2.30pm, 7-10.30pm	Sunday lunch £10.50

The Chequers has history and character crammed into every corner. A restored 16th-century coaching inn, it has played host to Samuel Pepys as well as Battle of Britain fighter pilots. Just above the front door is the inscription W.T.ANO.DOM.1675: in 1675 the occupant William Thrift had the inn renovated for his son. On the pub sign you will see both British and American pilots honoured, with the blue and white chequers of No.19 Sqdn. R.A.F. on one side and the red and white chequers of the 339th Fighter Group on the other.

> **history and character crammed into every corner... cooking borders on fusion cooking... friendly, young service, a garden full of roses and parasols...**

However, if you have come to the Chequers for food, the pub's history may be the last thing on your mind because the menu is far too distracting. The cooking borders on fusion cooking (prawns served with both aioli and Thai dipping sauce), without losing sight of the need for solid flavours and classic pub lunches. A Ploughman's, for example, can be one of the most tired, routine and overpriced of dishes. At The Chequers, it is served with matured Lancashire and Stilton cheese, duck rillettes, delicious home-made chutney, French bread and a tomato and cucumber salad. All for £4.25. Combine this with friendly, young service, a garden full of roses and parasols, and you have a perfect summer lunch. Inside the pub, log fires, beams, cushioned settles and different levels create a comfortable and attractive environment. There is an excellent, varied, albeit rather expensive wine list (cheapest white is Inkawu, a South African Chenin Blanc £11.40, cheapest red is a 1998 Gamay Touraine at £12.60), several real ales, an impressive malt whisky collection and freshly squeezed orange juice.

The Crown
budget, garden, rural peace

High Street
Little Walden CB10 1XA
Map ref: front H 5
Telephone: 01799 522475
Open Mon-Sat: 11.30am-2.30pm
(until 3pm Sat), 6-11pm,
Sun: noon-10.30pm

Food served Mon-Sat: noon-2pm,
7-9.30pm, Sun: noon-3pm
Credit cards except
American Express
Booking advised
Prices: £2.95-£12.95, Sunday
lunch £6.25 (one course)

Situated in a tiny village just outside Saffron Walden, The Crown is hard to miss: it is not only right on the road but it has a bright red door and sign which trumpet its presence. Which is a good thing because it is definitely worth stopping here.

The Crown is hard to miss... definitely worth stopping here... the garden is small but, like the pub, it overflows with colour... real ales... are always available as is real food...

Inside the pub the colours are just as bright: lots of red walls, blue cushions and pine tables create a warm yet open feel. The freehouse used to be three cottages, which explains the different levels and all the nooks and crannies, both indoors and on the terrace. Attractive mismatched tables and chairs add to the character. The garden is small but, like the pub, it overflows with colour.

The bar has casks at the back and serves directly from them. Three or four real ales, such as City of Cambridge Hobson's Choice and Adnams Regatta are always available as is real food. Though based on standard pub grub, the Crown's menu demonstrates individuality. Salads, for example, include salade niçoise, a likely summer soup is pea and mint and amongst the more usual sandwich fillings lurk more interesting options like smoked halibut. On a more traditional note fish and chips, steaks and pork fillet also feature on the blackboard. Everything is home cooked and made to order. The service is friendly and far removed from the snobbishness evident in some country pubs. You'll feel at home here whether you come from down the street or across the seas.

The Green Man
budget, rural peace

2 Lower Street
Thriplow SG8 7RJ
Map ref: front G 4
Telephone: 01763 208855
Open Mon and Wed-Sat: noon-
2.30pm, 6-11pm, Sun: noon-2:30pm,
7-10.30pm (closed Tue)

Food served Mon and Wed-
Sat: noon-2pm, 7-9pm,
Sun: noon-2pm
Booking advised: Fri-Sat
Credit cards except Amer Exp
Prices: bar food £3-£11

I love tales of Davids beating Goliaths, especially when
it's a case of an individual against a brewery. A pub for
over 300 years, The Green Man at Thriplow has obviously lived through quite
a bit, what with burning
down in the early 1800s
and being rebuilt in
1820. However, in the last
ten years it has only survived thanks to the deter-
mination of its now land-

**The inside of the pub...
resembles a Victorian
villa crossed with a
touch of Mexico... The
staff are very
laidback... Food, beer
and wine are all good**

lord, Roger Ward, who since 1992 has turned it into a
thriving real ale pub and restaurant, recognised in 1998
by CAMRA as Cambridgeshire Pub of the Year.

In 1991 the brewery tenant died and the brewery
decided, in the light of the dwindling figures, to try and
get a change of use and turn it and the surrounding
land into houses. Luckily, the change of use was refused
and the brewery were forced to sell the pub as a pub.
Roger's bid was accepted but the brewery were so reluc-
tant to sell that they stripped everything and Roger had
to rebuild the empty shell he was left with from scratch.

He has done a marvellous job. The inside of the pub
now resembles a Victorian villa crossed with a touch of
Mexico. The pictures, chairs and mirrors would fit easily into a home and the walls are painted in the bright
reds and greens of a warm country. It is a freehouse
and, in this case, the free seems relevant. The staff are
very laidback and there is room to lounge (armchairs
and sofas at the back), dine and drink without any particular activity preventing another.

Food, beer and wine are all good. Real ales predominate. The house bitter is Tim Taylor's Landlord and three
others are changed weekly. Food ranges from
lunchtime bar snacks, like a simple, homemade soup,
(Stilton and broccoli for example) served with a lovely
ciabatta-esque roll, or ham, egg and chips, to modern
English cooking and three-course meals in the
evenings. The owner is also the chef and he concentrates on fresh flavours and prime ingredients. One of
the most intriguing lunchtime choices is Deep Fried

Hell, a combination of all sorts of fried goodies served with a Cajun dip, which sounds like the perfect accompaniment to a beer or two. Everything is reasonably priced and in large portions. The wine list is very New Worldy and is selected by Oddbins, which is a fine pedigree since I consider it the best of the chains.

Every detail counts here, from the flowers in the window boxes to the Sunday newspapers by the comfy chairs. It feels more like a private home than a public house, one where everyone is welcome as a guest.

The John Barleycorn

business lunch, garden

3 Moorfield Road
Duxford CB2 4PP
Map ref: front G 4
Telephone: 01223 832699
Open Mon-Sat: 11am-11pm,
Sun: noon-10.30pm

Food served all day
Booking advised on weekends
Prices: main courses £6.15-
£12.95, 2-course Sunday roast
£8.95

The John Barleycorn was a coaching house from 1660 and was licensed in 1844. Its current name dates from around 1858-61. Over the last few years it has earned a reputation for good food from many noted pub guides and although the tenancy changed hands in January 1999, the new tenant plans to keep the standards just as high.

a lovely place to stop for lunch, dinner or some really good coffee

It is easy to see, even from the little things, that he knows what he's doing. The coffee is real, served in cafetières and with a free refill, there are no chips on the menu and even the simpler dishes, like salads, are slightly better than average: ham baked in brown sugar, smoked salmon marinated in herbs. There isn't a scampi or a sandwich in sight: starters include grilled sardines and hot black pudding with gooseberries; main courses include beef and Stilton pie and smoked haddock with poached eggs.

During the summer barbecues (around £7 per person) take place in the garden, in a brick chimney grill. As well as the usual slabs of meat, mussels with chilli and grilled prawns are on the menu. The wine list still bears traces of the previous (South African) owners and is reasonably priced and wide-ranging.

Outside there is a leafy, flower-filled garden, a timber barn, and gas heaters specially for English summer evenings. Inside the pub has the low ceilings and timbers you'd expect in such a thatched cottage. If you're on your way into or out of Cambridge, to or from the Imperial War Museum this is a lovely place to stop for lunch, dinner or some really good coffee.

The King's Arms

urban peace

INSIDER CHOICE

10 Market Hill
Saffron Walden CB10 1HQ
Map ref: front H 5
Telephone 01799 520350
Open Mon-Thu: 11am-3.30pm,
5-11pm, Fri-Sat: 11am-11pm,
Sun: noon-3.30pm, 7-10:30 pm

Music: Dixieland jazz,
first Sunday of the month
Booking advised on weekends
Prices: lunch £2.25-£9.50,
evenings main course £8.50-£11

Nothing on the outside of the King's Arms prepares you for what's inside. It looks just like any other pub: a few signs, a name, a door. But the frontage is simply the back of the wardrobe through which Narnia awaits. For the King's Arms is truly untouched and when you step inside you feel transported to a different time and place.

What distinguishes this pub is not simply a matter of aesthetics. Nor is this one of those nineties renovations that tries to recreate an original. It *is* the original. A plain oak bar greets you with a couple of pumps. The floors are wooden and crooked, the chairs are green and red leather covered armchairs, straight from a donnish study and the walls are covered in simple Vanity Fair prints (the original magazine not the glossy upmarket monthly). There is no noise except for the creak of the floorboards and the chat of the customers. Not even the hum of a fridge. No wonder it seems possible to imagine Cromwell's men drinking here.

> **when you step inside you feel transported to a different time and place... A beer in this freehouse is a very fine experience. A meal is even finer...**

Don't get me wrong, the pub is probably a little different from the 15th-century original. Its Georgian front for example doesn't match the Tudor interior and that is the fault of the Gibson bankers who used to own it and changed the pub's frontage to resemble that of their bank opposite. But this is one of the few places in the area that feels like a piece of history.

A beer in this freehouse is a very fine experience. A meal is even finer. The chef comes from Pau in South-Eastern France and the simple evening menu reflects classic French cooking: salade chèvre chaud aux noix; magret de canard and crème brûlée. At lunch times you will find a few traces of the chef's finest (boeuf bourguignon and moules marinières) alongside English pub food such as Newmarket sausages and mash, omelettes and sandwiches. The menu changes weekly and everything is freshly cooked. Just like any other good French chef, this one has no truck with the freezer to

Around-South

microwave trajectory found in some restaurants.

On the first Sunday of every month a Dixieland jazz band plays in the pub and other musical events are organised throughout the year.

For a brief moment, whether eating, drinking or listening to music, the King's Arms takes you back to a time when pubs didn't need the artificial crutches of noise, lights and lager promotions. Real character comes from good beer, interesting food and an atmosphere conducive to conversation and relaxation. This pub has it in armfuls.

The Pear Tree
budget, desserts, pets allowed, rural peace, veg choice, wines by the glass

❖ *DISCOUNT VOUCHER - £1.50 OFF A MEAL*

Hildersham
Cambridgeshire CB1 6BU
Map ref: front G 5
Telephone: 01223 891680
Open Mon-Sat: 11:45am-2pm,
6.30-11pm (until 6pm Sat),
Sun: noon-2pm, 7-10:30pm

Food served Mon-Sun: noon-2pm, 6.30-9.30pm (Sun: 7-9pm)
Credit cards except American Express
Prices: main dishes £3.25-£11.75

The village of Hildersham is picture-perfect, lush, rolling and green, and the Pear Tree fits in beautifully. A neat white building, facing gable-end onto the road, this is a pub where the interior lives up to the pretty exterior.

Just one bar, one fireplace and some window seats are more than enough to create a cosy and friendly atmosphere. Polished settles and smiles welcome locals and visitors, whether having a drink or a meal. The Pear Tree remains very much a pub: you can't make a booking for food and you won't find tables laid out for lunch. However, it does serve bar food at very reasonable prices. For example, scampi and chips costs £4.95, and a ploughman's is £3.75. There is also a more elaborate daily specials menu listing starters like crispy crab pancakes with sweet and sour dip and main courses such as breaded plaice with an asparagus, smoked salmon and cream cheese filling. There are two vegetarian dishes and traditional homecooked puddings, like treacle tart and fruit crumbles, are a speciality. IPA, Abbot, Triumph are the standard beers. There is an occasional guest ale and lots of wine by the glass.

🛈 The Queen's Head

budget, desserts, pets allowed, sandwiches, veg choice, wines by the glass

Cambridge Road
Newton CB2 5PG
Map ref: front G 4
Telephone: 01223 870436
Open Mon-Sat: 11.30am-2.30pm, 6-11pm, Sun:
noon-2.30pm, 7-10.30pm

Food served: noon-2:30pm,
6-9:30pm
Non-smoking area
No credit cards
Prices:(lunch) sandwiches, jacket potatoes, soup £1.80-£2.30,
eves/Sunday plates of cold meats, cheeses, smoked salmon £2.90-£4

This is, quite simply, a fabulous pub. There are no frills, no modern compromises, just a wooden bar, straightforward food and real ales. David Short's father bought the pub in 1962 and his son took over as landlord in 1971. A list of landlords by the bar takes you back to the first in 1728. Most of the building dates from 1680-1720 but arches in the cellars are even older. A loud clock ticks above the fireplace but not so loudly that you can't hear the chat and bustle of locals and visitors. Pictures cover the walls, mismatched chairs and settles cover the tiled floor and people crowd inside or onto the very few chairs out front.

> a fabulous pub. There are no frills, no modern compromises, just a wooden bar, straightforward food and real ales... The food, like the pub, is unpretentious

Only real ales are served, straight from the cask. Adnams Bitter, Broadside and Regatta are available all the time, plus Old Ale in the winter and Tally Ho, a barley wine, at Christmas. The food, like the pub, is unpretentious. Toast and beef dripping is the cheapest option at £1.80, sandwiches, mugs of soup and Aga baked jacket potatoes start around £1.90. Nothing costs very much and it's all served without fuss from the bar.

In the hallway there is a noticeboard, with details of a local tennis tournament. At the bar a young woman discusses her impending wedding the following day. Not only is this a wonderful pub for dropping into now and again, it is part of the local community. A rarity indeed.

The Sun

garden, urban peace

59 Gold Street
Saffron Walden CB10 1EJ
Map ref: front H 5
Telephone: 01799 506035

Open Mon-Fri: 3.30-11pm, Sat:
noon-11pm, Sun noon-10:30pm
No food served
No credit cards

The Sun is very much a sports pub but I'm a sportphobe
so that isn't why I like it. It has to be one of the most attractive pubs in Saffron Walden. Painted green and cream
woodwork, low brick chimneys as well as a brick porch
and a small, secluded
beer garden (with a
wendy house) make
this into an architectural gem. It is reputed
to be the oldest surviving pub in town and supposedly, the ghost of a man
who died in a fire haunts it. They don't serve food but the
beer is worth a journey since this is a Ridley's pub, serving IPA, Rumpus and ESX, ales not often seen in
Cambridgeshire. For sports fans there is a pool room and
all major events are shown on big screens.

**a sports pub... one of the
most attractive pubs in
Saffron Walden... reputed
to be the oldest
surviving pub in town**

The Temeraire

budget, garden patio

55 High Street
Saffron Walden CB10 1AA
Map ref: front H 5
Telephone: 01799 516975
Wheelchair access inc toilets

Open Mon-Sat: 11am-11pm,
Sun: noon-10.30pm
Food served: 11am-10pm
Prices: bar food £1.95-£7.95

Like many in the Wetherspoon chain, The Temeraire is a
massive pub, more hotel-like than anything else, and
somehow the building's
character remains despite
the corporate branding. It
is light and quiet (there is
no music played) and there
are plenty of separate sections for different groups, including a small outside patio.
There are lots of real ales, including Shepherd Neame's
Spitfire, B&T Dragon Slayer and something called Fudger.
On the day I visited Theakston's Best and Pilsner Urquell
were both on special offer at 99p per pint. The food is
equally varied and cheap with a two meals for £5 offer
running all day and a curry special (£4.99 for curry, naan
and a pint or soft drink). It is most definitely a chain: the
posters and magazines are on every surface advertising
the products, but the effect is still pleasant.

**a massive pub... light
and quiet... plenty of
separate sections for
different groups...
lots of real ales**

The Tickell Arms

garden

1 Old North Road
Whittlesford, CB2 4NZ
Map ref: front G 4
Telephone: 01223 833128
Open Tue-Sat: 11am-2.30pm,
7-11pm, Sun: noon-3pm, 7-10.30pm

No credit cards
Food served Tue-Sun:
noon-2.30pm, 7-10pm
Booking advised: weekends
Prices: food £4.75-£9

The Tickell Arms is very blue, probably the only blue pub in this county of pale thatched cottage inns. If you didn't know that this villa was a pub not a private house, you would probably drive past it. Which would be a shame because this is one of the few truly individual pubs in the region. The fact that it doesn't resemble any other on the outside is indicative of the differences on the inside.

> one of the few truly individual pubs in the region... Fresh flowers, rugs, antiques and paintings decorate every surface and classical music plays... beautiful but also cosy

For a start a notice on the door declares 'Thou shalt not enter nor be served upon these premises unless properly and cleanly dressed'. It continues with a list of the elements it obviously considers 'unclean' and 'improper' such as 'no tee shirts' and 'no bare feet'. The Tickell Arms doesn't believe in compromise. Once inside, that is if you're lucky enough to be correctly attired, you will realise that such an attitude is worth it.

Fresh flowers, rugs, antiques and paintings decorate every surface and classical music plays in the background. It is the perfect place for a relaxing Sunday lunch since it is not only beautiful but also cosy, thus making you feel at once pampered and at home. The food is of the same ilk: a little bit more complicated than home cooking without being fanciful or fussy. Pub staples are also available but the best food comes from the specials board, especially choices like lamb in Madeira sauce and fruit crumbles. Beer-wise you have a choice of Adnams or Adnams. There is no lager on tap.

The Tickell Arms is a pub which has, in every respect, more colour than most.

Around-South

Fat Jax

1st Floor Roysia House
Market HIll
Royston, Herts SG8 9JJ
Map ref: front H 2
Telephone: 01763 249 825
Open Fri-Sat: 9pm-2am
Entry fee: £2.50 before 10pm,
£5 after

No credit cards
No one under 18 admitted
Dress code: no trainers, over-
coats must be checked
Prices: fast food curries and
chili etc £6-£11.99. alcohol
(typical): beer, spirits, cocktails £2.20

Fat Jax is a small nightclub with just 180 capacity and
the feel of a discotheque. DJs Les Knott and 'Dancing'
Dave play a lot of 60s and 70s pop along with chart
music, keeping the place easy-going. The decor adds a
light touch, with some pop paraphernalia – Jumping
Jack Flash pictures – adding colour, but nothing as
heavy as a theme.

In addition to the Friday and Saturday openings, you
can get the weekend start-
ed early. Fat Jax runs a 70s
night on the last Thursday
of the month where
admission is free and
drinks are sold at reduced
prices. But it mainly gets
busy on weekends, when
after 11pm it may be hard

**a lot of 60s and 70s
pop along with chart
music, keeping the
place easy-going...
attracts a wide range
of people, with most
clubbers ranging from
18 up to 30**

to get in. That's in part because the club attracts a wide
range of people, with most clubbers ranging from 18
up to 30. The over-25s even have a lounge upstairs to
themselves.

Like all nightclubs, security is a concern. They seem
to have it in hand here – with CCTV and radio-linked
bouncers and a strongly anti-drug attitude. There's also
a good taxi service in Royston for those who have had
one too many.

If it is your birthday, be sure to bring your ID. Fat Jax
gives you free admission and a glass of champagne.

Surfer's Paradise Internet Café and Bar

budget, open early, sandwiches

168 High Street
Newmarket CB8 9AQ
Map ref: front D 7
Telephone: 01638 606160

Open Mon-Sat: 8am-5pm
No credit cards
Prices: sandwiches under £2, baked
potatoes £1.50, full breakfast £2.50

Seek no further for the cutting edge of the internet in Newmarket. Opened just months ago on the High Street, here you can access your email (a service popular with horse trainers in Newmarket for the races), 'surf the information super highway or just enjoy a byte to eat', as the blurb says.

> surf the information super highway or just enjoy a byte to eat

A byte might not be too filling but the menu offers a range of sandwiches and light meals – beans on toast, scampi and burgers for around £2 – along with drinks and alcohol. With five PCs for internet access, Surfers allows you to use the software for word processing, graphics, speadsheets, scanning and printing. You can also get some deals on computers and parts. Internet access is £1.25/15 minutes, £4.50/hour.

Brasserie 22

business lunch, children,
special occasion, veg choice

INSIDER
CHOICE

160 High Street
Newmarket CB8 9QA
Map ref: front D 7
Telephone: 01638 660646
Open Tue-Sat: lunch from
11.30am, dinner from 6.30pm

Non-smoking area
Booking advised
Prices: set lunch £9.95, starters
£3.75-£6.25, main courses £8.25-
£11.25, puddings £3.95-£5.25

You can't help but compare Brasserie 22 to its sister in Cambridge, Restaurant 22. They share a set of owners, but while the Cambridge 22 is all Victorian (see pp 41), Brasserie 22 is modern – a shop front on the high street behind a fogged glass window with a huge number 22 on it. Inside, the smallish two-level dining areas are bright with comforting exposed brick walls and wooden tables. There are no fussy decorations. You feel at ease coming in casual clothes.

> kind of snap-to-it attitude and easy dignity that wins friends... The food has a ght, fresh touch deserving f the brasserie name...

The brasserie, seating about 40, rises or falls on its

Around East

service and food. In these respects, it does exceptionally well. The staff display a kind of snap-to-it attitude and easy dignity that wins friends among customers and makes them feel special.

The food has a light, fresh touch deserving of the brasserie name. The meal begins with a bread basket – arranged beautifully – and olives, that arrive immediately. Along with a 38-choice wine list, (£9.25–£24.95), you can have daily fresh fish from the special menu, dishes like Newmarket sausages with apple mash and onion gravy or several pastas served as starters or main courses.

Dishes like the sautéed breast of chicken (£9.95) with olive, lemon and chili dressing come beautifully presented on a large white plate on a bed of carrot. Distinct flavours marked this delicious course. This is the Brasserie 22 style. You can taste the ingredients individually – and yet they work together subtly. This is a mark of gourmet food deserving of the name.

Sol Y Sombra Spanish Restaurant

special occasion

INSIDER CHOICE

❖ *DISCOUNT VOUCHER - £3 - £5 OFF A MEAL*

4-5 Crown Walk
Newmarket CB8 8NG
Map ref: front D 7
Telephone: 01638 668474
Open bar Mon-Sat: 11am-11pm
No Smoking

Food served Mon: noon-
2.30pm, Tue-Sun: noon-2.30pm,
6.30-10pm
Booking advised: weekends
Prices: tapas and starters £3.60-
£6.95, fish £7.95-£14.96, meat
£5.95-£20, set lunch £9.95

We are pleased to report that on a recent Saturday night, we made our pilgrimage to Sol Y Sombra only to find the restaurant so full that it could take no more diners and had reached it's capacity to serve food even at the bar. We can offer that as a recommendation, although we did not have the privilege of tasting the fare ourselves.

This smallish restaurant at the opening to a modern shopping centre has a dining room big enough for just 26 people and they all seemed to be having a jolly old time...

We could only look longingly at others enjoying their meals in the brightly lit, orange-walled dining room behind the bar. This smallish restaurant at the opening to a modern shopping centre has a dining room big enough for just 26 people and they all seemed to be having a jolly old time. Diners chose from at least 17 starters or tapas choices on the menu. These range from Pan de La Casa (£4.75), a toasted ciabatta with tomato, garlic and thinly sliced serrano hake to Mejillones Marinera (£5.50), mussels steamed open in wine, cream or wine and tomato sauce. The main menu included choices like Merluza a La Vasca (£10.95), cod with asparagus and prawn sauce and Cordonices Emborrachadas (£10.95), drunken quails stuffed with rice and apricots and with brandy sauce. It sounds delicious. We hope in future readers will have better luck in getting in.

You can also eat outside on the pavement of the shopping centre on warm days and just inside is a cosy bar, serving beer and wines in a pleasant Spanish decor – decorated with pictures of bull fights, ceramic tiles and notices. A massive trophy head of a bull, horns menacingly sharp, keeps vigil over drinkers.

Stocks Restaurant

business lunch, garden, special occasion

INSIDER
CHOICE

High Street	Credit cards except Amer Exp
Bottisham, CB5 9BA	Booking advised at weekends
Map ref: front E 6	Prices: Tue-Sat 2-course lunch
Telephone: 01223 811202	£10.95, 3-Course £14.95, á la
Open Tue-Sat: lunch from noon*,	carte main courses £12.95-
dinner from 7pm (last booking	£18.95 (*Tue-Sat lunch service
9pm); Sun lunch: noon-2.30pm	suspended until Dec 1999)

Stocks restaurant, named after the punishment stocks that once stood on the same site, consists of several different rooms as well as a garden terrace. The Stavely, the first you enter from the street, is a stone-flagged dining room with beamed ceilings and walls, an open fireplace full of plants and pictures everywhere. That might sound a little quaint. It's not.

> **dressiness without prissiness... very modern English but without fuss... If I owned a restaurant, I would want it to be like this**

Through an ingenious blend of modern fabrics and antique structures (the building dates from 1470 and is the oldest in the village), the proprietor Amanda Stavely has created dressiness without prissiness. Tables are beautifully laid and the right distance apart: despite the relatively small size of this room there is still privacy.

And then there's the food, which again, is very modern English but without fuss. The lunch menu (a bargain at £10.95 for two courses) offers starters like Caesar Salad and Galantine of Rabbit, Pigeon, Venison and Chicken. The salad was nothing short of inspired, with fresh anchovies and thick grated parmesan (no

Around-East

delicate shavings here). And the bread, warm from the oven, was obviously homemade. The main course, Roast Duck with rosemary and garlic and a Madeira jus, was both crisp-skinned and yet moist, exactly how it should be.

If I owned a restaurant, I would want it to be like this. Upmarket without being intimidating, Stocks now provides pleasure not pain.

Swynford Paddocks Hotel and Restaurant

business lunch, garden, rural peace, special occasion

Six Mile Bottom CB8 0UE
Map ref: front E 6
Telephone: 01638 570234
Open: 11am-11pm,
Sun: noon-10.30pm
Food served: daily noon-9.30pm

Booking advised
Prices: tea from £2.25, lighter meals £3.50-£14.95, à la carte main courses £9.75-£18.50, 4-course table d'hôte £26.50, 4-course Sunday lunch £17.50

Sometime in July, on one of the hottest days of the year, I was driving around the county in an overheated car, completely lost, totally frustrated and a perfect advert for which deodorant *not* to buy. Then I chanced upon a somewhat dilapidated sign for Swynford Paddocks Hotel and knowing nothing about it except that it was closer than anywhere else and likely to serve cold drinks, I followed the directions.

Sweeping up the drive of this grand country hotel (as far as it is possible to sweep in such a scruffy wreck) in

The effect is very much that of the private home it once was... this was the home of... Augusta, Lord Byron's half sister and forbidden love. Byron frequently spent time with her here, writing under a tree in the garden

a beaten-up car and beaten-up clothes, I felt a little out of place and somewhat overawed. Yet the lush green paddocks (it's not just a name you know) and white and black gabled mansion seemed a perfect antidote to the nasty heat of the A14. Shortly after arriving, sitting on a shady terrace with a couple of newspapers and a pretty flowered china teacup and teapot for company, the tarmac and maps I had been tussling with ten minutes before seemed miles away. I felt cool, calm and restored to normality, even if I still looked like a crumpled tissue.

As I scanned my surroundings, such refreshment seemed inevitable as well as welcome. The hotel and restaurant are completely surrounded by greenery outside and inside the galleried hall and panelled corridors are elegant without being too grandiose. The effect is very much that of the private home it once was. Indeed, in the nineteenth century this was the home of Colonel George Leigh and his wife Augusta, Lord Byron's half sister and forbidden love. Byron frequently spent time with her here, writing under a tree in the garden. All that remains of such history is the huge paintings of the lovers that decorate the stairs. However, the romantic associations meld well with the character of the hotel and restaurant which are more than perfect settings for candlelit dinners or weddings. The à la carte menu is incredible, offering the vast choice combined with the attention to detail of a one-off chef, whereas the daily table d'hôte menu is, at £26.50 for four courses, unusually cheap for this standard in this location. Bar snacks, tea and coffee are served all day and again the prices are reasonable considering that you could pay more for a sandwich in a cramped, trendy bar in Cambridge.

What turns Swynford into a special occasion, however, is the service which is gracious and welcoming, whatever state you arrive in.

The Anchor

business lunch, children, desserts, garden, rural peace, special occasion, veg choices

 DISCOUNT VOUCHER - £8 BOTTLE OF HOUSE WINE

63 North Street
Burwell CB5 0BA
Map ref: front D 6
Telephone: 01638 741101
Open Mon-Tue: 7-11pm,
Wed-Sun: noon-2.30pm, 7-11pm

Food served: 7-10.30pm, noon-2.30pm (except Mon-Tue lunch)
non-smoking area
Booking advised,
essential in evenings
Prices: food £2.75-£15

The Anchor has been a pub since 1610, easily making it one of the oldest in the region. It is run by Thomas and Eileen Murray, who are friendly to everyone, not just the locals. Their openness makes the Anchor feel very welcoming. It is divided into three very different areas: the sports and TV bar at one end, with orange walls, high bar stools and a big screen; the central bar section which is more pubby, with wooden chairs, tables and a fireplace and finally a dining-room with a blackboard menu at one end. There is also outside seating and a children's play area next to the river behind the pub.

Owned by Greene King, IPA, Abbot and Triumph are on sale but since there's an Irishman behind the bar

> pub since 1610...
> very welcoming...
> Guinness is a definite
> feature... the Anchor
> prides itself on an
> extensive fish menu

Guinness is a definite feature: properly served and available from either an extra cold or normal draught pump. But the beer isn't the only reason to come here, for the Anchor prides itself on an extensive fish menu. Filleted trout, Dover sole, anchor smokies and paella are some of the options and if you only want a bar snack there are seafood platters and smoked salmon sandwiches. A £3.99 8oz rump steak special should satisfy the most devoted of carnivores and roast dinners are available every day. The atmosphere is pubby: open and relaxed and the food is worth investigating.

The Kings Head
garden, rural peace

Station Road
Dullingham CB8 9UJ
Map ref: front E 7
Telephone: 01638 507486
Open daily: 11am-2.30pm,
6-11pm (Sun till 10pm)

Food served daily: noon-2pm,
6-10pm
Prices: bar food £4.95-£11.95

The King's Head has an enviable position, looking out across the whole width of Dullingham's village green. It is a pink-painted pub with two bars, a back garden as well as seats in front, and a large car park.

a pink-painted pub with two bars, a back garden as well as seats in front... a classic pub interior

The interior combines brick and timber with dark tables and chairs, creating a classic pub interior. A Pubmaster tenancy, the King's Head offers two real ales as well as Boddingtons, Flowers IPA and Kilkenny. Food is available every day, both lunch times and evenings but this still remains a pub more than a restaurant.

Customers are a mix of visitors and locals, some enjoying the view of the village, others the food on offer. The printed menu offers hot and cold pub food and there are also interesting blackboard specials, such as beef stroganoff (£9.95), half a roast duck with black cherry and port sauce (£11.95) and veal Switzerland (£10.95). Desserts, like tiramisu and chocolate orange mousse, are all £2.95. Staff and customers are friendly and welcoming.

The Queen's Head

INSIDER
CHOICE

budget, business lunch, children,
garden, rural peace,
special occasion, veg choice,
wines by the glass

Kirtling CB8 9PA
Map ref: front E 8
Telephone: 01638 731737
Open Mon-Sat: 11.30am-
2.30pm, 7-11pm,
Sun: noon-2.30pm

Food served: noon-2pm,
7-9.30pm (not Sun eve)
Booking advised
especially weekends
Prices: main courses £8.50-
£14.95

Situated in Kirtling, one of those villages which has no
discernible beginning, middle or end, The Queen's
Head is an oasis. Surrounded by trees, removed from
traffic it manages to provide all the joys of modern
pubs and none of the horrors.

This big cream and green house is flanked on one
side by a car park, on the other by a leafy, sloping garden simply furnished with bench tables. The door from
the car park leads into a flint-walled hallway with
menus displayed and part of a printing press to the left.

Up the short flight of
stairs is the lounge, with
soft olive chesterfields,
light wood tables and
chairs, and a fireplace.
Just beyond this room is
the public bar, with a
tiled floor and the same

*an oasis... all the joys
of modern pubs and
none of the horrors...
Many pubs fall short of
their reputations. The
Queen's Head isn't one
of them*

light tables. By the fireplace, sandwiched between the
sofas, there is a low coffee table with a neat row of magazines and newspapers. The only noise comes from the
rustle of the trees that edge the garden.

The range and quality of food is such that for once
the obvious, most interesting selections don't jump out
from amongst the more standard choices. That's
because nothing is standard about this menu. Light
lunches may include asparagus and pea risotto (£5.25),
warm salad with chicken, bacon, avocado and croutons
(£5.50 – bread is an extra £1) or a club sandwich and
there is also a more substantial menu which changes
regularly. Chips are hand-cut and chunky and made to
order. This is surely the only pub that offers lemon pos-
set for dessert. There are several wines available by the
glass as well as a couple of real ales.

Service is prompt and polite, the atmosphere
relaxed, quiet yet somehow upbeat, even without
music. Many pubs fall short of their reputations. The
Queen's Head isn't one of them.

Around-East

The Star Inn
business lunch, children, rural peace, special occasion, terrace

INSIDER CHOICE

❖ *DISCOUNT VOUCHER - £5 OFF MEAL FOR TWO*

The Street
Lidgate, CB8 9PP
Map ref: front E 8
Telephone: 01638 500275
Open daily: 11am-3pm,
5-11pm (10.30pm Sun)

Food served daily: (except Sun eve) noon-2.30pm, 7-10pm
Booking advised
Prices: lunch special 1-course £5.50, 2-courses £8.50, main courses £9.50-£18, 3-course, Sunday lunch £13.50

The Star Inn is a real gem. This 500 year-old building has been a pub for the last 100 years, and a notable one for the last five. Ever since Maria Axon took over, its reputation has been growing locally and nationally.

The Star Inn is a real gem... one of the gastronomic highlights of the region... The food is mostly Spanish, though boeuf Bourguignon and lasagne also appear

Steps from the car park lead up to the front garden which has a few tables and lots of colour. Inside, the wooden floors, the bar billiards and the darts board all suggest that this is a classic English pub. But there is something distinctly continental about the jazz seeping gently into the room, the brightly painted earthenware plates hanging above the fireplace and the heavy serving bowls. The owner, Maria Axon, is Catalan and her Spanish roots and business experience (she owned and ran a restaurant in Barcelona and a wine bar in Great Chesterford) have turned what could be just another country pub into one of the gastronomic highlights of the region.

The food is mostly Spanish, though boeuf Bourguignon and lasagne also appear. Starters include Mediterranean fish soup (£4.50), Catalan salad (lettuce, eggs, olives, spring onions, tomatoes) which is big enough for lunch (£4.50). There are lots of fish main courses, including paella Valenciana (£10.50) and whole grilled lobster (£18.00). There is also a fixed-price lunch available (one-course £5.50; two-course £8.50),

Greene King beers are available though a jug of sangria (£15) seems more appropriate. The wine list includes lots of specially imported Spanish wines from both new and established wine areas. In the winter, the pub sells cremat (£2.50 each), a sort of flambéd drink: coffee, brandy, rum, sugar, lemon and cinnamon are mixed together and then set alight.

Whenever you visit, you will find a friendly environment and good food. The Star lives up to its name.

Waggon & Horses

wines by the glass

36 The High Street
Newmarket CB8 8LB
Map ref: front D 7
Telephone: 01638 662479
Open Mon-Sat: 11am-11pm,
Sun: noon-10.30pm

Food served Sun-Thu: noon-9,
Fri-Sat: noon-7pm
Credit cards except
American Express
Prices: pub food under £6

The Waggon and Horses is a beer drinker's pub. Serving
up to 13 real ales at a time, many directly from the keg,
the pub serves a lot of beers like Flowers Original and
Adnams Best along with the
range supplied by Hogshead
Pubs, part of the Whitbread
group. You can also order 26
wines, many by the glass.

> a beer drinker's
> pub. Serving up
> to 13 real ales at
> a time...

At least a century old, the Waggon & Horses was
once a hotel with its own garden, stables and outbuild-
ing. The sense of age remains, with low ceilings, beams
and a handsome hearth surrounded by horse paraphernalia. There are fruit machines and satellite TV, but the
main attraction is the good drink. At lunch and just
before the horse races down the street, the pub is full
to bursting with punters downing a pint.

The White Hart Hotel

High Street
Newmarket CB8 8JP
Map ref: front D 7
Telephone: 01638 663051
Open Mon-Sat: 11am-11pm,
Sun: noon-10.30pm

Food served daily: noon-8pm
Prices: pub food under £6,
lager £2.20, real ales about
£1.75

The White Hart Hotel stands out for the crowds spilling
from its open front on to the High Street pavement on
a warm day. A café bar by concept, the open inside
space features a long
brass and wood bar
with lots of room for
people standing around
with drinks. In the
back, a score of tables
make a comfortable

> ands out for the
> owds spilling from its
> en front on to the
> gh Street pavement...
> s a buzz – and a
> odern, classy feel

space for eating from menu choices ranging from jacket potatoes to pasta and vegetable tagine (Moroccan
style chunky vegetables in sauce).

At noon, it is a popular café at with the office lunch
crowds. It takes on more of a bar persona by night,

Around-East

especially busy on weekends, when music booms loudly for the people on their way to nightclubs. The White Hart Hotel has a buzz – and a modern, classy feel helped by its renovation two years ago by Banks's of the Wolverhampton & Dudley Breweries. It is one of nine pubs in the group's collection.

The White Pheasant

rural peace, veg choice

Market Street
Fordham, CB7 5LQ
Map ref: front C 7
Telephone: 01638 720414
Open Mon-Sat: noon-3pm,
6-11pm, Sun: noon-3pm,
7-10.30pm

Food served: noon-2.30pm,
6-10pm (7pm Sun)
Credit cards except
American Express
Booking advised on weekends
Prices: main courses £5.95-
£13.32

From the road, the 17th-century White Pheasant doesn't look very exciting. It sits snugly beside some houses and next to the Burwell road. But once through the door, the Fens are replaced by the Highlands of Scotland, or at least what soft Southerners like me imagine exists north of the border. Tartan curtains, wooden floors covered with the odd rug, walls decorated with paintings, fishing and hunting paraphernalia and the odd bit of armour all create a warm environment. Add to that the combination of chapel chairs and restored commodes (thankfully made into comfortable seats), the blue and peach paint in different rooms, and the tongue and groove bar and you have an inn which combines a modern pub sensibility with traditional style.

combines a modern pub sensibility with traditional style... The food here is accomplished and adventurous, yet retains an awareness of tradition and local produce

The food here is accomplished and adventurous, yet retains an awareness of tradition and local produce. Typical dishes include Newmarket sausages with mash and onion and mustard gravy (£5.95), East Coast Cod Steak with herb crumb topping and pesto sauce (£12.95) and Norfolk Chicken Breast wrapped in bacon served with tomato and basil sauce (£10.95). Blackboards offer several fish and meat choices daily as well as a good range of desserts (all £3.70).

The inn is a freehouse and offers Theakston's Best, Courage Directors as well as a regular guest, like Hook Norton. The wine list has house bottles at £9.25 going

up to £16.95 for a Macon-Lugny. Apparently, if you only
drink half the bottle you will only be charged half the
price.

The White Pheasant is run by the same group who
own The Crown and Punchbowl in Horningsea. If you
know and like one, you will probably like the other.
Even though they each have a distinct style, they are
similar in certain, rather important respects: each offers
good food, lovely service and an attractive setting.

De Niro's Night Club
& Pacino's Wine Bar

146/146a High Street
Newmarket CB8 9AQ
Map ref: front D 7
Telephone: 01638 660031
Open (De Niro's) Thu-Sat:
9pm-2am, (Pacino's) Thu-Sun:
7-11pm/events midweek
No credit cards

Entry fee (De Niro's only) Thu:
£0.80-£5, Fri: £4-£6, Sat: £5-£7
No one under 18 admitted
No admittance after midnight
Dress code: (De Niro's only) smart
casual, no t-shirts or trainers
Bar snacks only
Prices (typical: spirits £1.65-£1.85,
pint £2.10-£2.40 (less at Pacino's)

At this writing De Niro's is about to become the largest
nightclub in the region. In November 1999, it shuts for
reconstruction, turning this venue for 700 people into
one with capacity for 1,800, putting it on the scale of
big   nightclubs   in
London. We are told the
spirit of De Niro's and its
feeder pub, Pacino's Wine
Bar, will endure. The now
seven year-old club attracts
a variety of people, ranging
in age from 18 to 35 who
girate and drink to DJed
commercial   party   and

**a classy show...
tiered main room...
mirrored walls and
gangster murals
around a central
dance floor... broad
mix of ages seems to
give the nightclub a
mellow feel**

dance music in the main club and to 70s and 80s music
after 11pm, when Pacino's closes as a wine bar and
reopens as part of the nightclub.

DeNiro's puts on a classy show. From the roof of the
circular building, a multi-beamed search light shoots at
the stars, Hollywood-like. Inside, the dimly lit, tiered
main room rises in mirrored walls and gangster murals
around a central dance floor. You get your drinks at the
bar at the back and top and then slither down to the
dance arena if you dare. A chatty DJ was on duty when
I visited, who was great fun – adding a casual note to
the atmosphere. The fairly broad mix of ages gives the
nightclub a mellow feel that some nightclubs lack.

Pegasus Nite Club

109-111 High Street
Newmarket CB8 8JH
Map ref: front D 7
Telephone: 01638 669771 Open:
Fri-Sat 9pm-2am
No one under 18 admitted,
No admission after midnight

Entry fee Fri: £8-£10, Sat: £1
before 10:30, £3 before 11, £5
after
Dress code: 'no effort, no
entry' smart trainers accepted
Prices (typical): beer £2,
spirits £2.60

Formerly the White House, Pegasus Nite club occupies a big, old theatre done up grandly. From the apex of the arched ceiling, coloured spots and a lava light projection shine down on a mini skating rink of a dance floor. This is surrounded by half walls with counters behind them. You lean up against them with your drink and peer over the wall at the writhing masses below (unless, of course, you are among them, in which case you feel like a performer on a crowded stage).

occupies a big, old theatre done up grandly... 'uplifting' House music and big name...DJs... are invited to run the show

It's got style. The main room is done up in purples, with huge clothes banners sliding down from above where giant gold cerubs on clouds overlook the scene. Whoever did the place up had a sense of humour, but not much sympathy for tired legs; seating is at minimum. But then who comes to a nightclub to sit down? Not this crowd. Mostly about 25 years old and under, they fill the 550-capacity main room and basement, girating to the pulsations of the DJ in each. On Fridays the music is 'uplifting' House music and big name DJ's like Boy George, Danny Rampling and Jeremy Healy are invited to run the show (hence the hefty prices). Saturdays are more commercial, chart music and R 'n' B setting the mood for the dance floors.

Stanley's Nite Club

44 The High Street
Newmarket CB8 8LB
Map ref: front D 7
Telephone: 07775 927310
Open: Fri-Sat 9pm-2am, Sun
(karaoke) 8-10.30pm

Entry fee Fri: 9-11pm £1, £5 after
11, Sat: 9-10pm £1, £5 after
10pm (member discounts), free
admission to Karaoke
No credit cards
No one under 18 admitted

Stanley's is a nightclub behind a pub called Oliver's. The smallest of the Newmarket clubs with a capacity of 250 people, it celebrates the comic duo (and a lot of other comics) in pictures and mementos on the walls of the long, dimly lit room. The bar occupies two-thirds of this space, and at the back, the DJ oversees a virtually postage-stamp dance floor with checkerboard black and white tiles that must get cosy at times.

In terms of music, Stanley's does 70s and 80s on Fridays, commercial dance tunes on Saturday and hosts something rare these days – a karaoke night on Sundays. This puts it on the more traditional end of things as clubs go, and no wonder it attracts a fairly wide mix of ages. This club exudes none of the anarchic-chic of some clubs. It's down to earth and fun.

on the more traditional end of things as clubs go... attracts a fairly wide mix of ages... down to earth and fun

Papworth Hotel

Indian

Ermine Street South
Papworth Everard CB3 8PB
Map ref: front E 1
Telephone: 01954 718851

Open daily: noon-2pm, 6-11pm
(Sun: until 10pm)
Booking advised Fri-Sat
Prices: from £4.95-£10.95
10% take away discount

If you live in Papworth Everard your opportunities for eating out are severely limited. So when the Papworth Hotel started advertising Indian food, something that was previously unavailable within eight miles of the village, I had to try it.

Though the hotel doesn't impress much in appearance, the Indian food is excellent. Very fresh ingredients, distinctive tastes and friendly staff characterise this restaurant. But with the lack of competition offered by its rural and isolated position, the Papworth Hotel is not a cheap curry house. A chicken korma, for example, which is usually one of the cheapest dishes, costs £5.95, a pound over the typical Cambridge price. So the cost of a meal can add up. But if you live in the new village of Cambourne, Papworth or are just in the area and don't want to go all the way to Cambridge or Huntingdon, it's worth the trip.

The Indian food is excellent. Very fresh ingredients, distinctive tastes and friendly staff characterise this restaurant

Around West

Tai Yuen

garden, Chinese

High Street
Toft CB3 7RL
Map ref: front E 2
Telephone: 01223 263337
Booking advised
at weekends

Open daily: 5-11pm
Credit cards except American Express
Prices: £14.50 all-inclusive 3-course
buffet, main dishes from £4.80
Service charge of 10% on meals
Take away dishes from £3.30

Tai Yuen looks vaguely like the pub it once was. However, what it offers is far removed from bar snacks and beer. For in the small village of Toft sits one of the best Peking and Szechuan restaurants in the region.

one of the best Peking and Szechuan restaurants in the region... everything is excellent and served in large portions...

The restaurant is classic Chinese style: a big, L-shaped room with a shiny bar near the entrance and lots of round tables ideal for groups. You can sit up at the bar and order very reasonable take aways (most dishes priced around £4) but dining in is the real treat. At £14.50 per head, for as many starters and main courses as you can manage, the all-you-can-eat meal is a bargain. It doesn't seem to matter how many choices you have: everything is excellent and served in large portions. Wandering Dragon (£6.70), for example, combines roast pork, king prawns and mixed vegetables in a garlic, black bean and soya sauce but manages to retain distinct flavours and textures. Similar dishes include Merry Paradise (£6.70) and Four Happiness (£6.70).

Service can be patchy (despite the service charge) but with this food and the incredible all-you-can-eat deal, a few glitches can easily be forgiven.

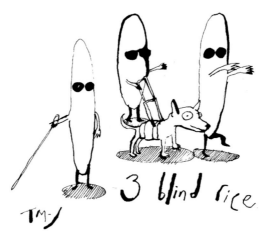

3 blind rice

TMJ

The Tudor Hotel & Thai Restaurant

INSIDER CHOICE

business lunch, garden, special occasion, veg choices

❖ *DISCOUNT VOUCHER - £10% OFF LUNCH*

High Street
Fenstanton PE18 9JZ
Map ref: front D 1
Telephone: 01480 462532
Open Tue-Sun: noon-3pm,
6-11pm

Non-smoking area
Booking advised at weekends
Prices: main courses £5.95-
£7.50, Sat buffet £15.50 per
person for 3-course meal, take
away, lunch salad bar

Cambridgeshire seems to have a rash of pubs offering Thai food, mostly out in the countryside and The Tudor is probably the best. From the outside it looks like many other pubs. Inside, you are transported to a little bit of Thailand. A display of Thai crafts and culture greets your eyes whilst your nose is met by the aromas of lemon grass, coconut and ginger. It seems strange to order a pint at the very English bar when, just across the other side of the room, there is another country.

> If you are not already a fan of Thai food this is an excellent place for an introduction... Ped Young... and her staff have done everything to make a very run-of-the-mill pub into a little haven of Thai serenity

If you are not already a fan of Thai food this is an excellent place for an introduction. If you are, then the Tudor will merely confirm that this is one of the greatest cuisines in the world. The Spicy fish cake (Tod Mun Pla) with cucumber and chilli sauce is truly delicious (albeit a tad pricey at £5.25 for a starter, compared to everything else). For a bit more variety, have the mixed starters which resemble those found in many Chinese restaurants except for the lovely biting chilli sauce. The main courses are all very reasonably priced. Moo Kraproa (stir fried pork with chilli and basil) and chicken green curry are standards on Thai menus but here they are exceptionally fresh and sharp, without any muddying of the various flavours.

What makes the Tudor even more special is that the owner, Ped Young, and her staff have done everything to make a very run-of-the-mill pub into a little haven of Thai serenity. There is a lovely garden, which you can eat in by request. The service is friendly and enthusiastic and the atmosphere is calming.

The Duke of Wellington

garden, special occasion

49 Alms Hill
Bourn CB3 7SH
Map ref: front E 2
Telephone: 01954 719364
Open Tue-Sat: noon-2.30, 6.30-
11pm, Sun: noon-3pm, 7-10pm
(closed: bank holidays)

Food served: noon-2.30pm (last
orders 2pm), 6.30-9.15pm
Booking advised at weekends
Prices: £2.95-£12.25, Sunday
lunch 1-course £6.95,
3-course £10.95

Billed outside as a country inn and restaurant, the Duke
changed hands recently and it is immediately obvious.
One of the bitters on offer comes from the Wolf
Brewery in Attleborough, something rarely found elsewhere. Just beyond the bar there is an intriguing hanging
arrangement on the wall. Modern art? No, the menu. The names
of the dishes on offer, such as spinach and sweet pepper tart,

> **Out front Jenny is friendly and efficient; in the kitchen her partner concentrates on producing wonderful food... exceptional quality... refined service**

lemon and lime cheesecake and poached fillet of
scotch salmon, are written onto small glass photo
frames. Asked about this, the owner Jenny Lund-Lack
explains that since they only use fresh ingredients and
can't always rely on a supply of particular produce,
they found that a more flexible, non-printed menu was
necessary.

Jenny and her partner used to be in the hotel business and although this freehouse is obviously a much
smaller operation, their customer service background
and experience shines through. Out front Jenny is
friendly and efficient; in the kitchen her partner concentrates on producing wonderful food. The asparagus
soup, containing several gently steamed fresh asparagus
tips, was a perfect blend of freshness and creaminess.
This isn't cheap food (at £9.75 the scampi was the most
expensive I saw on my travels), it's not groundbreak-
ingly different, but it is of exceptional quality.

If you can ignore the cartwheel and the carpet, rem-
nants of the pub's previous existence, you will find
refined service and a menu that is one step ahead of
those of many country pubs

The George and Dragon

budget, children, rural peace

41 Boxworth Road
Elsworth CB3 8JQ
Map ref: front D 1
Telephone: 01954 267236
Open Mon-Sat: 11am-2.30pm,
6-11pm, Sun: 11am-2.30pm

Food served Mon-Sat: noon-2pm,
6-9pm (Fri-Sat: until 9.30),
Sun: noon-2pm
Credit cards except
American Express
Booking advised at weekends
Prices: main course: £8-£15.50

The George and Dragon knows how to provide good food, and lots of it, at very reasonable prices.

At present an extensive à la carte menu, plus daily specials are on offer but The George plans to concentrate on fixed-price lunches and dinners. Throughout the week, both at lunchtime and in the evening, the pub has different set menus available. A starter, main course, dessert and coffee costs from £8.50 to £15, depending on the choice. My lunch menu (three courses for £9) began with oven-baked mushrooms served with a Stilton sauce. Although they looked suspiciously like they had been pinged in the microwave, what with the separating sauce, the mushrooms actually tasted of the cheese in question, not some cheaper blue alternative. This was followed by a whole Avon trout with buttered almonds and whole means whole: it was larger than the plate. Like the first course, the fish was well-presented and tasty. The portions are enormous and every main dish comes with a starch (potatoes in various guises) and salad or vegetables. I noticed, by eavesdropping on the table next to me, that even the already huge warm salads come with a side dish of chips or new potatoes. I had no room for dessert (either sherry trifle or spiced apple crunch with custard) and skipped to the coffee which was, as in most pubs, a bit disappointing.

The emphasis on food makes this more of a restaurant than a pub: most of the tables on a Wednesday lunchtime were reserved. You can eat outside but there isn't much of a garden. This isn't somewhere for a night's drinking or a romantic dinner for two, not that is if you're under 35. However, it's perfect for families and I certainly wouldn't be ashamed to bring my grandmother here.

> good food, and lots of it, at very reasonable prices... emphasis on food makes this more of a restaurant than a pub... perfect for families

The Golden Ball

**children, garden, rural peace
special occasion**

INSIDER
CHOICE

High Street
Boxworth CB3 8LY
Map ref: front D 2
Telephone: 01954 267397
Open daily: 11.30-3pm, 6.30-11pm
(Sun: 7-10.30). Food served daily:
noon-2.15pm, Mon-Thu: 6.30-9.30pm,
Fri-Sat: 6.30-10pm, Sun: 7-9pm

Booking advised
at weekends
Credit cards except
American Express
Prices: bar snacks £2.25-
£4.50, main course £6.95-
£10.25 (Sunday roast
£6.50)

A, shall we say, intriguing name for a pub? Probably because it's an intriguing pub. Boxworth is a village situated just off the main road from Cambridge to Bedford and, apart from allowing some of the best views of Cambridgeshire as you approach it from the A428, it isn't that memorable. Or wasn't. The Golden Ball's revival, under Hillary Paddock's management, may change that.

this 400-year old, white thatched cottage... welcomes anyone and everyone... There are several real ales on offer... and, instead of jacket potatoes, you spot chili, gnocchi ...and halloumi... Friendly and upbeat, chummy without being familiar

From the outside this 400-year old, white thatched cottage looks like many others. As you step inside from the sunny garden (long, secluded, with swings for children) your eyes might take a moment to adjust. Initially, you'll spot a traditional interior: carpet, those funny, ubiquitous chairs with spoke backs and a cartwheel detail, a fruit machine. Then, as your eyes become accustomed, you notice that some of the tables are made of a lighter, more sunny wood than others; that there are several real ales on offer, both noted and not so; that instead of the printed plastic menu offering jacket potatoes and gammon and chips that the decor might lead you to expect, you spot the words words chili, gnocchi and reduction nestling comfortably with tiger prawns and halloumi.

And then there's the staff. Friendly and upbeat, chummy without being familiar, you get the sense that this pub welcomes anyone and everyone. There are locals, of course, this is a village after all, but they don't create a scrum at the bar making the itinerant visitor feel out of place.

It is quite a feat to defy long-established and frankly outdated pub formulas. But in this pub's case it is even more incredible since a year ago it was saved from closure by a local resident. Like a phoenix, it is rising above its near-extinction with immense speed and style. A

major refurbishment is planned to make space for both
accommodation and a new layout and the Club Golden
Ball (which offers dining discounts and a free drive-you-
home facility to its members...who pay nothing to join)
is a mark of true customer awareness. This pub is a fine
example of a developing market trend: the light wood is
superseding the dead wood. From the customers' point
of view that can be nothing but encouraging news.

The Old Ferryboat Inn

children, garden, rural peace

Holywell PE17 3TG
Map ref: front C 2
Telephone: 01480 463227
Open Sat-Sun: all day, Mon-Fri:
11.30am-3pm, 6pm-11pm

Food served Mon-Sat: noon-2pm,
6.30-9.30, Sun: noon-2pm,
7-9pm (plus snack menu 3-5pm)
Booking advised on weekends
Prices: bar food £5.95-£12.30,
children's menu

Many pubs in Britain celebrate St. Patrick's Day with
green beer and a somewhat dubious connection to
Ireland. But at The Old Ferry Boat Inn in Holywell,
March 17th has an altogether different significance. It
was on this day in 1050
that Juliet, a local 17 year-
old, committed suicide for
the love of a local wood-
cutter. Her grave is part of
the Inn's granite floor and

**said to be the oldest
pub in Britain... has
riverside charm and a
cottage character... a
real ale pub**

the anniversary of her death is supposed to be one of
the best days to spot her ghost.

Juliet's 1000 year-old reign over this pub is nothing
for the Ferryboat is said to be the oldest pub in Britain,
dating back to the liquor sales first recorded here in
560 AD. It gets its name from the river ferry that used to
operate from the site, transporting both cargo and pas-
sengers. Hereward the Wake crossed the river at this
point during the Norman invasion of Britain and,
should the roads ever become impassable, the Inn still
holds the ancient right to operate a ferry.

In more recent times, its history has been chequered
by a fire in March 97 and two changes of ownership.
Now a Greene King pub, it still has riverside charm and
a cottage character (lots of low ceilings, timbered walls
and different drinking areas) but the service and food
are somewhat patchy. Beer-wise it fares much better. It
is a real ale pub and offers three resident beers, IPA,
Abbot and Marston's Pedigree as well as three guests
like Bateman's XXXB and Spitfire.

Hopefully, under its new regime, the pub will be
restored to its glory days.

Around-West

The Pike and Eel Hotel and Marina

children, garden, rural peace

Overcote Lane
Needingworth PE17 3TW
Map ref: front C 2
Telephone: 01480 463336
Open Mon-Sat: 11am-11pm,
Sun: noon-10.30pm

Food served daily: noon-2pm,
7-10pm
Booking advised at weekends
Prices: bar snacks from £3.25 -
£6.95, à la carte main courses
£8.50-£13.95

Overcote Lane is Memory Lane for me. When I was a child, my parents would sometimes take us for a special summer evening treat. We'd all get dressed up and drive to the Pike and Eel in Needingworth for scampi and chips and a glass of fizzy orangeade. Down a very, very long and narrow road, lined with cow parsley and sweet smells of hay, sits this huge, rambling pub. The fact that it was, and still is right next to a marina and endless little twists and turns of water made it all the more special in my mind.

Down a very, very long and narrow road... sits this huge, rambling pub... If you want something more than just a pub by the water, try heading out here

It still is special, although now it is the faded grandeur and endless armchairs that I notice, not the boats and hiding places. There are few places in the region that can claim such waterside seclusion. Sitting outside on an early summer's evening, there is no background roar of traffic, no sirens, no sulphurous glow. Maybe the slow gurgle of a boat engine and the hushed movements of weeping willows but not much more. Even cars arrive at a different pace here, slowed by the limited visibility of the road.

Wood pigeons, willows, wing chairs, this is England at both its most traditional and its most outdated. If you want something more than just a pub by the water, try heading out here. I wonder if they still sell fizzy orangeade.

The Trinity Foot

business lunch

Huntingdon Rd
Swavesey CB4 5RD
Map ref: front C 2
Telephone: 01954 230315
Open: Mon-Sat 11am-2.30pm,
6-11pm, Sun: noon-3pm

Food served Mon-Sat: noon-2pm,
6-9.30pm (Fri-Sat until 10pm),
Sun: noon-1:30pm
Booking advised: Sundays only
and large parties
Prices: £1.25-£12.50

Butterfish isn't something you encounter very often on any menu, let alone a pub menu. But The Trinity Foot isn't any pub: it is probably the most widely reputed for fish in the area. It even has its own fish shop (open Tue-Fri 11-2:30pm, 6-7:30, Sat 11-2:30 only). Of course, if you buy some then you can't sit and enjoy the efficient and friendly service. Nor can you smugly watch the roaring A14 traffic from the comfort of the airy, quiet conservatory.

the most widely reputed for fish in the area... The pub itself is quite traditional with lots of space

Lunch here was a huge slab of grilled butterfish (related to catfish apparently) with a side salad and plenty of tartare sauce. The menu obviously changes depending on what's available but you can be sure of finding several grilled fish (usually 15 different ones, many priced around £7.50), possibly a rare breed amongst the meat selections and all the usual pub staples like sandwiches and ploughman's. Not having fish here, however, seems almost a criminal offence.

The pub itself is quite traditional with lots of space and a big conservatory. Customers are a mix of pensioners, tourists and business people. Boddingtons is available.

Name index

Cross Listings by Cuisine

Budget Eating

Business Lunch
(see 'special occasion')

Children and Families

Café:

Courtyard

(see garden)

Desserts

(with or without
a meal)

Free Starter & Dessert

AL CASBAH RESTAURANT
Mill Road, Cambridge

SEE OVER FOR DETAILS AND CONDITIONS

Free £8 Bottle of House Wine

THE ANCHOR
North Street, Burwell

SEE OVER FOR DETAILS AND CONDITIONS

£5 Off Meal for Two

ANCHOR INN
Sutton Gault, Near Ely

SEE OVER FOR DETAILS AND CONDITIONS

Free Curry Worth up to £8

THE BENGAL RESTAURANT
Fitzroy Street, Cambridge

SEE OVER FOR DETAILS AND CONDITIONS

* Vouchers have limited validity – to 1 October 2001.
* This voucher is valid for for <u>one free starter and one free dessert.</u>
* This voucher can only be used for a booked table <u>for a minimum of TWO people dining Sundays to Thursday only</u>.
* Vouchers may not be used in conjunction with any other promotional scheme.
* No photocopies or any other kind of reproduction of these vouchers will be accepted.
* Vouchers are valid only for a pre-booked meal and the intent to use a voucher must be mentioned when booking.

* Vouchers have limited validity – to 1 October 2001.
* This voucher is valid for <u>one free bottle of house wine.</u>
* This voucher can only be used for a booked table <u>for a minimum of TWO people dining</u>.
* Vouchers may not be used in conjunction with any other promotional scheme.
* No photocopies or any other kind of reproduction of these vouchers will be accepted.
* The voucher offer may exclude use of the voucher at certain times of day, days of the week or with specific menus.
* If any restrictions are imposed, the establishment must advise customers of these at the time of booking and accept the vouchers at least 70% of the time the establishment is open.
* Vouchers are valid only for a pre-booked meal and the intent to use a voucher must be mentioned when booking.

* Vouchers have limited validity – to 1 October 2001.
* This voucher can be used only for a booked table <u>for a minimum of TWO people dining. Only ONE voucher per table.</u>
* <u>To be valid, both customers must choose two courses.</u>
* <u>This voucher excludes use for the £7.50 set lunch and may NOT be used on Friday evenings, Saturday, Sunday or bank holidays.</u>
* Vouchers may not be used in conjunction with any other promotional scheme.
* No photocopies or any other kind of reproduction of these vouchers will be accepted.
* Vouchers are valid only for a pre-booked meal and the intent to use a voucher must be mentioned when booking.
* The voucher's value is to be deducted from the final bill inclusive of VAT (and if applicable, service) with the participating establishment bearing the cost of the discount.

* Vouchers have limited validity – to 1 October 2001.
* This voucher can be used only for a booked table <u>for a minimum of FOUR people dining</u>.
* This voucher is valid for <u>one free curry excluding King Prawn.</u>
* Vouchers may not be used in conjunction with any other promotional scheme.
* No photocopies or any other kind of reproduction of these vouchers will be accepted.
* The voucher offer may exclude use of the voucher at certain times of day, days of the week or with specific menus.
* If any restrictions are imposed, the establishment must advise customers of these at the time of booking and accept the vouchers at least 70% of the time the establishment is open.
* Vouchers are valid only for a pre-booked meal and the intent to use a voucher must be mentioned when booking.

* Vouchers have limited validity – to 1 October 2001.
* This voucher is valid for <u>one bottle of house wine.</u>
* This voucher can be used only for a booked table <u>for a minimum of FOUR people dining on Sunday to Thursday only</u>.
* Vouchers may not be used in conjunction with any other promotional scheme.
* No photocopies or any other kind of reproduction of these vouchers will be accepted.
* Vouchers are valid only for a pre-booked meal and the intent to use a voucher must be mentioned when booking.

* Vouchers have limited validity – to 1 October 2001.
* This voucher can only be used <u>for TWO people dining</u>.
* This voucher is valid for <u>15% off up to two meals not including drinks.</u>
* Vouchers may not be used in conjunction with any other promotional scheme.
* No photocopies or any other kind of reproduction of these vouchers will be accepted.
* The voucher's value is to be deducted from the final bill inclusive of VAT (and if applicable, service) with the participating establishment bearing the cost of the discount.

* Vouchers have limited validity – to 1 October 2001.
* This voucher if <u>valid for a free glass of wine (175ml) worth up to £2.25.</u>
* This voucher can be used only <u>when TWO people dine</u>.
* <u>This offer is valid for up to four persons per voucher</u>.
* Vouchers may not be used in conjunction with any other promotional scheme.
* No photocopies or any other kind of reproduction of these vouchers will be accepted.
* Vouchers are valid only for a pre-booked meal and the intent to use a voucher must be mentioned when booking.
* The voucher's value is to be deducted from the final bill inclusive of VAT (and if applicable, service) with the participating establishment bearing the cost of the discount.

* Vouchers have limited validity – to 1 October 2001.
* This voucher can be used <u>only when a baguette, melt, baked potato or soup is also ordered</u>.
* This voucher is valid for <u>one free medium cappuccino</u>.
* Vouchers may not be used in conjunction with any other promotional scheme.
* No photocopies or any other kind of reproduction of these vouchers will be accepted.
* This voucher applies only to Canadian Muffin Company, Cambridge.

**10% Off
Set Meals**

*CHARLIE CHAN CHINESE
Regent, Cambridge*

SEE OVER FOR DETAILS AND CONDITIONS

**Free £8.85 Bottle
of House wine**

*CB2 INTERNET BISTRO
Norfolk Street, Cambridge*

SEE OVER FOR DETAILS AND CONDITIONS

**Free £7.50 Bottle
of House Wine**

*THE CRICKETERS ARMS
Melbourne Place, Cambridge*

SEE OVER FOR DETAILS AND CONDITIONS

Free Pint

*THE FIVE BELLS
Newmarket Road, Cambridge*

SEE OVER FOR DETAILS AND CONDITIONS

* Vouchers have limited validity – to 1 October 2001.
* This voucher can be used only for a table <u>for a minimum of TWO people dining for any day except Friday and Saturday</u>.
* This voucher is valid for <u>10% off set meals (except set economy lunches) ordered by the members of the dining party</u>.
* Vouchers may not be used in conjunction with any other promotional scheme.
* No photocopies or any other kind of reproduction of these vouchers will be accepted.
* Vouchers are valid only for a pre-booked meal and the intent to use a voucher must be mentioned when booking.
* The voucher's value is to be deducted from the final bill inclusive of VAT (and if applicable, service) with the participating establishment bearing the cost of the discount.

* Vouchers have limited validity – to 1 October 2001.
* This voucher can be used only for a booked table <u>for a minimum of TWO people ordering an evening meal from the diner menu.</u>
* This voucher is valid for for <u>one free bottle of house wine.</u>
* Vouchers may not be used in conjunction with any other promotional scheme.
* No photocopies or any other kind of reproduction of these vouchers will be accepted.
* The voucher offer may exclude use of the voucher at certain times of day, days of the week or with specific menus.
* If any restrictions are imposed, the establishment must advise customers of these at the time of booking and accept the vouchers at least 70% of the time the establishment is open.
* Vouchers are valid only for a pre-booked meal and the intent to use a voucher must be mentioned when booking.

* Vouchers have limited validity – to 1 October 2001.
* This voucher can be used only for a booked table <u>for a minimum of TWO people ordering an evening meal.</u>
* This voucher is valid for <u>one free bottle of house wine.</u>
* Vouchers may not be used in conjunction with any other promotional scheme.
* No photocopies or any other kind of reproduction of these vouchers will be accepted.

* Vouchers have limited validity – to 1 October 2001.
* This voucher is valid for for <u>one free pint on a Monday or Tuesday</u>.
* Vouchers may not be used in conjunction with any other promotional scheme.
* No photocopies or any other kind of reproduction of these vouchers will be accepted.

Free Pudding

THE FREE PRESS
Prospect Row, Cambridge

SEE OVER FOR DETAILS AND CONDITIONS

£3.75 Children's Meals Free

HOBBS PAVILION RESTAURANT
Park Terrace, Cambridge

SEE OVER FOR DETAILS AND CONDITIONS

Free Starter Worth up to £3

INDIAN GARDENS
Victoria Street, Littleport

SEE OVER FOR DETAILS AND CONDITIONS

£5 Off Restaurant Meals

JOLLY BREWERS
Fen Road, Milton, Cambridge

SEE OVER FOR DETAILS AND CONDITIONS

* Vouchers have limited validity – to 1 October 2001.
* This voucher can be used <u>only when more than £4 of food is purchased.</u>
* The voucher can be used only when food is being served: Mon-Fri: noon-2pm, 6-9pm, Sat: noon-2.30pm, 6-9pm, Sun: noon-2.30, 7-9pm
* Vouchers may not be used in conjunction with any other promotional scheme.
* No photocopies or any other kind of reproduction of these vouchers will be accepted.

---

* Vouchers have limited validity – to 1 October 2001.
* This voucher can be only used for <u>children under 10 years old accompanied by an adult who is ordering a meal. Orders must be placed by 6.30pm.</u>
* The voucher is valid for <u>a maximum of two children.</u>
* This voucher is valid for <u>a free Menu Enfant worth £3.75 for each child.</u>
* Vouchers may not be used in conjunction with any other promotional scheme.
* No photocopies or any other kind of reproduction of these vouchers will be accepted.

---

* Vouchers have limited validity – to 1 October 2001.
* This voucher is valid for <u>one free starter worth up to £3.</u>
* This voucher can be used only for a booked table <u>for a minimum of TWO people dining.</u>
* Vouchers may not be used in conjunction with any other promotional scheme.
* No photocopies or any other kind of reproduction of these vouchers will be accepted.
* The voucher offer may exclude use of the voucher at certain times of day, days of the week or with specific menus.
* If any restrictions are imposed, the establishment must advise customers of these at the time of booking and accept the vouchers at least 70% of the time the establishment is open.
* Vouchers are valid only for a pre-booked meal and the intent to use a voucher must be mentioned when booking.

---

* Vouchers have limited validity – to 1 October 2001.
* This voucher can be used for a £5 discount only for a booked table <u>for a minimum of TWO people dining.</u>
* Vouchers may not be used in conjunction with any other promotional scheme.
* No photocopies or any other kind of reproduction of these vouchers will be accepted.
* Vouchers are valid only for a pre-booked meal and the intent to use a voucher must be mentioned when booking.
* The voucher offer may exclude use of the voucher at certain times of day, days of the week or with specific menus.
* If any restrictions are imposed, the establishment must advise customers of these at the time of booking and accept the vouchers at least 70% of the time the establishment is open.
* The voucher's value is to be deducted from the final bill inclusive of VAT (and if applicable, service) with the participating establishment bearing the cost of the discount.

INSIDER GUIDES

Free Drink
Worth up to £1.30

THE LITTLE TEA ROOM
All Saints Passage, Cambridge

SEE OVER FOR DETAILS AND CONDITIONS

INSIDER GUIDES

Free Afternoon Tea
Worth up to £6.95

OCTAGON LOUNGE - University Arms
Regent Street, Cambridge

SEE OVER FOR DETAILS AND CONDITIONS

INSIDER GUIDES

Free Tea/Coffee

MARTIN'S COFFEE HOUSE
Trumpington Street, Cambridge

SEE OVER FOR DETAILS AND CONDITIONS

INSIDER GUIDES

Free Bottle of
House Wine

NEEDHAMS FARM RESTAURANT
Main Street, Witchford

SEE OVER FOR DETAILS AND CONDITIONS

* Vouchers have limited validity – to 1 October 2001.
* This voucher is valid for <u>one free drink Monday through Friday only</u>.
* <u>This voucher can only be used when a meal and dessert are also ordered</u>.
* Vouchers may not be used in conjunction with any other promotional scheme.
* No photocopies or any other kind of reproduction of these vouchers will be accepted.

* Vouchers have limited validity – to 1 October 2001.
* <u>This voucher can only be used when FOUR afternoon teas are also ordered.</u>
* This voucher is valid for <u>one free afternoon tea worth up to £6.95 consumed in the Octagon Lounge of the De Vere University Arms Hotel.</u>
* Vouchers may not be used in conjunction with any other promotional scheme.
* No photocopies or any other kind of reproduction of these vouchers will be accepted.

* Vouchers have limited validity – to 1 October 2001.
* <u>This voucher can only be used with meals of £4 and over.</u>
* This voucher is valid for <u>one free coffee or tea</u>
* Vouchers may not be used in conjunction with any other promotional scheme.
* No photocopies or any other kind of reproduction of these vouchers will be accepted.

* Vouchers have limited validity – to 1 October 2001.
* This voucher is valid for for <u>one free bottle of house wine.</u>
* This voucher can be used only for a booked table <u>for a minimum of TWO people dining.</u>
* <u>This voucher is not valid on Saturdays.</u>
* Vouchers may not be used in conjunction with any other promotional scheme.
* No photocopies or any other kind of reproduction of these vouchers will be accepted.
* Vouchers are valid only for a pre-booked meal and the intent to use a voucher must be mentioned when booking.

Free Dessert

NO 1 KING'S PARADE
King's Parade, Cambridge

SEE OVER FOR DETAILS AND CONDITIONS

Free £9.95 Bottle of House Wine

PALM TREE CARIBBEAN
Norfolk Street, Cambridge

SEE OVER FOR DETAILS AND CONDITIONS

£1.50 Off

THE PEAR TREE
Hildersham, Cambs

SEE OVER FOR DETAILS AND CONDITIONS

Free Bottle of House Wine

RAINBOW VEGETARIAN CAFE
Kings Parade, Cambridge

SEE OVER FOR DETAILS AND CONDITIONS

* Vouchers have limited validity – to 1 October 2001.
* This voucher is valid for <u>one free dessert.</u>
* This voucher can be used only for a booked table <u>for a minimum of TWO people eating two-course meals.</u>
* Vouchers may not be used in conjunction with any other promotional scheme.
* No photocopies or any other kind of reproduction of these vouchers will be accepted.
* The voucher offer may exclude use of the voucher at certain times of day, days of the week or with specific menus.
* If any restrictions are imposed, the establishment must advise customers of these at the time of booking and accept the vouchers at least 70% of the time the establishment is open.
* Vouchers are valid only for a pre-booked meal and the intent to use a voucher must be mentioned when booking.

---

* Vouchers have limited validity – to 1 October 2001.
* This voucher is valid for <u>one free bottle of house wine.</u>
* This voucher can be used only for a booked table <u>for a minimum of FOUR people dining.</u>
* Vouchers may not be used in conjunction with any other promotional scheme.
* No photocopies or any other kind of reproduction of these vouchers will be accepted.
* The voucher offer may exclude use of the voucher at certain times of day, days of the week or with specific menus.
* If any restrictions are imposed, the establishment must advise customers of these at the time of booking and accept the vouchers at least 70% of the time the establishment is open.
* Vouchers are valid only for a pre-booked meal and the intent to use a voucher must be mentioned when booking.

---

* Vouchers have limited validity – to 1 October 2001.
* This voucher can be<u> used only when ordering a main course and dessert.</u>
* Vouchers may not be used in conjunction with any other promotional scheme.
* No photocopies or any other kind of reproduction of these vouchers will be accepted.
* The voucher's value is to be deducted from the final bill inclusive of VAT (and if applicable, service) with the participating establishment bearing the cost of the discount.

---

* Vouchers have limited validity – to 1 October 2001.
* This voucher is valid for <u>one free bottle of house wine.</u>
* This voucher can be used only for a booked table <u>for a minimum of FOUR people dining, each ordering a main course.</u>
* Vouchers may not be used in conjunction with any other promotional scheme.
* No photocopies or any other kind of reproduction of these vouchers will be accepted.
* The voucher offer may exclude use of the voucher at certain times of day, days of the week or with specific menus.
* If any restrictions are imposed, the establishment must advise customers of these at the time of booking and accept the vouchers at least 70% of the time the establishment is open.
* Vouchers are valid only for a pre-booked meal and the intent to use a voucher must be mentioned when booking.

£1 Off
Per Person

SALA THONG THAI RESTAURANT
Newnham Road, Cambridge

SEE OVER FOR DETAILS AND CONDITIONS

£5 Off
Meal for Two

RUPERT BROOKE
Broadway, Grantchester

SEE OVER FOR DETAILS AND CONDITIONS

£3 to £5 Off

SOL Y SOMBRA
SPANISH RESTAURANT
Crown Walk, Newmarket

SEE OVER FOR DETAILS AND CONDITIONS

£5 Off a
Meal for Two

THE STAR INN
The Street, Lidgate

SEE OVER FOR DETAILS AND CONDITIONS

* Vouchers have limited validity – to 1 October 2001.
* This voucher is valid for <u>£1 off per person dining for set menu B, C or D only.</u>
* This voucher can be used only for a booked table <u>for a minimum of TWO people dining on Tuesday, Wednesday, Thursday and Sunday evenings.</u>
* Vouchers may not be used in conjunction with any other promotional scheme.
* No photocopies or any other kind of reproduction of these vouchers will be accepted.
* Vouchers are valid only for a pre-booked meal and the intent to use a voucher must be mentioned when booking.

* Vouchers have limited validity – to 1 October 2001.
* This voucher can be used only for a booked table <u>for a minimum of TWO people dining.</u>
* Vouchers may not be used in conjunction with any other promotional scheme.
* No photocopies or any other kind of reproduction of these vouchers will be accepted.
* Vouchers are valid only for a pre-booked meal and the intent to use a voucher must be mentioned when booking.
* The voucher offer may exclude use of the voucher at certain times of day, days of the week or with specific menus.
* If any restrictions are imposed, the establishment must advise customers of these at the time of booking and accept the vouchers at least 70% of the time the establishment is open.
* The voucher's value is to be deducted from the final bill inclusive of VAT (and if applicable, service) with the participating establishment bearing the cost of the discount.

* Vouchers have limited validity – to 1 October 2001.
* This voucher can be used only for a booked table <u>for a minimum of TWO people dining and is valid for £5 off food in the restaurant dining room and £3 off food served at the bar.</u>
* Vouchers may not be used in conjunction with any other promotional scheme.
* No photocopies or any other kind of reproduction of these vouchers will be accepted.
* Vouchers are valid only for a pre-booked meal and the intent to use a voucher must be mentioned when booking.
* The voucher offer may exclude use of the voucher at certain times of day, days of the week or with specific menus.
* If any restrictions are imposed, the establishment must advise customers of these at the time of booking and accept the vouchers at least 70% of the time the establishment is open.
* The voucher's value is to be deducted from the final bill inclusive of VAT (and if applicable, service) with the participating establishment bearing the cost of the discount.

* Vouchers have limited validity – to 1 October 2001.
* <u>This voucher is valid for £5 off.</u>
* This voucher can be <u>used only for a minimum of TWO people dining</u>
* <u>This voucher can be used only for dinner or à la carte lunch.</u>
* Vouchers may not be used in conjunction with any other promotional scheme.
* No photocopies or any other kind of reproduction of these vouchers will be accepted.
* The voucher's value is to be deducted from the final bill inclusive of VAT (and if applicable, service) with the participating establishment bearing the cost of the discount.

15% Off a Meal

STICKY FINGERS
Regent Street, Cambridge

SEE OVER FOR DETAILS AND CONDITIONS

10% Off Lunch

THE TUDOR HOTEL AND
THAI RESTAURANT
High Street, Fenstanton

SEE OVER FOR DETAILS AND CONDITIONS

Free Coffee

VARSITY RESTAURANT
St Andrew's Street, Cambridge

SEE OVER FOR DETAILS AND CONDITIONS

INSIDER GUIDES

Free 'Kir Royales' Worth £10

"venue"
Regent Street, Cambridge

SEE OVER FOR DETAILS AND CONDITIONS

* Vouchers have limited validity – to 1 October 2001.
* <u>This voucher is valid for 15% off a meal Tuesday through Friday.</u>
* <u>This voucher applies only to food items.</u>
* Vouchers may not be used in conjunction with any other promotional scheme.
* No photocopies or any other kind of reproduction of these vouchers will be accepted.
* The voucher's value is to be deducted from the final bill inclusive of VAT with the participating establishment bearing the cost of the discount.

* Vouchers have limited validity – to 1 October 2001.
* <u>This voucher is valid for 10% off one meal at lunch only.</u>
* <u>This voucher applies only to food items.</u>
* Vouchers may not be used in conjunction with any other promotional scheme.
* No photocopies or any other kind of reproduction of these vouchers will be accepted.
* The voucher's value is to be deducted from the final bill inclusive of VAT (and if applicable, service) with the participating establishment bearing the cost of the discount.

* Vouchers have limited validity – to 1 October 2001.
* <u>This voucher is valid for one free coffee when a main course is also ordered.</u>
* Vouchers may not be used in conjunction with any other promotional scheme.
* No photocopies or any other kind of reproduction of these vouchers will be accepted.

* Vouchers have limited validity – to 1 October 2001.
* <u>This voucher is valid for two "venue" Kir Royales.</u>
* <u>This voucher can only be used when TWO people order a 3-course meal each.</u>
* Vouchers may not be used in conjunction with any other promotional scheme.
* No photocopies or any other kind of reproduction of these vouchers will be accepted.

ORDER FORM FOR
THE MILLENNIUM COLLECTION

🍴 Order now to ensure early delivery.

Item	Price	P & P	Quantity	Sub total
1. Millennium Dish 310 mm diameter, 58 mm deep	£49.99	£4.00	....	£ ....
2. Millennium Sideplate 210 mm diameter	£29.99	£3.00	....	£ ....
3. Millennium Eggcup 50 mm diameter, 48 mm high	£ 9.99	£1.50	....	£ ....
4. Millennium Mug 77 mm diameter, 90 mm high	£16.99	£2.50	....	£ ....
			Total	£ ....

To: Cardozo Sanluis Designs Ltd, PO Box 21, St Neots, Cambs PE18 9GQ
Telephone/Fax 01480 811131

❏ I enclose a cheque/PO made payable to Cardozo Sanluis Designs Ltd,
or, I am paying by ❏ Master Card ❏ Visa ❏ Switch ❏ Delta. £ ....

Card No. [ ][ ][ ][ ][ ][ ][ ][ ][ ][ ][ ][ ][ ][ ][ ][ ][ ][ ][ ]

Exp.date [ ][ ][ ]   Switch Issue No. [ ][ ]

Signature ....

Name ....

Address ....

....

Postcode ....   Date .... /.......... 1999   TCI/BRC1

THE MILLENNIUM COLLECTION

PRICES AND ORDER FORM SEE OVERLEAF

Cardozo Sanluis Designs Ltd is delighted to be able to offer you its fine Millennium Collection of porcelain that will appeal to both traditional and modern tastes.

The porcelain has been subtly designed using the alphabet as the pattern, highlighting the Roman numerals 'MM' in gold to commemorate the Millennium. The lettering, in capitals and italics, is in Delft blue and is on white Swiss porcelain of the highest quality.

The Cardozo Kindersley Workshop, which created the set at its workshop in Cambridge, England, has sought perfection in the design and cutting of letters for over fifty years, following an age-old tradition of craftsmanship. It has created unique works for individuals and for institutions, such as the British Library. Now we invite you to share in the tradition by collecting this timeless design.